Working on the Margins

Black workers, white farmers in postcolonial Zimbabwe

Postcolonial Encounters

A Zed Books series in association with the International Centre for Contemporary Cultural Research (ICCCR), Universities of Manchester and Keele.

Series editors: Richard Werbner and Pnina Werbner

This series debates the making of contemporary culture and politics in a postcolonial world. Volumes explore the impact of colonial legacies, precolonial traditions and current global and imperial forces on the everyday lives of citizens. Reaching beyond postcolonial countries to the formation of external ethnic and migrant diasporas, the series critically theorises:

- ✪ the active engagement of people themselves in the creation of their own political and cultural agendas;

- ✪ the emerging predicaments of local, national and transnational identities and subjectivities;

- ✪ the indigenous roots of nationalism, communalism, state violence and political terror;

- ✪ the cultural and religious counter-movements for or against emancipation and modernity;

- ✪ the social struggles over the imperatives of human and citizenship rights within the moral and political economy.

Arising from the analysis of decolonization and recolonization, the series opens out a significant space in a growing interdisciplinary literature. The convergence of interest is very broad, from anthropology, cultural studies, social history, comparative literature, development, sociology, law and political theory. No single theoretical orientation provides the dominant thrust. Instead the series responds to the challenge of a commitment to empirical, in-depth research as the motivation for critical theory.

Other titles in the series:

Richard Werbner and Terence Ranger, eds, *Postcolonial Identities in Africa* (1996).

Pnina Werbner and Tariq Modood, eds, *Debating Cultural Hybridity: Multicultural Identities and the Politics of Anti-Racism* (1997).

Tariq Modood and Pnina Werbner, eds, *The Politics of Multiculturalism in the New Europe: Racism, Identity and Community* (1997).

Richard Werbner, ed., *Memory and the Postcolony: African Anthropology and the Critique of Power* (1998).

Itty Abraham, *The Making of the Indian Atomic Bomb: Science, Secrecy and the Postcolonial State* (1998).

Nira Yuval-Davis and Pnina Werbner (eds), *Women, Citizenship and Difference* (1999).

Working on the Margins

Black workers, white farmers in postcolonial Zimbabwe

Blair A. Rutherford

In Zimbabwe and South Africa:

Weaver Press Ltd, P O Box A1922, Avondale, Harare, Zimbabwe

In the rest of the world:

Zed Books Ltd, 7 Cynthia Street, London N1 9JF, UK and
Room 400, 175 Fifth Avenue, New York, NY 10010, USA

Distributed in the USA exclusively by St Martin's Press, Inc,
175 Fifth Avenue, New York, NY 10010, USA

© Blair A. Rutherford, 2001

The moral right of the author of this work has been asserted by him in
accordance with the Copyright, Designs and Patents Act, 1988

Typeset by Fontline Electronic Publishing, Harare

Cover designed by Danes Design, Harare

Printed and bound in Mauritius by Préci-ex Limited

A catalogue record for this book is available from the British Library

US CIP data is available from the Library of Congress

ISBN: 0 7974 2241 2 Pb (Weaver Press)

ISBN: 1 84277 001 2 Pb (Zed Books)

ISBN: 1 84277 000 4 Hb (Zed Books)

Contents

Southern Africa

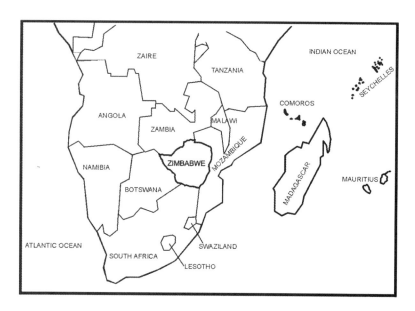

Hurungwe District, Zimbabwe

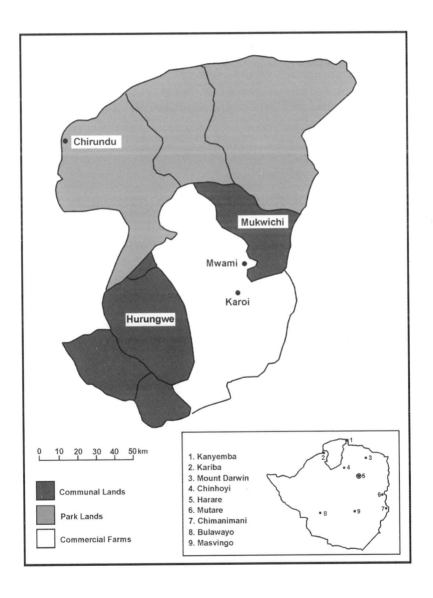

Chirundu

Mukwichi

Mwami •

• Karoi

Hurungwe

0 10 20 30 40 50 km

Communal Lands

Park Lands

Commercial Farms

1. Kanyemba
2. Kariba
3. Mount Darwin
4. Chinhoyi
5. Harare
6. Mutare
7. Chimanimani
8. Bulawayo
9. Masvingo

Urungwe District, 1947

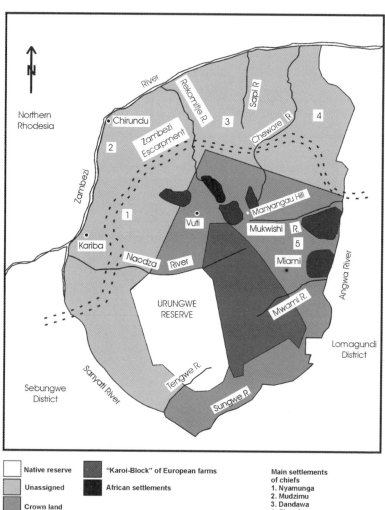

Native reserve	"Karoi-Block" of European farms
Unassigned	African settlements
Crown land	

Main settlements
of chiefs
1. Nyamunga
2. Mudzimu
3. Dandawa
4. Chundu
5. Kazangarare

source: based on S2805/2000, land for Natives,
memo from ANC, Urungwe, October 1947

Living structures on Chidhadhadha Farm

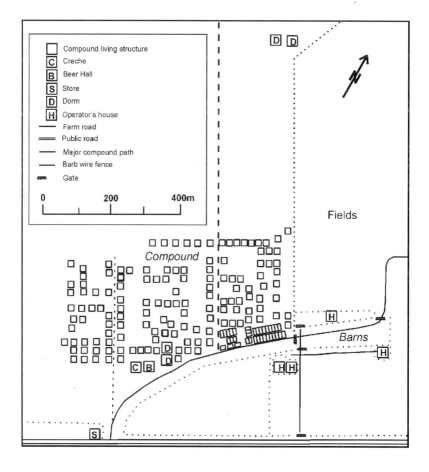

Kinship Tree of the "Big Family" on Chidhadhadha

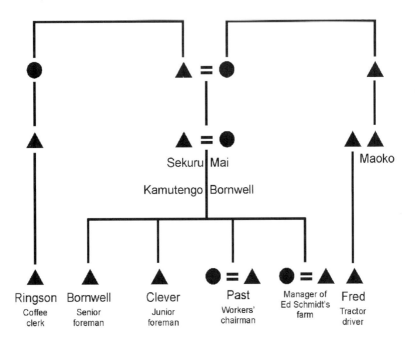

Agritex	Department of Agricultural, Technical and Extension Services
ALB	Agricultural Labour Bureau
CFU	Commercial Farmers Union
ESAP	Economic Structural Adjustment Programme
GAPWUZ	General Agricultural and Plantation Workers' Union of Zimbabwe
ICA	Intensive Conservation Area
MDC	Movement for Democratic Change
RNFU	Rhodesian National Farmers Union
RNLSC	Rhodesian Native Labour Supply Commission
VIDCO	Village Development Committee
ZANU(PF)	Zimbabwe African National Union (Patriotic Front)
ZCTU	Zimbabwe Congress of Trade Unions
ZTA	Zimbabwe Tobacco Association

A year after the publication of the University of Rhodesia economist Duncan Clarke's magisterial overview of working and living conditions of farm workers in colonial Zimbabwe, a civil servant in the Rhodesian Ministry of Agriculture who had worked on issues concerning farm labour wrote a critical review of it in *Zambezia*, the University of Rhodesia social science journal. F.P. Du Toit's 1978 review is highly dismissive of Clarke's political economy analysis and argument that farm workers' living and working conditions need to be transformed away from the 'quasi-feudalism' of white paternalism to a more modern policy and regulation regime to tackle farm worker poverty and the larger issue of rural development. For Du Toit and, he claims, for the 'farmer and the agriculturalist who live with the subject treated by Dr Clarke', Clarke totally misrepresents not only the industry of white commercial farming but also the developmental level of farm workers to which white farmers need to accommodate their management policies. Moreover, Du Toit constantly reiterates in his review that life on the farm is an improvement for farm workers compared to life in the 'tribal areas', the then Tribal Trust Lands (formerly native reserves). Just to give one example, Du Toit rebutted Clarke's condemnation of the lack of economic security for farm workers by suggesting that he ignores the broader social security white farmers provided to their labourers: 'Ever since the establishment of White commercial farming (as distinct from 'subsistence farming') the Black farm-worker enjoyed a far greater measure of territorial security than did his ancestors when at the mercy of tribal conflict and factional disputes. Until only a decade ago his "place" on the farm was unchallenged, provided he maintained allegiance to his employer. This may seem feudalistic, but we are talking about Africa, not Europe' (Du Toit 1978:78-79). Written during the height of the liberation struggle, when casualty levels were increasing on both sides, including in the white farming areas, Du Toit's review likely resonated with many supporters of white farmers inside and outside Rhodesia.

There are two issues relevant to my book that I want to draw out from this exchange. Firstly, Du Toit has a point in that Clarke was misapplying 'modern' standards to evaluate a labour regime that was shaped by other concerns. Indeed Du Toit's critique was not only a defence of the tradition of this labour regime on white farms but also exemplified the informing discourses of the regime: that white farmers should not be expected to provide 'European' standards of labour and living conditions to their workers because African farm workers have yet to fully evolve out of their traditional wants and desires. In fact, this line of reasoning continues to the present day amongst those who suggest that white farmers should be praised for the 'care' they give their workers, as it helps them adjust to modern life. However, in contrast to Du Toit's claims, I do not find Clark's analysis to be somehow 'false' in terms of explaining this regime of what I call 'domestic government'. Rather, his book can be understood as part of an emerging and competitive project of modernization of farm workers, of treating them as 'workers' who have the same rights and responsibilities as any other worker and whose lives should not be subject to white paternalism. While a version of this competitive project was being adopted by the leadership of white farmers at this time, it really came into official prominence after Independence when the new, nominally Marxist-Leninist ruling party and former liberation group, the Zimbabwe African National Union (Patriotic Front), began seeking to change what was widely viewed as the racist colonial legislative and socio-cultural inheritance of postcolonial Zimbabwe.

But my book, my argument, my narrative, is not simply about progress, about modernizing attempts, about the successes and failures of development. For if there indeed was a major break as Zimbabwe became postcolonial – a departure from the white paternalism of 'settler rule' and an entrance into the African nationalist era in which the leadership of the postcolonial nation will enable all Africans to improve their lives – why then have farm workers been the main targets of the violence led by liberation war veterans who have been occupying many hundreds of commercial farms since early 2000? Why have these war veterans and the leadership of ZANU(PF) and its media outlets described farm workers as 'sell-outs' – those whose interests lie with the 'settlers', white farmers and their international supporters – and simultaneously as people who still suffer under white racist paternalism, twenty years after Independence? At the same time, why do many white farmers, who are also targets of this intimidation and occupation, talk of the interests of their 'labourers' as converging with their own and characterize any alliance of farm workers and occupiers as an example of disloyalty or brain-washing?

I suggest that these on-going events indicate the poverty of understanding the labour regimes on commercial farms through a teleology of modernization, of a narrative of 'coming to' some higher plateau of material and cognitive living; simultaneously, they indicate the strength of these very discourses in helping to marginalize farm workers in terms of government policy and political practice. Domestic government has played a dominant role in postcolonial Zimbabwe, although it has been in dialogue and dynamic interaction with a range of practices and discourses, some supportive and some antagonistic, from the government, from ZANU(PF), from opposition parties, from some farmers, and from neighbouring small-scale peasant farming areas. In this book, I strive to provide an understanding of these interactions, practices and discourses, and a critique of many of them, arguing that they have cumulatively helped to marginalize farm workers in terms of their working and living conditions, their access to state services, and more generally their ability to improve their lives on and off commercial farms. This leads to the second point I want to draw from Du Toit's reaction to Clarke's book.

It is a commonplace to say that authors cannot predetermine the reception of their arguments, and that there are different ways in which their ideas will be received. But analogous to the timing of Duncan Clarke's book, mine is being published during an era of great upheaval, flux, and economic uncertainty for many Zimbabweans, particularly those whose livelihoods depend on commercial farming. It is a highly politicized period in Zimbabwe and among those interested in the country from afar, as people take sides between ZANU(PF) and the new and dominant opposition party, the Movement for Democratic Change; a time of politics and a time of *hondo* (war), which for most farm workers I know are equivalent – *mapolitikisi ihondo* (politics is war) – as I discuss in the Afterword.

Given all of this, there is a strong possibility that my arguments on a topic that touches on the political rhetoric concerning the status and citizenship of 'white farmers', will be massively misconstrued. It is in this political climate that I hope that a foregrounding of the partiality of my understanding and critique, of trying to undermine epistemological certainty and of insisting on the heterogeneity of points of view, particularly amongst farm workers, will assist in tempering any attempts to use this book to further political ends that I may find objectionable. I am sure that some – farmers, farm workers, policy-makers, politicians, academics, staff of trade unions and NGOs, friends and strangers alike – will take exception to my arguments; but I hope that in so doing they engage with them and do not simply dismiss them as ignoring the 'reality' on the farms, privileging their epistemological authority to mask their particular perspectives and to ignore other possible courses of understanding and action.

Some readers and reviewers may say this is not a time for the nuance that characterizes my analysis, critiques and suggestions (and which is very much a part of the orthodoxy of the theoretical streams of North American and European socio-cultural anthropology in which I am situated). It is during times of upheaval, however, when new possibilities emerge for farm workers, possibilities pregnant with potential for both improvement and harm, and I am aware of some such movements occurring right now in Zimbabwe, initiated by farm workers, NGOs, individual politicians, and white farmers. But as Marx reminded us in the eloquent introduction to his classic study of revolutionary times,

> *Men make their own history, but they do not make it just as they please; they do not make it under circumstances chosen by themselves, but under circumstances encountered, given and transmitted from the past. The tradition of all the dead generations weighs like a nightmare on the brain of the living. And just when they seem engaged in revolutionizing themselves and things, in creating something that has never yet existed, precisely in such periods of revolutionary crisis they anxiously conjure up the spirits of the past to their service and borrow from them names, battle cries and costumes in order to present the new scene of world history in this time-honoured disguise and this borrowed language* (Marx 1987 [1869]:15).

I hope that my critical understanding of the traditions that have shaped the lives of farm workers and how these have been tied to larger processes of nation-building and profit-accumulation, strategies of improvement and practices of marginalization, will resonate with some readers, pointing to issues of inequality, desires and, especially, power. By examining the ways of living of those working on the margins of discourses and practices of development, nationalism, and farm management, I hope to raise questions and ideas that may have some use to the growing number of people trying to improve the situation of farm workers in one way or another.

Although the responsibility for the opinions, arguments and explanations lies solely with me, I have developed them through discussions with a great range of people in Zimbabwe, Canada and elsewhere. Firstly, I thank the many farm workers, commercial farmers and their respective families – particularly those who have lived on what I call Chidhadhadha farm in Hurungwe – for sharing with me their thoughts, hospitality and arguments. You will remain anonymous because of the risk of retribution, but my debt is enormous. Thanks also to everyone in the non-farming community of Hurungwe who helped me in many ways. I have had the pleasure of being associated with both the Faculty of Law and the Institute of Development Studies at the University of Zimbabwe during my research. The late and missed Kempton Makamure was instrumental in facilitating my initial research and in constantly providing provocative insight and enthusiasm. Lloyd Sachikonye, Kwanele Jirira and, especially, Brian Raftopoulos have also provided much assistance and a broader context in which to situate my research. Rene Loewenson, Godfrey Magaramombe, Dede Amanor-Wilks and Sam Moyo have shared their vast knowledge, experience and scholarly resources, helping to shape my interpretations in many ways. Government officials in Hurungwe, Harare, and Mashonaland East have all been welcoming and helpful in dealing with my inquiries and requests. Friends such as Susan Wilkinson, Isaac Maposa, Alan Brewis and Anderson Mutemererwa constantly provided support and helpful suggestions whenever I found myself in Harare. I want to thank Victor Jagi, Phineas Jundukwa, Felistus Makama and Tichaona Mudzikitiri for assisting with my survey in 1993 and Ingrid Mukondwa for helping me in interviewing people in 1999 and 2000. I am especially grateful to Rinse Nyamuda for all the assistance, friendship and interpretations he has given me since 1992.

In North America, both McGill University and the University of Regina have supported me in carrying out different phases of this research. The Social Sciences and Humanities Research Council of Canada has generously provided most of the financial support for my research and I hope that this book helps to demonstrate the importance of continuing to fund individual social science and humanities research projects by Canadian scholars. Many, many scholars here and in Europe have also been influential in my thinking. To be brutally brief, let me just note the contributory roles played by John Galaty, Jim Faris, Udo Krautwurst, Jocelyn Alexander, Bill Derman and Donald Moore. Eric Worby deserves special mention as he has guided so much of my research and understandings with his friendship, advice and writings.

I have received tremendous support from my publishers. Dick Werbner has been a strong advocate on my behalf and a critical and constructive editor. Robert Molteno, Louise Murray, and Farouk Sohawon have helped to nurture my book in London while Murray McCartney and Irene Staunton in Harare have provided much assistance in copy-editing and in making more substantive comments.

I also want to note my gratitude to Mike Chimba, one of the first farm workers to befriend me and to show real enthusiasm for my research. His keenness, particularly to read any book to come out of my research, helped to motivate me to publish this book. Tragically, he died in the mid-1990s, a victim of malaria and/or witchcraft, a victim of the dangers facing so many farm workers who live on the margins of an increasingly deteriorating health care system and within the constant tensions of power in their lives. Finally, I am indebted to my parents, Al and Wanda Rutherford, my sister, Kate, and her family, my in-laws, Robert and Ann Farquharson, and especially my wife, Laura Farquharson, and our children, Clara and Ry, for their immeasurable and innumerable forms of support, indulgence, and insight.

Chapter 1

Re-presenting commercial farm workers in Zimbabwe

The margins of rural Zimbabwe

A narrative: North-west along the main highway from Harare to Karoi during the wet season stretch expansive fields of tobacco and maize, intermixed with lush green pastures for cattle and, occasionally, (farmed) wildlife. Driving past these predominantly white-owned commercial farms gives a fleeting impression of farm workers, black men, women and children dressed in overalls or torn clothes working in the fields; or one may glimpse their homes on the farms, rows of small brick houses on the 'better' farms or, more typically, poorly constructed mud and grass houses packed into a small, barren area. These farm workers, comprising nearly a fifth of the total population, are the people whose labour sustains the commercial farming sector as the backbone of the Zimbabwean economy. Yet they are also the people who work and live in generally poor conditions and about whom little is known, 'forgotten' by the wider society...

This introduction is typical of a common genre for discussing farm workers in Zimbabwe in the 1990s. The growing number of reports, mainly written by members of non-governmental organizations (NGOs), have all drawn attention to the farm workers' general 'lack' of development. The reader is carried into the very visible contradictions of commercial agriculture in Zimbabwe and given, both literally and figuratively, a point of view on its social landscape (e.g. Mugwetsi and Balleis 1994, McIvor 1995). This viewpoint portrays farm workers as being hidden away, living in the margins of Zimbabwe. Accordingly, such reports reveal *who the farm workers are*, typically in terms of their working and living conditions, the history of the political economy of commercial agriculture, and the need for assistance by NGO development programmes, government-provided social services, and increased trade union activities.

These reports represent a new-found interest in farm workers. The University of Rhodesia economist Duncan Clarke wrote a groundbreaking book in 1977 for the then fledgling Catholic Commission for Justice and Peace, a few articles about workers' public health appeared during the 1980s, and Rene Loewenson (1992) wrote about the political economy of farm workers globally and in Zimbabwe. Otherwise, farm workers in Zimbabwe were generally ignored by social scientists and policy-makers. In the 1990s NGOs and even government officials and ministers have had a growing interest in farm workers' conditions. Not only are more NGO programmes directed towards farm workers, but the NGOs are also trying to establish various self-run structures to help farm workers negotiate with farmers over social development issues. Moreover, advocacy on the workers' behalf by the main trade union and NGOs has increased. These initiatives have resulted in farm workers recently (late 1997) receiving the franchise in local government elections and – in a dramatic *volte-face* – in government ministers and official policies on land redistribution recognizing farm workers as entitled to benefit from the land resettlement exercise which will redistribute land from white to black Zimbabweans.

This book contributes to the growing interest in farm workers and also problematizes that new-found visibility. The points of view bringing farm workers to light, so to speak, have perspectives that need to be situated in wider forms of power and discursive authority. More importantly, the same is true for farm workers themselves who have been working in the social, economic, and political margins; it is necessary to unpack both the discursive means and the political and economic processes by which they have been marginalized. We have to understand the conditions of farm workers but even more we have to understand the dominant and specific forms of thought and power which enmesh them on the farms and in broader policy and administrative structures. Their economic, political and social conditions have been well documented (e.g. Loewenson 1992, Mugwetsi and Balleis 1994, Amanor-Wilks 1995). By contrast, little is known of how they have been 'imagined' (cf. Ranger 1993b) in official discourses and how this has affected both their material conditions and their daily activities and struggles.

Before making farm workers in Zimbabwe visible, letting them 'speak', I want to give some necessary background. This situates how they have been thought about by wider powers and what are the politics and positioning of those, including myself, representing farm workers in the political economy of discourse. Here I follow Foucault. Whereas Marx taught us to recognize the weight of history on the minds of the living (e.g. Marx 1987; see Roseberry 1991), Foucault urged us to attend to how that history is thought and taught, to question how subjectivities and identities are inscribed into our understanding of particular domains and groups (e.g. Foucault 1983).

Commercial farm workers in Zimbabwe have largely been imagined through a dualistic space, now called commercial farms and Communal Lands. This divide *is* rural Zimbabwe for many policy-makers, development experts and academics. The colonial-era legal distinction between a private, freehold-property zone reserved for 'European' ownership and occupation and an amalgam of customary and state-controlled property areas for 'Natives' has continued to inform divisions between these two entities in official discourses of postcolonial Zimbabwe. Both sides of this divide in rural Zimbabwe are attributed to, and the divide itself enforces, what may be called a 'spatial order of things' (Pigg 1992, Malkki 1995). The predominantly white-owned large-scale commercial farms and the African occupied Communal Land smallholder farms are commonly thought of as operating and existing in two different spaces. These are contrastingly defined by the teleological terms Modern/Traditional or Developed/ Un(der)developed which, in turn, blend into the social identities of '(white) commercial farmer' and 'African peasant'. Although up to a fifth of the commercial farmers are now black (and their reputation amongst farm workers in terms of living and working conditions is often worse than that of the white farmers[1]), the sector is still largely thought of as being 'white' by national and international policy-makers, farm workers, commercial farmers, and other Zimbabweans. It is on these identities that official commentators and decision-makers have anchored their analyses, administrative structures, and development interventions within rural Zimbabwe.

Over three hundred thousand farm workers and nearly two million people live and work on Zimbabwe's commercial farms. By having a liminal identity within the entrenched official imagination of Zimbabwe – they are neither white farmers nor African peasants – farm workers

---

[1]   See, for example, comments by the representatives of the farm workers' trade union in "Black farmers sack 200,000 labourers." *Financial Gazette* February 6, 1992.

have been marginalized from development policies, political rights, and social programmes: being rural Africans living outside of Communal Lands, they have had limited access to government schools and clinics; not being property owners, they were unable to vote in local government elections until 1998; and working for rural rather than urban industries, their working conditions were the least regulated in formal employment sector (Herbst 1990, Loewenson 1992, Amanor-Wilks 1995). This book is about these people working in the margins, how they have been marginalized, and how they work against the processes of marginalization.

Working on the margins: methodological considerations

Through archival and ethnographic research in Hurungwe District, part of the 'tobacco belt' of northern Mashonaland, I learned about the lives of people working in the margins.[2] In 1992-93, I spent a year living on a tobacco farm in Hurungwe. I talked with men while they reaped tobacco under the eyes of foremen, picked coffee alongside unmarried women with children strapped to their backs, chatted with families after work in their pole and mud houses in the farm compound, interviewed farm operators in their family rooms, discussed policies with government officials in their offices, talked with my research assistant, Rinse Nyamuda, and carried out other planned and incidental activities over a year on what I call Chidhadhadha farm and surrounding commercial farms and Communal Lands. From this, I gained an understanding of how the dual space produced within official discourses has marginalized commercial farm workers and, at the same time, how these farm workers, differentiated by gender, job type, and marital status, subvert, transgress, and take advantage of this spatial order of things.[3]

For farm workers, working in the margins does not mean being unable to negotiate, struggle, or parlay (see Moodie 1994). What it does mean is that there are dominant discourses and power relations which script their identities and life trajectories and make it difficult for others to acknowledge, let alone work with, such actions. For

---

[2]   I gratefully thank the Social Sciences and Humanities Research Council of Canada as well as the Social Sciences Grants Sub-Committee and the Centre for Society, Technology and Development of McGill University for funding to carry out this research in 1992-93. A standard research grant from the Social Sciences and Humanities Research Council of Canada has also enabled me to carry out further research in Zimbabwe starting in 1998.

[3]   From 1998-2000, I returned to Zimbabwe three times to carry out research on 'civil society' organizations working with farm workers in Mashonaland East province. During each visit, I briefly returned to Chidhadhadha farm.

researchers like myself, working on the margins entails attending to the ways the marginalizing processes and discourses also shape the research process itself (e.g. Tsing 1993, Torres 1997).

Having a pigmentation which usually falls under the category of 'white',[4] it was often assumed, by both workers and farmers, that I would identify with the white farmers. Many workers on Chidhadhadha farm thought, even by the end of my stay, that I was training to be a commercial farmer,[5] even though I was taking more of an interest in their lives than other white farmers and trainees they had known. In turn, many white farmers I met assumed I would share their outlook on the world, which they broadly defined as 'modern', although some also presumed (and worried) that I would have a more liberal attitude towards 'race' relations (read 'black versus white') than them, given that I was born and raised in Canada.

To carry out my research amongst farm workers, I initially relied heavily on Rinse to be a broker for me, partly because of my linguistic limits at that time, but also due to the assumption held by many workers that I was working for the *varungu* (Europeans, farmers, bosses). I, and Rinse in a more articulate manner, would try to assuage their fears and discuss my association with the University of Zimbabwe and stress that I was not working for the farmers. For many, however, particularly the older workers who may have spent their entire lives on farms working for white people, that meant very little. I thus rarely taped or took notes during these early meetings, relying on Rinse's interpretation of responses. As my chiShona fluency improved, I talked with workers as they undertook their daily activities and wrote notes afterwards. I used a tape recorder only during formal interviews, which were translated and transcribed by Rinse. Unless otherwise stated, most of the quotations in the text are reconstructed from my field notes. Throughout the remainder of the book, I comment more reflectively about the research process and its link to my analysis.

---

[4]   The adjectives 'white' and 'black' are commonly used in Africa to denote people whose ancestry lies in Europe or sub-Saharan Africa respectively. There is a tendency in academic literature to treat these labels as more 'natural' indices of human differences (i.e. of phenotypical variation) than, say, biological 'races' and thus somehow not culturally constructed (Wade 1993). Although I will not place quotation marks around these terms in the remainder of the text, I want to stress that this does not mean that they are somehow outside of culture any more than the terms 'European' and 'African'.

[5]   There is a common practice of white farmers sending sons to neighbouring farms to work as managers in order to learn about running a commercial farm, including dealing with labour issues (Von Blackenburg 1994).

Betwixt and between: commercial farm workers and rural development

Throughout the book, I will tack back and forth between dominant assumptions of farm workers in Zimbabwe, the ways in which they have been imagined in the nation of Zimbabwe through the media, policy documents, and even in conversations with non-farm working Zimbabweans, and my interpretations of fieldwork, the ethnographic examinations, explanations and descriptions of the 'locale' in Hurungwe district. A significant way in which farm workers have been understood in the administration of, and belonging to, the nation has been through official discourses of rural development. Before summarizing these, I will indicate some of the limitations of the dominant assumptions by describing a few of the farm workers I knew in 1992-93 (and will discuss periodically later) and their strategies for improvement.

John was a junior foreman in his early thirties. He had been working at Chidhadhadha farm – where I conducted most of my research – for five years, moving up the ranks with the help of his friend George, the senior foreman. Much of his salary went to cover the living expenses of himself, his wife, three young daughters, his mother and a sister. But he also invested some in buying goods from Kariba and Zambia (where his deceased father was born), for resale in the surrounding farms in Hurungwe and in Harare. He also was actively seeking to get a *musha*, a piece of land in the neighbouring Mukwichi Communal Lands. He hoped that once he secured a *musha* he, like other 'big workers' on the farm, would be able to get interest-free loans and cheap agricultural inputs from the owners of Chidhadhadha to invest in both subsistence crops and cash crops. Although the white farm owners were wary about lending too much, given their own cash flow problems, they also felt it their duty to help out some of the workers who showed promise and were loyal, as a way to help develop Africans more broadly. According to John's planning, a *musha* would provide many benefits: a home for his mother who no longer wanted to work on a commercial farm; food he would not need to purchase; and more income for his family. Although his wife, who like him spent her entire life on commercial farms, was not too enthusiastic about moving to a *musha* during the rainy season to help out with the farming, he was sure that he could convince her, especially as he could hire someone in Mukwichi to help out once he started to get more income from the farming.

Mai Chido, a single mother in her forties, had also been working on the farm for five years and had already acquired a field in Mukwichi. She and the three of her four children who lived with her on Chidhadhadha (in quarters reserved for single women workers) went to their land on weekends and occasional evenings to weed and harvest. Although her yield of maize was not large, it was an important supplement to their diet for she had access to even fewer resources than male general workers. According to the rules of the farm (which were common on many commercial farms), women could not be permanent workers (except in domestic work) and as she was unattached to a male permanent worker she lived in poor housing, and had difficulty in getting loans or subsidized maize-meal from the farm owners. She was anxiously trying to find more land for herself and her family in the hopes that she could eventually leave commercial farms for good and live full-time on a *musha*.

This is exactly the strategy of Chimpeto, a farm worker who was in his late fifties or early sixties. After coming to Southern Rhodesia in the early 1960s from Tete province in Mozambique, he had worked on several commercial farms. In late 1992 he retired to live full-time with his wife and some of his children and grand-children on a *musha* in Dunga, an area of state land that had been slowly incorporated into the administration of Mukwichi Communal Land during the 1980s. Ever since he found the *musha* in the early 1980s, he had his wife had grown maize and groundnuts for their own consumption, and kept goats; the *musha* acted as a place of retirement for him and a base for his children between their jobs on the surrounding commercial farms.

Mai Coni came from Hurungwe Communal Land, where she was born, in 1992. She was nearly twenty and had a baby daughter, Coni. Following a dispute with the baby's father she came as a single mother to stay with a friend on Chidhadhadha and work in the coffee fields, which provided her with some money to buy food and soap. She moved in with a young man who was working on the farm, thereby gaining more living space and access to his income. They were young, and their horizons were limited to working on commercial farms.

These strategies for improvement were clearly shaped by the social contours and power relations on commercial farms regarding gender, class, age, race, marital status and job rank. They also were intimately involved with events and activities in the nearby

7

Communal Land. This presents some difficulty for the dominant way policy-makers and other commentators have imagined farm workers in terms of rural development, predicated as it is on a sharp division between commercial farms and Communal Lands.

The bifurcated space that constitutes rural Zimbabwe in many policy and academic studies takes the form of a 'dual economy' in which neo-liberals and political economists tend to anchor their analyses and prescriptions. Neo-liberals divide rural Zimbabwe into traditional, subsistence-oriented peasant areas and modern cash-oriented commercial farms. If mentioned at all in these celebrations of commercial agriculture (which, in these writings, epitomizes praiseworthy modernity), farm workers are viewed largely as beneficiaries of paid employment, although the impression is given that this is a temporary affair as commercial farms will mechanize and more rural workers will be absorbed into the urban labour market (e.g. World Bank 1981, Muir et al 1982, Ranney 1985, von Blackenburg 1994, Muir 1994). Political economists distinguish between the capitalist sector, including commercial farms, and the pre-capitalist sector, embracing underdeveloped peasant areas *cum* labour reserves where pre-colonial social relations function to underwrite the low-wage reproduction of African labour. Farm workers are viewed as super-exploited by settlers/farmers, as people who are denied the chance to become full-time peasants themselves (e.g. Arrighi 1967, Bush and Cliffe 1984, Weiner et al 1985, Weiner 1988). The dual economy model not only explains rural Zimbabwe but carries within it a prescription for its future development: Africans will 'modernize' by becoming either full-time workers in the capitalist sector, or self-sufficient peasants enjoying government support and land redistributed from the commercial farms. In short, farm workers will progress by becoming what they are not: urban workers or full-time peasants.

Within these dominant narratives, there is a fundamental contrast between 'commercial farmers' and 'African peasants.' The former are characterized as completely dependent on capitalist relations and norms, and as epitomizing the 'modern' economy (evaluated either positively or negatively, depending on the perspective of the commentator). The latter are seen either as evolving capitalist farmers or as productive farmers stymied by colonial land policies.

Commercial farm workers do not easily fit into this 'modern-traditional' duality. Although their work falls within the modern, 'commercial' economy, they themselves are not completely part of it. They share the 'rural' with 'peasant farmers' but, at least according to the parameters of official discourse, they are not quite as integrated into the 'modern' economy as are urban African wage-earners and proletariat. They earn wages but they also live in the countryside (e.g. Muir et al 1982). Through their location on commercial farms and thus being both rural and not rural, modern and traditional, commercial farm workers have until recently been largely ignored in discussions of development and policy.[6]

In this sense, farm workers have been 'betwixt and between' in rural development discourses. I use this metaphor in several ways. In terms of the commonsense notion of a triadic comparison, commercial farm workers are neither Communal Land 'peasants' nor urban 'workers' so they fall 'betwixt and between' this dichotomizing development discourse, and are placed on the margins of the power relations that emerged in the administration of development during the colonial period.

I use 'betwixt and between' deliberately, and perhaps ironically, to echo Victor Turner's usage of 'rites of passage.' Expanding on the work of Van Gennep (1909), Turner (1979 [1964], 1967) focuses on the transformative power of transition, via rites of passage, from one state to another. The climactic moment for this power, according to Turner, is the 'liminal' (or 'marginal') stage, at which the subject is suspended between the old state and the new. These initiates are 'betwixt and between' – '[t]hey are at once no longer classified and not yet classified' (1979:236) – and thus are viewed as dissolving their old culturally ascribed state and acquiring a new one. Like other ambiguous categories, the 'betwixt and between' state is surrounded by strong sentiments of marginalization (such as taboo and pollution) as it challenges the normalcy of the categories from which it is in transition. But, according to the temporal and teleological logic of the rite of passage, its danger and potency is fleeting. Liminal status is merely a stage in a process from one state to the next.

In my use, 'betwixt and between' refers to this notion of liminality of farm workers in official discourse – they are no longer 'African peasants' nor are they yet 'African workers'. They do not fit the

---

6   This is seen in the government's cursory treatment of farm workers in their Second Five-Year National Development Plan, 1991-1995 (Zimbabwe 1991a) and their neglect of health care reform (Herbst 1990). Rene Loewenson has been the sole consistent commentator who has discussed farm workers in newspapers, articles, and in a book (e.g. 1986, 1988, 1992).

dominant narratives of modernization that place 'peasants' as the anchor of rural Africa and 'workers' as the foundation of urban capitalism. Farm workers have thus been marginal, penumbral to most official discourse on 'development'.[7] At the same time, I want to challenge the assumption that some transformative action is taking place; that 'farm workers' will become truly 'modern' in either the liberal or socialist sense; that they will become true proletarians or authentic peasants. For me, such transformative claims help to marginalize farm workers by steering official inquiries into the dynamics of 'development' along the framework of a dual economy discourse and by ignoring the conditions of 'farm workers' as historically and discursively situated, including through this dual economy narrative itself.[8] Although farm workers have been understood through this narrative as either benefiting from the money and exposure to modernity offered by commercial farms, or as being (super-)exploited and denied the right to become peasants, no one has examined how it helps to shape particular power relations, forms of administration, and policies.

This marginalization, this liminal status, of farm workers is not simply due to less inclusive categorization within official discourses. Rather, I am going to argue, it is the effect of the particular form of 'government', in Michel Foucault's sense, that postcolonial Zimbabwe inherited from (Southern) Rhodesia. This, in turn, is related to the power relations that are constitutive of most other development projects and state formation in Africa and in the South (Mitchell 1988, Ferguson 1990a, Manicom 1992, Escobar 1995, Werbner 1999). The power relations that constitute this governmentality are themselves dependent on particular spatial distinctions, or what Stacey Pigg (1992) calls 'social territories,' and what Gupta and Ferguson term an 'identity as place.' As Gupta and Ferguson explain, 'the identity of a place emerges by the intersection of its specific involvement in a system of hierarchically organized spaces with its cultural construction as a community or locality' (Gupta and Ferguson 1992:8). For someone who wants to critically understand the situation of farm workers, the question then becomes: how does one engage with such a social territory to challenge some of its hierarchies?

---

[7]   For similar discussion of 'peasants', see Ennew et al 1977, Roseberry 1989, Trouillot 1989, and of 'workers', Ferguson 1990b, 1999, Cooper 1992, 1996.

[8]   This is not to say that if only 'official discourse' investigates farm workers as farm workers 'really are', their conditions will improve. Changing vocabularies is key for alternative ways to approach situations but this does not automatically change situations, *contra* rationalist assumptions that the proper words, often epistemologically guaranteed, will lead to the proper results (see Sloterdijk 1987).

Postcolonial critique: towards a political ethnography

Commercial farm workers in Zimbabwe are ineluctably tied to official discourses, both as a historical consequence and as contemporary reality. Interpretative practices, dominant in policy, media and academic institutions, help to sustain the conditions which keep commercial farm workers relatively disempowered. These official discourses provide the identities, based on an amalgam of race, gender, and evolution, that inform decisions, attitudes and practices contributing to the marginalization of commercial farm workers.

But these official identities are *not* the same as the distinctions of identity that pervade daily life on commercial farms. Although official identities strongly shape local distinctions and contestations, they are also shaped by local practices. An important point made by postcolonial writings on Africa is that the official identities, while imposing powerful fictions, are constantly transformed, subverted, and played with by Africans in their everyday lives (e.g. Cohen and Odhiambo 1989, Mbembe 1992, Ranger 1993b, Hecht and Simone 1994, Werbner 1996).

Local discourses are, for me, neither completely independent of official discourses nor identical with them. 'Local' distinctions and arrangements are not mere reflections of larger forces and narratives, but they are often shaped by these wider discourses, including my own (Tsing 1993). In fact, the 'local' takes on its meaning here specifically through my representation. As recent critiques of ethnography have suggested, the understanding of 'the local' field in ethnographic writing is very much shaped by the rhetorical mechanisms and theoretical presumptions of the genre (Fabian 1983, Clifford 1986, 1988, Tyler 1987, Thomas 1991, Gupta and Ferguson 1992). Accordingly, 'local discourses' refers to the understandings and knowledge which I learned about in the encounters, meetings and events that comprised my 'field research' in Zimbabwe. By attending to the varied and often contradictory responses and activities of my field-site, I reject a familiar usage that privileges the 'local' as some repository for homogeneous knowledge, politics, or morality, as the resisting opposite of what is taken as the homogeneous and hegemonic, official, extra-local force.[9]

---

[9]   For example, Dorothy Smith (1990) essentializes 'woman's standpoint' in the everyday world in contrast to male, extra-local relations of ruling; Michael Taussig's (1992) writings on the 'Nervous System' occasionally proffer a different form of embodied cognition as a base for understanding capitalist poetics; Stephen Tyler's (1987) critique of the anthropological project offers a therapeutic immersion in 'commonsense reality' as an alternative. For an astute critique of such rhetorical strategies in explaining 'local' knowledges in non-Western places, see Tsing (1993).

'Official discourses' refers to the overlapping knowledges and practices that implement and shape policies, interventions and representations in socially powerful institutions: 'official' because the knowledges and opinions are mutually constituted of institutional networks of power and control (e.g. bureaucracies, academia, hospitals); 'discourse' because the distinctions of meaning are taken seriously. Understandings and actions are not explainable through some underlying or separate sociological or psychological 'structure'. These modern 'relations of ruling,' resting on both textual and metaphysical means, have more capacity to control, impinge on, and conduct actions of others than do 'local' discourses (Mitchell 1988, Smith 1990).

'Official discourses' are intimately linked to what Michel Foucault has called 'government', the institutional and discursive prescription and restriction of certain fields of action. Foucault employs an older notion of government which not only covered 'the legitimately constituted forms of political or economic subjection, but also modes of action, more or less considered and calculated, destined to act upon the possibilities of action of other people. To govern, in this sense, is to structure the possible field of action of others' (Foucault 1983:221). Government, for Foucault, has been intimately connected to 'the state' in Europe since the eighteenth century. This is not to say that power relations, the capacity of 'acting upon an acting subject or acting subjects by virtue of their acting or being capable of action' (1983:220), derive from the state. Rather, the diverse networks of power 'have been progressively governmentalized, that is to say, elaborated, rationalized, and centralized in the form of, or under the auspices of, state institutions.' (1983:224; see also Hindess 1996).

I approach both official and local discourses, and the distinction between them, by valorizing 'politics' over 'epistemology' (Hirst 1979). In my usage, 'politics' is more akin to potentially effective opinion. It is close to Michael Oakeshott's definition of 'politics' as an activity that, within the (hegemonic) traditions of behaviour for a community, attends and amends general social arrangements. These arrangements compose a pattern and at the same time they intimate a sympathy for what does not fully appear. Political activity is the exploration of that sympathy; and consequently, relevant political reasoning will be the convincing exposure of a sympathy, present but not yet followed up, and the convincing demonstration that now is the appropriate moment for recognizing it (1962:124; quoted in Mouffe 1993:16).

My politics challenge those arrangements of official discourses that lead to the marginalization and disempowerment of Zimbabwean farm workers. For 'local discourses,' I argue that they help form particular localized arrangements, informed by official discourses, that have particular consequences in terms of farm workers' access to resources (land, wages, housing, etc.). These are consequences that perhaps have not been assumed by other participants in these encounters. Yet, what I take to be consequences are provisional, open to (political) argument, and not anchored to an underlying structure (guaranteed by some epistemology) which, if grabbed, will lead to a form of empowerment (Faris 1992). Instead, I provide a narrative that attempts to provoke the reader into thinking about altering particular 'arrangements', in Oakeshott's sense. I want to challenge some of the meanings and arrangements, not in a way that doubts their veracity but by assigning consequences to them. This is not an identification with either official or local discourses, but a point of view on them, an invitation to debate. It strives to be a form of responsible criticism, as Talal Asad has termed it, "a point of view, a (contra) version, having only provisional and limited authority" (1986:157; see, also, Scott 1999). My writing is provisionally authorized criticism, not a universal declaration of empowerment.

Many others have publicly declared what farm workers *should* be doing based on their determination of what is in their best interest: for the longest time, these others have been white farmers, but they now also include black commercial farmers, trade unions, NGOs and – as the violence towards farm workers by the ruling party and its surrogates during the build-up to the parliamentary elections in June 2000 has shown – political parties. My aim is to critically situate some of these forms of representation, and review their effects on the lives of different farm workers. Rather than dismissing them out of hand I will suggest that they have both limits and adverse consequences regarding the possibilities for farm workers to improve their lives in the manner they intend.

****

In the next chapter, I argue that colonial jural distinctions of land tenure based differences of race and class began to mark very different forms of administration and power for 'European farms' and 'native reserves.' Through these state policies and power relations, the spaces of land tenure have become saturated with

13

racial, gendered, and sociologized identities; identities that, when infused with the administrative categories of 'population' and 'citizenship,' have constituted different forms of control; indeed, they have taken on lives of their own as political and social subjectivities in official discourses. Such identities become jural identities: differentiated politics, procedures of surveillance, and hierarchical relations emerged through the figures of the 'rural African cultivator' and 'the European farmer.'

From the 1940s onwards, a 'development apparatus' (Ferguson 1990a) emerged nationally and internationally for the modernization of the African figure, while a 'democratic' apparatus emerged for the already 'modern' European figure. Farm workers fell into a system of administration that was largely outside the scope of the state. Save for the concern about labour supply, and a periodic and unsustained interest in productivity, 'farm workers' were viewed less as a government responsibility and more as a domestic responsibility of European farmers themselves. It is a responsibility that depended on a gendered and racial depiction of white and black households which underpins what I shall call the 'domestic government' of commercial farms. The government is 'domestic' in two senses: by officially promoting the 'private' over 'public' domain – the rule of the farmer over that of state officials – and by administratively valuing paternalistic relations between male workers and their families and between farmers and 'their' workers. This is not to say that farm workers were outside the colonial government's sphere of influence; rather, that domestic government has been part and parcel of the colonial and postcolonial governments' modernizing projects, but through a mode quite different from that experienced by those identified as 'peasant farmers.'

In the remaining chapters, I problematize local discourses in the part of Hurungwe District where I conducted my research. My guiding question is: how do the social distinctions and arrangements on the farms respond to, replicate, resist, and transgress the hierarchy of jural identities within the domestic government of commercial farms? I show how such distinctions differentially affect access to and struggles over resources for farm workers such as wages, housing, credit, food, agricultural means of production, and land. I explore the binding and the fraying – the forms of regulation, the opportunities provided, and the precipitated dialogues – within this intersection of official and local discourses, by dividing the chapters thematically around sites which tend to compel particular assumptions about Zimbabwean farm workers within both official and local discourses.

In Chapter Three, I discuss the production of a 'European identity' on commercial farms in Hurungwe through the cultural inscription of particular spatial boundaries and the telling of certain histories and stories. The social architecture and the discourses about 'being European' produce and sustain the notion that farm workers are the domestic responsibility of white farmers, who in turn become the bearers of modernity on commercial farms.

The next three chapters examine the forms of supervision, discipline and rewards of (socially differentiated) farm workers which derive from these notions of domestic responsibility. Chapter Four sketches out the entailments, distinctions, and antagonistic relations that comprise the 'management' *cum* governmental practices of permanent farm workers, who are predominantly black men. In the following two chapters, I show the very different pressures and opportunities women farm workers face. Chapter Five argues that domestic government marginalizes women in general, and single women in particular, from resources on commercial farms available to men farm workers. Turning to the farm compound, in Chapter Six, I look at the ways in which the social spaces create both common identities for certain farm workers, such as 'women farm workers,' and differences within these identities, such as married versus single women. The crucial features of the arrangement of domestic government on commercial farms are shown to be the giving and receiving of credit. The various entailments of marriage, a strong marker of the domesticity and family life of which the compound is supposed to house, are also investigated.

Chapter Seven examines how the boundaries of the bifurcated space resonate with local practices, primarily among farm workers who are also farmers in Mukwichi Communal Land, particularly in Dunga. This final ethnographic chapter examines how such people threaten the identities that help to constitute development in rural Zimbabwe.

In each ethnographic chapter, I present a critique of the various modernist discourses informing the power relations of social territories which locate Zimbabwean farm workers. I do so by pointing to changes within the local discourses and thus I aim to unsettle conventional assumptions about farm workers, modernization, and development in Zimbabwe; assumptions which help to produce the sites in which power operates.

Without a critical understanding of these relations of rule, and of the way lives are shaped within commercial farms, the recent interventions by Zimbabwean and international development professionals with the aim of helping 'farm workers' may, however inadvertently, reinforce current power relations. A reflexive examination of the enduring discursive frames for understanding farm workers and how they have shaped the forms of government on commercial farms may lead to other tactics and strategies for challenging arrangements on commercial farms. I return to this deeper issue in chapter eight.

Throughout the book, I argue that these sites of the spatial order of things are not naturalized entities but are identities produced by an intersection of local and official discourses. Hence, as identities of place, they can be engaged and unsettled. More broadly, I seek to challenge some of the arrangements of power informing the situation of Zimbabwean commercial farm workers through provisional, not epistemological, critique.

Chapter 2

Situating farm workers in Hurungwe: development and the administrative space of (European) commercial farms, 1940s-1990s

Urungwe and colonial state formation – 1940s

On October 2, 1940, Mr T. de Beer, a Southern Rhodesian government land inspector, wrote a memo to his superior describing the farms he had just demarcated. After briefly talking about the progress he was making, he turned to more troubling topics: 'I am gravely concerned about the Native squatters spread over the areas described above... Certain timbered areas on the higher ridges have been cut in the usual native fashion and cultivated. Fresh river and ridge lands are being extended by these natives for the coming season.' Noting that he had raised this issue before in other reports, he concluded with a directed plea:

> I have no authority to stop the present Native squatters from
> opening up new land before my eyes, land which I know to
> be valuable seed bed sites and excellent tobacco soil. I would
> therefore ask if a very early decision can be arrived at for the
> timely removal of natives at least from 'K' farms 1 to 12 and
> the adjoining area marked in red [on an accompanying map]
> before the Natives hoe and sow their crops.[1]

The 'K' farms refer to the Karoi-block of farms in the north-western part of the colony, which at that time was part of the sub-

---

[1] S2588, Native Squatters on Crown Land: Lomagundi District: 'K' farms, Assistant Chief Native Commissioner to Native Commissioner, Lomagundi, October 15, 1941. Unless indicated otherwise, all archival sources refer to the Zimbabwe National Archives. The other sources used here include 'MLGRUD', the Ministry of Local Government, Rural and Urban Government. 'MLGRUD' refers to the Ministry's Harare offices, though if specified as 'MLGRUD, *Karoi*', it refers to the Ministry's Hurungwe District offices.

district Urungwe within Lomagundi District.[2] These farms were being demarcated and, where possible, having boreholes drilled and some land stumped, with the aim of giving them to European soldiers returning from World War Two. The 'K' Block was the largest area being prepared by the Southern Rhodesian government for what was to become their Land Resettlement Scheme No. 1 for Rhodesian Ex-Servicemen.[3] The 'native squatters' whom de Beer complained about were subsequently removed by the Native Affairs Department's Assistant Native Commissioner in Urungwe and his 'native messengers' in 1942. This operation removed some 4,600 black farmers from their lands and placed them in Urungwe Reserve in the southern part of the district.[4]

Until these events, Urungwe was more known in the local colonial imagination for its hunting and tsetse fly.[5] When it became a separate District in 1944, it was home to about ten European farmers, considerably more European mica miners and approximately 19,000 Africans – 8,600 living in the Reserve, 8,000 living in unassigned land, and 2,200 on Crown Land (see Map 3).[6]

Before 1890, the year when the area came under direct administration of the British South African Company (BSAC) for the British Crown, people living on the Urungwe Plateau had been farming and engaged for centuries in various forms of mercantile trade and production (largely copper, ivory and gold) with Swahili, Portuguese, Munhumutapa and Changamire traders (Fagan 1969, White 1971, Lancaster and Pohorilenko 1977). In 1914-15, Urungwe Reserve was created in the southern part of the sub-district and 69 white settler farms were also demarcated.[7] Urungwe already contained a BSAC farm and another farm granted by Cecil Rhodes to one of the original pioneer settlers in the 1890s (Black 1976:72).

---

2   Shortly after Independence, 'Urungwe' District was changed to 'Hurungwe', its old district capital 'Miami' to 'Mwami', 'Lomagundi' District to 'Makonde' District, its district capital 'Sinoia' to 'Chinhoyi', and the capital city 'Salisbury' to 'Harare'. The colony was called 'Southern Rhodesia' until 1963 when it became 'Rhodesia'. In 1979, it was called 'Zimbabwe-Rhodesia' before becoming just 'Zimbabwe' in 1980. I will use the particular spellings for the time period I am discussing.

3   "S1194/190/28/1, Crown Land proposed for utilisation for post-war settlement, Memo from Under Secretary, Department of Lands to Secretary, Department of Agriculture and Lands, January 4, 1944.

4   S1563, Annual Report, Assistant Native Commissioner, Urungwe, 1942.

5   A map from a 1932 publication on European settlement described the north-western part of the colony which included Urungwe as an 'area rendered untenable [for European settlement] by the tsetse fly' (Darby 1932:193; see also White 1971, Edwards 1974, Black 1976).

6   S1563, Annual Report, Assistant Native Commissioner, Urungwe, 1944.

7   S2129, Report of the Unsurveyed Land NNW of Sinoia, between proposed Urungwe Native Reserve and Angwa River, June 29, 1914. See also Palmer (1977:259).

Most of these farms remained unsettled due largely to the presence of tsetse fly, poor transportation routes into the area, the relatively small size of the European population in the colony, and poor agricultural terms of trade for both maize and tobacco. Rather, European settlement in the area grew around the mica mines at Miami, the then administrative centre of Urungwe, and fluctuated with the global demand for the mineral.

By the early 1940s, tobacco had become an economically viable crop in the colony and the sandy loams that comprise the soil of the centre belt of Urungwe made it ideal for this crop. Tsetse control officials had been pushing back the fly to the major river valleys by killing much of the large game in the area. Southern Rhodesian politicians were expecting a considerable rise in European settlement after the end of World War Two and the 'K' Block was designated to become a new home for some of them. This policy quickly transformed all black farmers in this area into 'squatters' and shaped the geography of Urungwe through the identities that were crystallizing in the emerging relations of power during the 1940s.

Of course, these issues did not emerge in a vacuum: many strands and hints of what occurred in Southern Rhodesia during the 1940s were found in the practices of the earlier colonial state (Phimister 1988, Drinkwater 1991, Alexander 1993) as well as in other colonies (e.g. Feierman 1990, Cooper 1996, Mamdani 1996). But at the same time, as many officials themselves declared, the 1940s in Southern Rhodesia were the start of something different.[8] It was a time of political and economic expansion, both predicated on each other. While the Southern Rhodesian government and its civil servants began to give strong support to European industrial and agricultural activities in the name of national growth, they also extended the presence and coercive powers of the state administration into the lives of Africans in the name of 'native development'. As part and parcel of this expansion, particular forms of power consolidated and helped to form two very different rural spaces around the identities of 'native' and 'European'.

By the end of World War Two, substantial changes occurred within the government of Southern Rhodesia and the power relations associated with the state and other institutional bodies. Administratively, certain groups of Africans found themselves placed

---

[8]   An internal government report described the 'unique' Southern Rhodesian approach to 'native administration', following a path between putting 'native interests' paramount, as in the British colonies to the north, and the white supremacy in South Africa. S520, Survey of Native Policy in Southern Rhodesia, Internal Memorandum, 1950.

under greater state control in the name of the emerging field of 'development', whereas more and more Europeans played a greater role within the state through their own self-elected, representative organizations. The contrasting identities of 'European' and 'native' began not only to justify these political and administrative relations but they also started to privilege 'domestic' as opposed to 'public' procedures of labour relations on European farms. The forging of such relations become apparent in the 1940s and may be illustrated by examining the development of administrative relations in Hurungwe.

Below, I outline the crystallization of three spatially differentiated spheres of government activity in the 1940s: what may be called 'administrative development' of rural Africans, 'administrative politics' for Europeans, and 'domestic government' of farm workers, with a specific focus on Hurungwe District. I then trace how these spatial forms of power have provided enduring frames of reference for institutional arrangements up to the early 1990s.

I emphasize here the weight of official discourses and spatialized power relations at the district and national levels and some of the resulting institutional arrangements regarding administrative relations and politics rather than detailing the events, individuals and conjunctures that shaped them. The formation of these spaces and identities in official discourses did not result from a simple singular agent such as the homogenous 'state', but was the result of various differentiated, overlapping, and competing projects by various government departments, international agents, and organized groups and individuals (see, e.g., Murray 1970, Phimister 1988, McKenzie 1989, Drinkwater 1991, Alexander 1993). Moreover, the meaning and boundaries have never been fixed in and of themselves. Rather, they are contested and retooled by various social forces and projects (see, e.g., Worby and Rutherford 1997, Moore 1998, Worby 1998, Hirsch 1998). Despite such contestation, these discursive spaces do have a stable presence, situated within particular institutional arrangements, social processes, and dominant assumptions (Mitchell 1991). It is the formation of these enduring discursive frames of the relations of rule regarding farm workers which I outline in this chapter, only touching on some of the important events, groups and individuals which helped to shape them. In the remainder of the book, I discuss how they have shaped and have been shaped by the actions of those I met during my fieldwork.

'Administrative development' for Africans in reserves

In 1944, the Assistant Native Commissioner, Urungwe, held his first agricultural meeting with African farmers in Urungwe Reserve. There were only eight 'plotholders'[9] present at the meeting, indicating for the government official the backwardness of the district: 'it will take a couple of seasons for results to react favourably on the minds of those who still think that the old method of hand tillage and the higgledy-piggedly manner of cultivation is good enough.'[10]

Undeterred by this lack of 'rational' order, the head government official in charge of 'natives' in Urungwe arranged for the start of cattle sales, and agitated for more clinics and, especially, more missionaries to improve the 'morals' of the Africans. Over the next few years, the number of Native Affairs department technical officers increased as Urungwe Reserve began to be 'planned' according to 'proper' development standards, whilst more weirs and dams were built allowing a greater concentration of Africans in the reserve. By 1947, the same official commented on the great strides taken by listing, as material evidence of progress, the number of agricultural implements present – 250 ploughs, 16 cultivators, a few scotch carts – and the increasing number of 'development' staff whose 'value to the fast awakening Reserve natives is of inestimable worth and it is a joy to see the development of the Reserve taking shape and the signs of growing prosperity in the lives of many, who until a few years ago, were indigent, ignorant and without purpose.'[11] The euphoria of conversion through the secular power of development had reached Urungwe.

Until the 1940s, government officials disregarded the sub-district in its first 'development' effort: land centralization promoted by the American missionary turned Native Affairs department official, E.D. Alvord, as a solution not only for 'civilizing' Africans but also for improving agricultural productivity and stopping erosion on Native Reserves (see Drinkwater 1989, 1991, Alexander 1993). As the Native Commissioner, Lomagundi, wrote in respect of Urungwe and Sipolilo sub-districts in 1934, 'I am personally of the opinion that [native agricultural] demonstrators in those remote places are not necessary or required at the present time.'[12] But the 1940s saw a significant shift of that assessment, given that Urungwe was the site of rapid expansion of European settlement and that 'native development' was

---

[9] This was the second highest rung of the four stages that the Native Affairs Department used to mark the modernising 'development' of African cultivators.
[10] S1563, Annual Report, Assistant Native Commissioner, Urungwe, 1944.
[11] S1563, Annual Report, Assistant Native Commissioner, Urungwe, 1947.
[12] S1563, Annual Report, Native Commissioner, Lomagundi, 1934.

now being promoted actively as an important component of government policy and (colonial) nation-building.

In the 1940s, 'natives' were also becoming more of a concern for colonial administrations and governments throughout Africa. There were increased demands by war-ravaged, metropole governments for more efficient production in their colonies and more frequent political claims to self-determination by African leaders, including more widespread labour disputes on the continent. In addition, a greater emphasis by colonial administrators and international organisations such as the International Labour Organisation on the edifying mission of Europeans, shaped a growing concern for establishing an order of stable urban-working and rural-farming communities of Africans (Cooper 1989:752ff, 1996).

Relations between the colonising and colonised countries began to be defined through the paradigm of 'development', as the International Monetary Fund and the World Bank targeted the newly defined 'Less Developed Countries' with money and plans. Their objectives were to try to mimic European success in such countries through planned industrialization and opening up markets for northern industries, while trying to prevent communism from taking root in impoverished nations (Escobar 1995, Crush 1995, Shenton and Cowen 1996). As Arturo Escobar points out, 'Development, as a mode of thinking and a source of practices, soon became an omnipresent reality' (1988:430).

In Southern Rhodesia, the decade ushered in a crystallization of new political and power relations. Development went hand in hand with the extension of state practices (Ferguson 1990a). Not only did the government expand and play a larger role within the country, it achieved a greater cohesion and a greater administrative capacity (Arrighi 1967). Government became the key player among other white organizations in influencing the power relations of the colony (Murray 1970). The role of government planners became elevated in stature. As contemporary observers proclaimed, 'state planners ...are in some way our modern colonizers and developers' (Thompson and Woodruff 1954:35). Planners focussed particularly on 'natives'.

The Native Commissioners and other Native Affairs department officials had increasing power over Africans based on their constitutional responsibility to represent 'native interests' in government decisions. This position depended on the department 'being accepted in European society that it had the capacity and right to do so, and this was taken to arise, in the first place, from the knowledge gained by officials of what tended to be termed the "African Way of Life'" (Murray 1970:279; see also Holleman 1968:27).

Post-war state planners in Southern Rhodesia, as in other newly defined 'developing countries', increasingly began to justify interventions into African lives in the name of 'modernization' and 'technical development'. Responding to demands from European settlers and officials to ensure that more Africans can fit on the reserves, and resting on the epistemological authority of Western science, and the common anthropological assumption of the time that African society was 'traditional' in contrast to European society, these plans were explained as a means to assist the evolution of Africans into the 'modern' world (Worby 1995).

Such plans legitimated the central tenet of racial segregation laws that Africans and Europeans were at different stages of social 'evolution'. They also justified coercive state interventions in the lives of Africans. These included the removal of tens of thousands of black farmers from land designated for European use (Palmer 1977, Moyana 1984); mandatory conservation and agricultural measures introduced in the reserves (Beinart 1984, Ranger 1985, Phimister 1986, Page and Page 1991, Drinkwater 1989, 1991, Alexander 1993); and paternalistic control over urban-based (including, eventually, mining) African workers and residents (Raftopoulos 1992, Scarnecchia 1994, Raftopoulos and Phimister 1997). During this decade, bureaucratic apparatuses were strengthened in native reserves. Their policies and plans helped to generate racial and gendered identities as the natural end-points for 'evolving, modernising Africans' (e.g. Worby 1992, Ranchod-Nilsson 1992). In reserves and townships, 'development' was to be achieved through bureaucratic control nurturing Africans along this prescribed evolutionary track. For example, an internal government review of 'native policy' in Southern Rhodesia at the end of the 1940s noted:

> [the] government's desire to intensify the development of the
> Native areas and their inhabitants while they [Africans] are
> in a state of tutelage and [there is a] recognition of the need
> of special measures to equip them speedily to play a fuller
> part in the national life and economy... This policy appears
> to be influenced by the belief that under direct rule and
> European control the African can be to some extent advanced
> despite himself until he treads the path of progress of his

> *own volition, and by the fear, which there has been little so*
> *far to dispel, that the removal or relaxation of direct authority*
> *would result in stagnation or retrogression, which neither the*
> *Europeans, who intend to stay in and develop the Colony,*
> *nor Africans can afford.*[13]

African areas were defined principally as Native Reserves.[14] 'Development' of the reserves concentrated more power within the Department of Native Affairs and increased governmental presence in the reserves (Holleman 1968). Although such post-war administrative structures and identities associated with conservation and development plans were not accepted uncritically by Africans (e.g. Ranger 1985, Ranchod-Nilsson 1992, Alexander 1993, Worby 1995), they did help to situate a spatial division between rural and urban areas. They also facilitated the consolidation of administratively defined 'traditional leaders', i.e. chiefs, headmen and kraal-heads; the establishment of a form of local government called Native Councils, which was viewed as a synthesis of 'modern' and 'traditional' forms of politics (see Howman 1962 (1953), Rutherford 1996:96ff); and the emergence of various African organizations (farmers clubs, women's clubs, etc.) in the reserves. All these organizations were predominantly under a form of government tutelage and were (theoretically) oriented to the 'modernizing' goal of the emerging development plans (Garbett 1966a, Holleman 1968, Alexander 1993). For colonial officials, the 'administrative development' of Africans in reserves, and through sanctioned organisations, was supposed to act as a substitute for autonomous African political activities (e.g. Fields 1985). It did not, however, turn out that way as their responses to such policies and practices were also shaped by local concerns and politics (e.g. Alexander 1993).

In bureaucratic correspondence, African farmers in Urungwe district increasingly became regarded as numbers of 'natives' who were to be moved or were to remain on the land they were currently farming, depending on its assessed suitability for European settlement; or as a sufficient mass which would act as a human tsetse fly barrier for the newly settled European farms.[15] Approximately 4,600 Africans were removed in 1942 from land designated for European settlement and placed in Urungwe Reserve.

---

[13] S520, Survey of Native Policy in Southern Rhodesia, 1950.
[14] The Native Purchase Areas, the place for African freehold farming, were generally neglected by policy-makers until the 1950s (Cheater 1984:8).
[15] See the various Annual Reports of the Assistant Native Commissioner, Urungwe during this period.

24

With the decision to do this, Native Affairs department staff began to concentrate on 'planning' the agricultural methods and living arrangements of Africans farming there. This was done along the lines of the emerging conservation and development criteria, in order to ensure that the area could hold more people. However in practice such plans were implemented slowly and were often resisted by those who were said to be the beneficiaries.[16]

Spatial division resting on the sociological attributes of evolving Africans came to situate the procedures and objectives of 'native development'. In 1946, the Chief Native Commissioner announced a plan which would create full-time peasants on the reserves and full-time workers in towns by making a final allocation of land and prohibiting rural-urban labour migration.[17] Such a plan rested on the ability to drastically re-engineer African lives. With the institutionalization of the technical view over the administrative one within the Native Affairs department (Alexander 1993), the culmination of the coercive interventions of 'native development' in the name of 'modernization' was the passing of the Native Land Husbandry Act in 1951. As other scholars have noted, this self-declared 'development plan' sought to enforce centralization and 'stabilize' a proportion of Africans on the land, through distributing and controlling the disposal and transfer of permits for cultivation and stock holdings to as many individual Africans as allowed by the 'carrying capacity' of the reserve (e.g. Floyd 1959, Drinkwater 1991). Land centralization was now viewed by policy-makers as 'a powerful instrument of rural community development which adopted the traditional units of the family group, the village and the headman or sub-chief as its basis.'[18] Although ultimately failing as a policy when it was discontinued in 1961 due to growing resistance by African nationalist groups, traditional leaders, and more administratively oriented staff within the Native Affairs department, the Native Land Husbandry Act significantly shaped African lives, agriculture and politics (see Holleman 1968, Drinkwater 1991, Alexander 1993).

Urungwe was only included in this development plan at its end, in the late 1950s. In 1949, the Land Settlement Board opened up Crown Land farms to the general European public (not just to ex-servicemen). An outpouring of demand for land led the Department

---

[16] See, for example, the complaints of the Assistant Native Commissioner, Urungwe that the 'natives' are uninterested in improving themselves in S1563, Annual Reports, Assistant Native Commissioner, Urungwe, 1944, 1948.

[17] S1563. Annual Report, Chief Native Commissioner, 1946.

[18] S520. Survey of Native Policy in Southern Rhodesia, 1950.

of Lands to expedite surveying Crown Lands and to pressure the Native Affairs department to remove Africans to reserves. Until the late 1950s, relocation of Africans had a higher priority than implementing the Native Land Husbandry Act in Urungwe.[19]

Although the population of Urungwe Reserve was increasing in the 1940s as more African farmers were forcibly moved there, more than half the population of the District in 1947 still lived on Crown Land in the Zambezi Valley, including people farming in Chief Kazangarare's area north and east of Miami. They were however under surveillance by officials of the Native Affairs department in terms of their farming styles, their potential for 'development', the suitability of their land for European agriculture, and their potential role as labourers on the construction of the Kariba Dam.[20] By 1950, though, the officials said they too were 'tribal populations' that had to be relocated.

In 1950, an amendment to the Land Apportionment Act was passed that granted an extra 3.7 million acres for 'native occupation on a communal basis' called 'Special Native Areas', technically Crown Land but administered as reserves (Christopher 1971). This was the start of intense Native Affairs department activity to remove African 'squatters' and occupants from Crown Land and alienated land.[21]

After ensuring it was not suitable for European settlement, Crown Land adjacent to Urungwe Reserve became separate Special Native Areas. All remaining 'populations', defined by chief or by headman on the Crown Land, were to be removed to Urungwe Reserve. In 1950, officials estimated that 7,800 Africans and 3,060 livestock

[19] On (at least) one occasion in Urungwe, the Native Affairs department over-rode the Native Land Husbandry Act policy of centralization and encouraged settlement on a 'shifting cultivation' basis in the river valleys in the western part of Urungwe Reserve and the adjacent Special Native Area as this type of land-use was believed to push back tsetse fly. S2827/2/2/5, The Reclamation of Land from Tsetse and Its Relation to Native Settlement in the Urungwe Native Reserve and Special Native Areas, R. Goodier, Entomologist, May 15, 1958; and S2827/2/2/4, Annual Report, Native Commissioner, Urungwe, 1956; S2827/2/2/5, Annual Report, Native Commissioner, Urungwe, 1957.
[20] See, for example, S2895/2000, correspondence between Native Commissioner, Urungwe and Provincial Native Commissioner, Mashonaland, October 1947.
[21] S2588/2004, Removal of Natives from the European Area, Chief Native Commissioner Circular No. 71, July 12, 1950. See also S1194/190/27/6/1, Report of the Committee Appointed to investigate the Question of Additional Land for Native Occupation, June 1948; S190/21, Memorandum Submitted by the Lands Department and Land Settlement Board to the Select Committee on the Assignment of Lands, January 18, 1951. By 1960, the government estimated that 113,000 Africans had been forcibly relocated in the colony since 1945 (Passmore 1971).

would be 'relocated'.[22] After an initial delay in the removals – given an outbreak of tsetse fly infestation and a lack of administrative development in the reserve (e.g. few water supplies, the lack of centralization), plus the constantly changing order and location of the removals – more than 11,000 people were moved to Urungwe Reserve and the adjacent Special Native Area 'A' in the 1950s.[23] But others, including those deemed to be under Chief Kazangarare, were eventually told to remain where they were, with their land converted into Special Native Area 'C' that became Mukiwchi Tribal Trust Land (the new name for native reserves) in the early 1960s.

In contrast to the government-directed 'modernization' of 'natives' on reserves which marked these Africans as needing 'assistance' and the (European) government as those who would provide it, through force if necessary, for European farmers a sphere of government very different from 'administrative development' was taking shape during this period.

'Administrative politics' of European farmers

Starting in 1940, the Department of Lands began demarcating farms in what was called the Karoi Block in Urungwe. The 'K' Block was the largest area being prepared by the government for what was to become the Land Resettlement Scheme No. 1 for Rhodesian Ex-Servicemen, a scheme reserved solely for 'European' ex-servicemen.[24]

---

[22] S2588/2004, Removal of Natives from the European Area, Assistant Native Commissioner, Urungwe to Native Commissioner, Lomagundi, August 21, 1950.

[23] S2808/1/32/2, 1958 Movements and the April 1955 Plan, Native Commissioner, Urungwe to Under Secretary, Native Lands and Settlement, December 17, 1957. In 1950, approximately 2,200 people under Chief Mujinga were moved into the south-eastern part of Urungwe Reserve. S2588/2004, Removal of Natives from the European Area, Assistant Native Commissioner, Urungwe, to Native Commissioner, Lomagundi, August 21, 1950. In 1953, approximately a thousand people under Headman Mzilawempi 'voluntarily' accepted a Native Affairs department offer to move from a Gwelo (Gweru) farm to central-eastern Urungwe Reserve after the owner altered their labour agreement. S2805/2000, Movement from Bushy Park to Urungwe, 1953. In 1956, approximately 1,923 people under Chiefs Nyamunga and Mudzimu moved from the Kariba area to western part of Urungwe Reserve to make way for the damming of the Zambezi River at Kariba Gorge. S2827/2/2/4, Annual Report, Native Commissioner, Urungwe, 1956. In 1957, approximately 790 people from Sipolilo (Guruve) District were moved to the western portion (Rengwe) of Special Native Area 'A', south of Urungwe Reserve. S2827/2/2/5, Annual Report, Native Commissioner, Urungwe, 1957. In 1958, approximately 2,412 people under Chief Dandawa from the Zambezi Valley by the Rekomitje [Rukomeche] River were moved to the western portion (Rengwe) of Special Native Area 'A' and 469 moved to Urungwe Reserve. In 1959, approximately 2,250 people under Headman Matau were moved from Crown Land near Manyangau Hill to the western part of Urungwe Reserve. S2827/2/2/7, Annual Report, Native Commissioner, Urungwe, 1959. See Map 4, which itself is based on a map drawn by the Assistant Native Commissioner, Urungwe for the planning of these forced removals.

[24] There was a scheme for 'Coloured' ex-servicemen with fewer benefits and only 14 took advantage of it (see Weinmann 1975:192).

By January 1944, 103 of the 186 farms ready for this scheme were in the 'K' Block, with a total of 313,193 acres, or an average of 3,000 acres per farm.[25]

The European ex-servicemen farmers in Urungwe occupied nine farms in 1945 and 79 by 1950.[26] Like others assisted by the Land Settlement Scheme No. 1, they held them on a lease-hold basis with the option to purchase after seven years (later reduced to five). In addition to receiving delayed interest loans up to £3,000 on reasonable terms or outright grants, these farmers received agricultural advice and acclimatised cattle[27] from the Karoi Experiment and Demonstration Farm.

This settlement scheme for Europeans reflected a bias towards European farmers over African farmers due to racial and evolutionary assumptions of the British colonial government more generally, and Southern Rhodesian administration more particularly, about different capabilities of African and European farmers (see, e.g., Palmer 1977, Page and Page 1991). By the early 1900s in Southern Rhodesia, there was a broader government policy of promoting European agriculture as part of a larger colonial development scheme for European settlers (Rukuni 1994). This led to a policy of land segregation which, after it was systematically legislated for in 1930, initially provided half the arable land to European farmers (the minority) in the form of freehold farms and gave usufruct rights in reserves to African men who could claim membership to a 'tribe' deemed indigenous to the colony. It also led to extensive government support to, and investment in, European agriculture in terms of inputs and output markets as well as research and development (Rukuni 1994, Muir and Blackie 1994).

In the early 1940s, many government officials were concerned about the state of European agriculture and the productive use of Crown Lands. Such concern was generated, in part, by a report by

---

[25] S1194/190/28/1, Crown Land Proposed for Utilisation for Post War Settlement, Memo from Under Secretary, Department of Lands to Secretary, Department of Agriculture and Lands, January 4, 1944.

[26] S/AG 065, Report of the Land Settlement Board, 1945, 1950. In 1950, Urungwe was the district with the highest concentration of the 496 ex-servicemen settled in the colony (Weinmann 1975:192). The distribution of these farms rested with the Land Settlement Board, an advisory body to the Minister of Agriculture and Lands set up in 1944 to govern the settlement of Crown Lands. S/AG 065, Report of the Land Settlement Board, 1947, 1950.

[27] Most of the cattle were bought by the Cold Storage Commission from African farmers living in tsetse fly free areas close to the 'K' Block, although the Secretary of Agriculture did not want to advertise their origins. S2496/1949/28, Letter from Secretary of Agriculture to Natural Resources Board Chairman, November 17, 1944.

the newly formed Natural Resources Board which noted that conservation practices for most European farmers were poor,[28] and, in part, by a sudden decrease in maize production.[29] However, since European farmers were considered to be 'modern' in contrast to 'natives', the government used different procedures of administration to deal with these problems. To encourage sound conservation practice and increased maize production, the government adopted policies that revolved around monetary incentives and administrative devolution, not bureaucratic control as for Africans in the reserves.[30] 'Planning', as the Natural Resources Board declared in regards to European agriculture, 'should be for the benefit of those planned and NOT the Planners'.[31]

The administration that developed to implement these policies thus emphasized local self-governing structures. These local organisations managed to keep supervisory duties away from the bureaucracy and in the hands of the farmers and to effectively pressure the government for better treatment of their constituents (Murray 1970).

The newly formed Rhodesian National Farmers Union (RNFU, founded in 1942) strongly advocated this position. The RNFU quickly became an exceptionally strong interest group that increasingly had a say in governmental programmes and policies, given its compulsory membership, personal and administrative ties to government, and its visible representation of that important figure in (European) nationalist discourses, 'the European farmer/pioneer' (e.g. Joerg 1932; see Leys 1959, Murray 1970, Clarke 1977, Kennedy 1987, Lowry 1997). Despite the growing economic importance of manufacturing and other urban-based businesses after the War,[32]

---

[28] S990, Memorandum on the Position of European Farmers in the Colony by Chairman of the Natural Resources Board, December 21, 1942.

[29] For instance, the government began to favour European maize producers over tobacco farmers in the distribution of agricultural inputs (Roberts 1951).

[30] In order to 'facilitate the switch-over from mining the soil to conservation farming or good husbandry', the Secretary of Agriculture and Lands wrote regarding white farmers, 'it will be necessary, so far as possible, to make good farming as lucrative as soil exploitation.' S955/298, On Conservation Payments, Secretary of Agriculture and Lands to Chairman of Natural Resources Board, November 14, 1944. For examples of some of the subsidies given to white farmers, see S955/233, Progress Reports of Food Production Committees, 1942-1949.

[31] S1217/2, Points from Reports, Natural Resources Board; emphasis in original.

[32] This was partially driven by an increase of European immigration. From 1941-46, the net balance of European migration was +2,058. From 1946-51, it was +47,187, most of whom settled in the growing towns of the Colony (Thompson and Woodruff 1954:62). The economy also was driven by increasing diversion of foreign, particularly British, investment to Southern Rhodesia manufacturing and mining industries from South Africa after the Afrikaner-based National Party won elections in the Republic in 1948 (Arrighi 1967).

European farmers continued to have considerable strength in the government. The RNFU had representatives on the growing number of marketing boards and committees, including those that decided prices of commodities such as maize. Its success can be noted by the differential government spending, even at a time when 'Native development' was a policy priority: between 1945/46 and 1953/54, the government spent £12 million on research, extension advice, and infrastructure on European farms compared to £2 million on African agriculture in the same period (Dunlop 1971:59).

With the assistance of the RNFU, the government established local and national bodies of farmers to help enforce a variety of war-time policies and to disburse loans, grants, fertilizer, oxen, tractors, and forced labour gangs to farmers according to their conservation practices and cropping mixtures (Food Production Committee 1943). The Intensive Conservation Area committees (ICAs) emerged as the most enduring of these bodies. ICAs were formed upon agreement of the majority of farmers in an area and were under the aegis of the Natural Resources Board. The main duties of ICAs were to ensure that proper conservation practices were followed by farmers in their area and to distribute the growing number of government subsidies and grants for conservation works, premised on the assumption that Europeans as a 'race' respond best to monetary incentives.[33] In 1944 there were two ICAs; by 1950, there were 72.

Given that the ICAs were run by local European farmers as a form of self-administration and formed a line of communication to government, they were flexible in implementing policies. Although ICAs had legislative power to enforce conservation, persuasion was the preferred method for compliance, with government consent given the larger goal of establishing a viable European agriculture sector.[34]

In the 1940s, tobacco surpassed gold as the number one export of the colony, largely due to preferential treatment for Rhodesian

---

[33] See S987/2/1, Recommendations from the Natural Resources Board enquiry into farming in the Colony, 1942; and S990, Memorandum on the Position of European Farmers in the Colony by the Chairman of Natural Resources Board, December 21, 1942.

[34] As the Natural Resources Board Chairman explained in 1944: 'It is suggested that the most effective way of ensuring the preservation of the farming areas of the Colony is through the efforts of the farmers themselves, with technical assistance and, during the initial reclamation period, a measure of financial assistance from the government.' S2384/16, Notes on Conservation Policy, Natural Resources Board, September 20, 1944. See also S955/298, On Conservation Payments, Secretary of Agriculture and Lands to Natural Resources Board Chairman, November 14, 1944 and S2558/2004, memo from Mr. C.A. Murray, Director of Conservation and Extension to Secretary for Agriculture and Lands, March 1951.

tobacco over American tobacco in the United Kingdom (Roberts 1951). Combined with the preferential subsidies and successful agricultural research and support programmes, European agriculture reached 'take off', to use the famous development metaphor of that period (Rostow 1952), in the 1950s, making it one of the most productive sectors in the economy (Rukuni 1994).

By 1947, there were over 300 European settlers established on the scheme. Most were located in the high rainfall areas of the north and central parts of the colony, with 65 living on the Karoi farms in Urungwe. These farms brought Urungwe into the realm of economics and productivity, as defined by official discourses at the time (see Mitchell 1998). As the Land Settlement Board Annual Report put it in 1948, 'The occupation of these 65 farms implies that approximately 162,500 acres of Crown Land which have been lying idle since the occupation have now been brought into profitable production.'

Although conservation and food production were equally impressed upon the settlers, the priority was on establishing European farmers rather than enforcing good husbandry. For example, given the administrative weight of monetary inducements as the official conservation strategy for European farms, the Land Settlement Board encouraged tobacco production on farms in Mashonaland, 'in the initial stages to build up capital and facilitate the ultimate development of the farm on correct lines'. This despite the putative policy emphasis on maize production at that time.[35]

The post-war European settlers of Urungwe lobbied for and received a range of government support such as matching grants for road construction, aid during droughts, and compensation for cattle killed by trypanosomiasis.[36] They also quickly established their own organisations to interact with the emerging administrative practices. In 1946, the Miami Farmers' Association was established as the district organization of the RNFU. In 1948 the white settlers of Urungwe formed their own ICA. In 1950, the Karoi ICA advocated for and won grants from the government to build dams on 50 European farms in Urungwe.[37]

---

[35] Report of the Land Settlement Board, 1945.

[36] See S992/2, Karoi Road Council, 1949; Black (1976:30), S1194/190/28/2, Settlement of Discharged Servicemen on the Land, Scheme No. 1 (as amended), 1949.

[37] The farmer paid half to two-thirds of the costs and the government picked up the remaining expenses for the ICA's mechanical unit to dig out dams (as well as loaning some farmers their proportion of the costs). 1090/1/3, Karoi Watershed Scheme, 1950.

With such support, European settlement of Urungwe grew and the local organizations, as part and parcel of national groups, became effective political bodies promoting the cause of 'European farmers'. Situated in the middle of the ex-soldier settler scheme, the village of Karoi emerged as the service centre of these farmers and soon became the administrative capital of Urungwe, replacing Miami whose population waned with the drop in world mica prices in the 1950s. From this point onwards, 'Karoi' has become a metonym of the now dominant European farming sector with the institutional presence of an ICA, a RNFU body, and government agricultural officials. One issue strongly advocated by these groups was the need for the state to help to recruit workers.

Bureaucratized labour recruitment, not labour relations

The new white settlers in Urungwe demanded extensive state assistance in their efforts to recruit more farm workers.[38] The state was already helping white farmers in the area by facilitating the migration of African workers from northern colonies, providing forced labour during the war, and, in 1946, resurrecting its foreign labour recruiting agency, the Rhodesian Native Labour Supply Commission (RNLSC).[39]

The RNLSC recruited workers primarily from Nyasaland (colonial Malawi). It placed workers under a bureaucratized system of power relations, which included classifying and distributing them according to their physical body size.[40] Yet farmers were generally hesitant to use the RNLSC because they had to pay a capitation fee and deal with the RNLSC's bureaucracy as well as the uncertainty of obtaining the contracted workers (see Rubert 1990:34). Foreign-born workers comprised more than half of the farm workers from the 1940s to the mid-1960s, but only a small proportion of them came from the RNLSC (Clarke 1977:31 *passim*).

The ex-soldier settlers on the Karoi farms, however, relied heavily on foreign workers. With an increased local demand and a colony-wide shortage of labour after the War, farmers themselves illegally

---

[38] For example, S1051, Annual Report, Assistant Native Commissioner, Urungwe, 1945.
[39] In terms of the facilitation of migrant labour, see P. Scott (1954), Vickery (1989), Rubert (1990, 1998). For insight into the formation of the RNLSC (its precursor closed down in the early 1930s), see S1215/1060/16, Report on Conference to discuss the Formation of a Native Labour Organization, February 22, 1944.
[40] The few 'A's, the 'good physique' workers, mostly went to the coal mines while the lower paid 'D's, the 'poor physique' workers, tended to be placed with farmers. S957/2, Circular 10 to all ICA Committees, December 1, 1951.

recruited Africans from the colonies to the north.[41] In the face of this action, the Assistant Native Commissioner was ambivalent about enforcing the law against fellow white men, or what he called 'public opinion': 'No little tact had to be employed in handling several delicate situations and I hope higher circles do realise the difficulties and unpleasantness rural district officials have to contend with when applying government's policies in the face of unpopular public opinion.'[42] Whereas the state played an active role in assisting farmers to recruit workers, the ambivalence of the official's 'public opinion' reflected the government's hesitancy in playing a role in the administration of labour relations on European farms. Instead, in the 1940s European farmers were being officially sanctioned as the administrative overseers of farm workers.

Administration by paternalism: the construction of the 'European farmer'

Official discourses attributed particular capacities and responsibilities to the European farmer. The identity of the 'European farmer' was gendered as masculine and pre-supposed a set of domestic relations that subordinated both the wife and the workers of the white farmer. As most farms were operated by individual farmers, who lived on the farm, the work place was closely linked with 'home'. The combination of 'home' and 'work' meant that the wives of white farmers played an important role on the farm, given that 'home' was valorized as a crucial site for 'wives' in state and academic discourses (Kirkwood 1984a). White farming women were 'incorporated wives', defined as integral parts of the farmer's domestic authority in his 'family' and his farm and not, for instance, as independent economic agents in themselves.[43] They not only kept his house orderly by supervising domestic workers, they also contributed to his farm (or 'domestic') economy through gardening and dairy sales and by providing the proper nurturing to his workers' welfare. Management rested on the domestic and dependent ties between farmer and wife and between them and the workers and their families. As Deborah Kirkwood (1984b) has observed,

---

[41] After the war, private recruiters were banned as the RNLSC became the monopoly recruiter of foreign workers.

[42] S1563, Annual Report, Assistant Native Commissioner, Urungwe, 1947.

[43] There were some farms operated by widowed white women and there was a Land Settlement Scheme for European ex-servicewomen, but it only provided loans to purchase farms on the open market and only two women took advantage of it. See S1194/190/28/2, Settlement of Discharged Servicewomen on the land, Scheme No. 3, 1949. For discussion of 'incorporated wives', see Callan (1984).

> *it is clear that a [farmer's] wife's attitude to workers and their*
> *families could be crucial. If she handled morning 'clinics' [of*
> *providing first-aid to workers and their families] and other*
> *encounters with patience, sympathy and interest a genuine*
> rapport *developed between the two worlds of white and black;*
> *a readiness to interest herself seriously in the health and*
> *education problems of workers' families was undoubtedly*
> *appreciated.*

This domestic view of the European farmers was made explicit in a pamphlet issued by the National Rehabilitation Board in 1944 for post-war agricultural occupations of soldiers.[44] The pamphlet not only provided a similar description of the 'suitable' settler wife as above, but it also laid out the 'inherent' characteristics necessary for an ex-soldier to become a Southern Rhodesian farmer. The largest section for this topic, almost equal in size to the other six sections, was devoted to a European man's ability to accommodate the 'restricted mental outlook, the un-European characteristics and the inherent irresponsibility of the average native labourer'. The relationship of the farmer to his workers should be 'towards developing his [the worker's] best qualities and an interest and pride in the work'. The objective of this edification was purely instrumental – 'if a more reliable type of farm labourer is gradually to evolve' – but the means were purely personal, being dependent on the presumed racially endowed attributes of the 'European'. For example, the pamphlet noted that the European farmer was responsible for ensuring good communication with farm workers given 'his immense advantage in intelligence and education'. If he was unwilling to learn the workers' own language and lacked the 'knowledge of and ability to handle natives', he would jeopardise the success of the farm:

> *In most cases a native will not attempt to explain his*
> *difficulties to an employer who cannot understand and speak*
> *the native's own language. Failing this he usually regards*
> *the employer as unsympathetic and unapproachable and*
> *discontent and friction are thus inevitable.*

Whereas discipline in the reserves was to become formalized in rules and laws and internalized by Africans progressing to a stage of economic and domestic maturity, discipline on farms largely rested on European farmers' acceptance of the proper paternal responsibility over his workers. Government officials identified European

---

[44] All references are to Southern Rhodesia (1944).

paternalism as the source of governance as well as of improvement of farm workers. Removed from any direct control over farm workers, government officials discussed how to impress upon the European farmer his duty to edify Africans and his obligation to 'take the trouble' to control their activities. The Assistant Native Commissioner, Urungwe invoked this domestic responsibility when his office had to deal with labour relations on numerous European farms for the first time in 1945: 'The native is in transition. There is a need for a fundamentally new attitude towards him and I think he would respond to a more personal, unselfish interest being displayed in his welfare.'[45]

Whereas a bureaucratic administration was being developed for urban workers (Murray 1970),[46] no such regulation was occurring for farm workers. Rather the type of edification promoted rested on strict white control over black behaviour through discipline and surveillance of their bodies. The discipline was not to come from some symbiotic relation between European techniques of planning and the evolving African, but rather from direct European male control. For instance, the Native Commissioner, Lomagundi, noted that as 'gaol is not felt to be a deterrent to native mind, corporal punishment is felt to be healthy and effective'.[47] One of the requirements of the Land Settlement Board for granting title to white lessees of Crown Land was that buildings should be solidly constructed 'in accordance with the nature of the farming activities in progress and should be conveniently sited so as to entail economy in the working of the property and in European supervision'.[48] The implied objects of this white supervision were the black workers. White farmers, not administrative bodies, were in charge of supervising the development of Africans working on farms. This domestic responsibility of European farmers over farm workers became one of their defining features within the Rhodesian public. Being a white farmer meant, in part, being a responsible authority over black workers.

---

[45] S1051, Assistant Native Commissioner, Urungwe, Annual Report, 1945. See also S1563, Assistant Native Commissioner, Urungwe, Annual Report, 1946, 1947, and 1948. In 1938, there were only 350 Africans employed in the sub-district, and most of them were employed at the mica mines. With the post-war decline of the international market for mica and the increase of farmers and labour recruitment in the north and within Urungwe District, by 1948 employment increased to 5,000 Africans on farms compared to 1,500 on mines. S1051, Assistant Native Commissioner, Urungwe, Annual Report, 1945. See also S1563, Assistant Native Commissioner, Urungwe, Annual Report, 1948.

[46] An internal history of the emerging bureaucratic system can be found in S28243/5/2, Native Labour Advisory Board Meeting, February 20-21, 1952.

[47] S1563, Annual Report, Native Commissioner, Lomagundi, 1940.

[48] S955/182, Memorandum prepared by the Land Settlement Board on Beneficial Occupation of a Holding, July 28, 1948.

Edification by intimate coercion: European responsibility and farm workers

In 1946, European agriculture was the largest employer of Africans. There were 3,975 white farms in the colony employing 141,822 men and 8,267 women.[49] This was equivalent to 39 per cent and 61 per cent of male and female African employees respectively. In addition, European agriculture employed 15 per cent of the European population.

During this period, there was increased discussion about the type and intensity of European responsibility over Africans – the driving theme in official discourses on 'Native Policy'. The emerging consensus was that on white farms it should lie with the (male) farmer (and his family) and not any government authority. The assumed moral bonds of familial dependency became the primary means of administration. For example, in a 1943 inquiry about the Native Affairs Department control over Africans, the Natural Resources Board chairman asked the Chief Native Commissioner, 'You control them in the Reserves but not natives on farms?' The Commissioner replied, 'We have practically no control over those – actually less than the landowner'. This was not a concern, he reflected later, since the 'natives live generally under better conditions and their activities can be controlled by the farmer if he takes the trouble to do so'.[50] The assumptions underlining this form of administration, which I call domestic government, are clearly presented in the following passage from a 1950 government memo on 'native policy':

> *The system at its best is valuable as providing the landholder with a stable labour supply and providing opportunities for development of the personal relationship between the employer and the old retainer which is conducive both to efficiency and good race relations, and on many large estates and ranches there has been built up a permanent pool of labour of Africans who have confidence in their employer and can feel secure in the knowledge that while they fulfill their obligations they may trust him to allow them to exercise all rights necessary for a contented existence.*[51]

---

[49] Dunlop (1971:61), Thompson and Woodruff (1954: 64-5). This figure excludes the 69,943 African men living under 'labour agreements', a form of labour tenancy, with European farmers in 1946. S2806/4396, Labour Agreements Memo from Secretary of Native Affairs, 1948.

[50] S2384/16, Verbatim Report of Chief Native Commissioner to Natural Resources Board over Soil Conservation at Chiduku Reserve, January 20, 1943.

[51] S520, Survey of Native Policy in Southern Rhodesia, Internal Memorandum, 1950.

Farmers were seen in official circles not only as the administrative body over labour agreements but also over labour relations. In this way, they were treated differently from other European employers.

Being outside the urban areas and industrial sites, farm workers were seen to be outside the sphere of state-directed 'modernization' in which officials were locating most other African workers during this period. Unlike the workers in towns, on the railways, and (eventually) on the mines, farm workers were commonly viewed by colonial officials and commentators as 'still raw'.[52] Rather than falling under the rudimentary labour legislation being created for other categories of African workers and their organisations, farm workers were still governed by the Masters and Servants Act which, among other things, prohibited them from forming organisations. Farm workers were under not a labour agreement or an administrative arrangement but what amounted to a codified domestic relationship under the European farmer.

The Masters and Servants Act depended on institutionalized paternalism as the form of governance (see Du Toit 1993). The close bond between master and servant that this Act presupposed was emphasized by the inclusion of harsh penalties for any action by the servant that challenged the personal authority of this compact. For example, disobeying a master's command, missing work without permission, neglect of duty, or abusive behaviour towards master or his family could result in a prison term if the convicted worker could not pay the court-imposed fine. A conviction did not break the contract of service, for a servant could not escape the bonds of his master (at least until the contract expired). Rather the farm worker was obliged to return to finish the contract and make up for the time spent in prison. For the master, the law only set out his responsibility to provide adequate welfare to the servant.[53] Administration over the act's enforcement rested with the courts and not with any administrative body.

Transition to Independence

The power relations and official discourses that crystallized in the 1940s shaped the government interventions, academic assumptions and social geographies that have emerged since. The 'social

---

[52] S2824/5/1, Native Labour Advisory Board meeting, January 14, 1947. See also Rubert (1990:331).

[53] Masters and Servants Act, Chapter 247, Revised Statutes of Rhodesia, 1974.

territories', the 'identities of place', of European farms differentiate them from Africans living in the reserves in terms of institutional arrangements, which constitute social identities. 'Politics' and self-representation have been the major defining attributes of European farmers while the administration of 'development' has been a determining factor in the lives of rural Africans.

This difference was largely based on the assumed distinction between Europeans and Africans, or, as Mahmood Mamdani (1996) puts it, between 'citizens' and 'subjects': official discourses assumed that Europeans had the capacity for self-governance, whereas Africans, lacking that capacity, had to be administered by European forms of control. Self-selected white farming organizations not only managed to keep supervisory duties away from bureaucratic entities but they were also able to effectively pressure the government for better treatment of their members. Africans living in reserves were subjects of the bureaucracy and officially sanctioned traditional leaders. Although the 'interests' of various state projects converged and diverged with different individuals and groups in both these spaces at different times and in different places, this was the broad distinction between the two social territories.

As for (African) farm workers, they were subjects to European farmers under the administration of 'domestic government', the paternalistic relationship between the white farmer and his farm workers. Personal interest, provision of recreation, strong discipline, and effective supervision were the key themes for the proper European care of farm workers. Responsibility rested within the private, domestic parameters of the farm.[54] African workers were not passive spectators with these developments. As I argue in the following chapters, African farm workers have deployed various techniques and strategies of resistance to better their lives.

The shape of the different jural identities in official discourses during the remainder of the colonial period was predominantly based on this spatialization of power relations (see Rutherford 1996:89ff). African peasants were targeted by several development initiatives concerned with moulding them into productive colonial subjects and

---

[54] For example, farms were excluded from the 1948 Factories and Work Act, which was legislated to permit government inspections of industrial working conditions. Shortly after it was passed, the former Chief Inspector of factories in South Africa prepared a report for the Southern Rhodesian government which suggested to change this exclusion. Yet the Minister of Labour ignored the advice. S482/102/1/48, Labour Regulation, August 16, 1948.

undercutting the growing nationalist demands of African leaders (Alexander 1993). White farmers were still provided with various forms of state support to underwrite their growing economic importance in the colony. Farm workers were continuously excluded from the labour relations machinery applicable to most other workers, falling as they did under the patronizing, occasionally violent, rule of white farmers, with support from government officials.[55]

Meanwhile, African protests and proposals for change were increasingly met by oppression and intransigence from the settler government, fostering frustration and support for an alternative means of struggle 'in the bush' (see Lan 1985, Kriger 1992, Bhebe and Ranger 1995a, 1995b).

The growing war had a dramatic impact on Urungwe, particularly in the 1970s. The number of vacant farms increased as the droughts of the early 1970s and intensifying guerrilla attacks drove Europeans off their farms. One newspaper reported that instead of having aeroplanes, five figure incomes, and selling farms for a profit, Karoi farmers and the town itself were all living on credit with an estimated 50 farms already abandoned (*Rhodesia Herald*, February 7, 1973). Increased attacks by ZIPRA fighters (ZAPU's armed wing) and the corresponding increased call-up of European farmers for civil defense and army units disrupted production on the farms (Caute 1983). Meanwhile, the fighting in the Tribal Trust Lands in Urungwe led to the eventual abandonment of any form of administration in those areas (Rutherford 1996:139ff).

Following the strictures of domestic government and given the foreign origins of many farm workers, the guerrillas were ambivalent towards them. Farm workers were closely identified with the farmers, particularly as farmers organised some workers into auxiliary defence forces. They also viewed them as foreigners who did not have a right to land in Zimbabwe. At the same time, guerrillas saw them as Africans

---

[55] A labour relations case from a Karoi farm in 1973 is a good illustration of the agreement of government officials and farmers on farm workers during this period. An Industrial Relations Officer found that the complaints of twenty farm workers in Karoi concerning non-payment for over three months, being over-worked and subject to assaults, were true: 'The employer admitted that the workers had been forced to work until midnight on many occasions and that he had found it necessary to assault certain individuals in an effort to make them carry out his instructions.' In the face of such violations of the Masters and Servants Act and criminal law, the official chose the 'penalty' of threatening to withhold his help: 'Arrangements were made for the payment of wages due and the employer was warned to change his management technique in future if he expects to receive assistance from the industrial relations officer.' MLGRUD 32.25.7f, 164077 LAB/1/1 Vol IV.

exploited by white settlers and encouraged them to abandon the farms, not only to hurt the farms' production but also to enable them to get land for themselves (e.g. Kriger 1992:147-148). Yet given their identity as 'Africans', many farmers and army units were also suspicious of them as potential guerrilla sympathizers. For example, many farmers followed the government's suggestion and increased surveillance of their workers. They made them sleep in barns and restricted their rations to isolate them from guerrilla attacks and requests for assistance. While Urungwe farmers literally fortified their own houses, armed themselves and their families, and established militia patrols with some of their workers as a way to protect themselves from the 'terrs' (as in 'terrorist', the common term farmers used to describe guerrillas) beyond their farms, they had a growing unease during the war about the loyalty of their own workforce: were they 'domesticated' or 'infiltrated'? Were the bonds of domestic government as secure as they imagined? According to the memories of farm workers with whom I talked, this ambivalence translated into both an increased concern to demonstrate their 'care' towards farm workers to ensure their loyalty and a heightened preparedness to punish, often physically, any transgressions committed by workers. In the context of African nationalist arguments of the guerrillas and their attacks on farms, and the Rhodesian nationalism built in part around the figure of the white farmer espoused by the Smith regime, the boundary between 'us' and 'them', farmers and workers, white and black, became accentuated and a source of anxiety for farmers and workers.

Yet, in a sense, the white farmers were better prepared for Independence than the farm workers. By the mid-1970s European farmer organizations like the RNFU were able to ready themselves for Independence. For example, they developed a consciously 'professional' attitude towards labour relations, promoting 'modern' management techniques on the farm. 'Management' emerged as an organizational trope to replace 'domestic responsibility' in the RNFU's literature on farm workers. Its Labour Committee was converted into the Agricultural and Labour Bureau (ALB) in February 1975. It had a mandate to deal with the question of labour shortages and future political developments. It had representatives on many advisory bodies to the government and it actively lobbied for legislative changes concerning farm workers based on their model of 'labour stabilization'.[56]

---

[56] See 1975, 'Loss Control in Agriculture', ALB Paper No. 1; November, 1975, ALB's 'The Concept of Ideal Farm Labour Management'. These initiatives complemented a series of reports by Conex on labour and equipment planning (de Jong 1975) and labour productivity and housing (Du Toit 1977).

The ALB's version of 'labour stabilization', however, still relied on an intimate, domestic relationship between farmer and worker; a relationship that now included skill differentials, worker safety, housing and amenities, and public education. Farm workers did not play a role in this governance. In fact, the RNFU was still against recognizing the unofficial trade union, the Agricultural and Plantation Workers' Union, that had been agitating for legal recognition since the early 1960s.[57]

The ALB was so confident in its new 'modern' role that it eventually advocated for the inclusion of farm workers under the Industrial Conciliation Act. On April 27, 1979 an Industrial Board was set up for the agricultural industry. It clearly favoured the employers as almost all of its initial regulations came directly from the ALB.[58]

Substantial shifts were also occurring over the land question. The RNFU, and later the government itself, began to formulate a policy of economic justification for the retention of white farmers on the land. Explicit justification in terms of racial rights slowly disappeared within official discourses. By early 1979, the racially defined land legislation was repealed, with support of the RNFU (Baker 1979). The RNFU strategy was directed towards the international community, stressing the economic role and the apolitical nature of farmers (McKenzie 1989).

Like other Africans, farm workers in the colonial period were politically disenfranchised and were seen officially as a 'population' that had to be developed through European supervision. Yet, black farmers in the Tribal Trust Lands and black people living and working in towns began getting vague, albeit top-down, forms of political and industrial representation and forms of government that sought to control and supervise their 'development' during the last decades of colonial rule. In contrast, male farm workers were viewed principally as being under the government of the European farmer and his wife while female and juvenile farm workers were under the authority of their husbands and fathers. However, the shifts in the 1970s that resulted in the inclusion of farm workers in the formal industrial relations machinery, an increasing emphasis on 'management' of

---

[57] RNFU Annual Congress Report, 1972. The illegal union, the Agricultural Plantation Workers' Union, had petitioned the Minister of Labour and Social Welfare many times from the late 1960s onwards to include farm workers under the Industrial Conciliation Act but received either no reply or outright dismissals. Their members were also detained by the Police, imprisoned, and harassed and fired by employers (Clarke 1977:188-195, 275-280; Davies 1975:430-431).

[58] RNFU Annual Congress Reports, 1978, 1979.

'labour relations', and the 'economic' importance of 'commercial' (read 'European') farms did lead to some amalgam of 'domestic' and more bureaucratic forms of control over commercial farm workers. But if this led to some uncertainty for farm workers, the end of colonialism gave rise to even greater ambiguity. Given their close association with Europeans under the regime of domestic government, as well as their being seen as 'foreigners' within the context of a liberation war waged in part for Africans and in part for the 'sons of the soil' (indigenous peoples), many farm workers were not sure what 'Zimbabwe' would hold for them.

Independence

Elections were held in early 1980 and were won by the former liberation group turned political party, the Zimbabwe African National Union (Patriotic Front), or ZANU(PF), under the leadership of Robert Mugabe. As Prime Minister, Mugabe pledged both a policy of 'racial reconciliation' and a socialist transformation where property would belong to 'peasants and workers'.

Land quickly emerged as the focal (and vocal) point for Zimbabwean politics. The liberation parties agreed to a constitution that prohibited compulsory acquisition of land, other than 'underutilised land', for agricultural resettlement. All other land had to be bought on a willing seller, willing buyer basis at full market values. This provision could only be altered by a two-thirds majority in Parliament after ten years.

'Land' areas became (re-)identified in official discourse according to the same dualistic division of the rural areas. However, the two identities of this division were now characterized as much by sociological-*cum*-economic attributes (which had been emerging in the 1970s), with a stress on the percentage of land owned and amount of 'economic value' produced, as by racial identities. Rather than the tribal/cash economy split, it was a division between the '(African) peasant sub-sector' and the '(European) commercial sub-sector'.

I will briefly examine how such spatialized identities have affected institutional arrangements and power relations for farm workers since 1980 in three (overlapping) areas: labour relations and social conditions on commercial farms; local government; and land resettlement. In each area, Independence initially seemed to usher in significant changes. But such promise soon dissipated to the extent that for many living in post-colonial Zimbabwe the 'post' seems to be out of place as colonial orders, assumptions and arrangements were re-asserted and imposed by the old and new elites.

Labour relations and social conditions on farms: continuity and change

Just after Independence in 1980, workers throughout the country demanded and agitated for improved working conditions, the removal of harsh white managers, and higher wages. In response to what was the strongest labour unrest in the country since the nationwide 1948 strike, the new ZANU(PF) government responded by introducing mandatory minimum wages for all sectors. They also clamped down on continuing labour action, and set up a Party-supported umbrella organization for trade unions, the Zimbabwe Congress of Trade Unions (ZCTU), to try to shape the labour movement in a way that accorded with (the Party-defined) 'national interests' (Zimbabwe 1984; see Sachikonye 1986, 1997, Woods 1988, Shadur 1994).

In the agricultural industry, white farmers were faced with a barrage of new legislation and political antagonism. Despite the state policy of racial reconciliation, white farmers were publicly criticized not only for stealing the land from Africans but also for the paternalism of domestic government. In speeches delivered by government and Party members, white farmers were commonly singled out, harshly condemned for their 'Rhodie' attitudes and threatened with expropriation if the new laws were disobeyed.[59] For instance, the government told farmers that they were no longer to provide rations but to remunerate workers fully with minimum wages and free accommodation for *all* workers.[60] Women were to receive the same wages as men, and child labour was prohibited (*The Herald*, December 23, 1981). The Ministry of Labour initiated labour regulations and set minimum wages more or less annually for farms, occasionally in consultation with the ALB and the Industrial Board for the Agricultural Industry.[61]

---

[59] For example, the Minister of Labour stated: 'If any farmer does not pay his farm labourers minimum wage, all we will have to do is to nationalize the farm – give it to the Ministry of Lands, Resettlement and Rural Development, so that it can become part of the resettlement programme' (*The Herald* December 23, 1981).

[60] Although the first statutory minimum wage in agriculture was introduced in 1979 with Statutory Instrument 917/1979 when farm workers were included for the first time in the Industrial Conciliation Act, the minimum wages imposed by the Zimbabwean government were higher than that of 1979 and were increased several times in 1980 alone, much to the displeasure of commercial farmers. See RNFU Annual Congress Report 1979, and CFU Annual Congress Report 1981.

[61] ALB Chairman Reports, CFU Annual Congress, 1982, 1983.

43

Initial enforcement of laws came less from the government and more from Party activists. Shortly after Independence, ZANU(PF) established Party cells, called village committees, on many commercial farms (Ladley and Lan 1985). In addition to enforcing allegiance to ZANU(PF) and acting as a preliminary judicial forum for civil disputes in the compounds, village committees played a large role in establishing worker committees and providing an entry for unions on farms, often challenging not only the farmer's authority but occasionally the authority of government labour regulations.[62]

The new legislation, and especially the activities of the Party on commercial farms, led to struggles among workers (along overtly political, generational, and factional divisions) and, especially, between workers and employers.[63] Many farmers reacted against these regulations by (illegally) firing workers and (legally) downgrading permanent workers to a seasonal or casual status (the distinction between different labour contracts was left to the discretion of the employer).[64] This worker unrest and government initiative in the early years of Independence forcibly challenged relations between white farmers and black farm workers on the farms, and at the national level, for the first time ever.

The new government assisted farm workers in another way. They gave citizenship to anyone who had been in the country for a specified number of years. Government and Party officials went from farm to farm granting citizenship cards to 'foreign' workers and informing them of their right to vote (in national elections) and get land rights

---

[62] For example, the local Industrial Relations Officer in Karoi complained of a man from an unregistered union (and local Party activist) who was disregarding the governing legislation and called upon his superiors to try and have this man stopped. MLGRUD, Karoi, Letter from Industrial Relations Officer, Karoi to Regional Industrial Relations Officer, Mashonaland. March 25, 1981.

[63] As the ALB Chair reflected in 1982, 'at times the situation [on commercial farms] became near chaotic with daily incidents such as strikes, slow work, absenteeism, poor quality of work, indiscipline, drop in productivity, etc. etc. – you name it – our industry had it'. ALB Chairman's address to CFU Annual Congress, July 1982.

[64] 'It has been noted that the general trend now in the Karoi Commercial Farming community is to fire employees who have not completed eight months and when a complaint is received the employers insist that these are seasonal workers... Most employees who are engaged even during the off-peak period when there is no pressure of work are made to sign seasonal contracts. With these pieces of paper, the officers are disarmed and the rampant dismissals are reaching alarming proportions as the employers are now hiding behind the term seasonal worker.' MLGRUD, Karoi, Monthly Report, Regional Industrial Relations Officer, Mashonaland, December 1985. See also *The Guardian*, UK, July 7, 1980. These contracts ranged between 'permanent workers' who received vacation and health benefits, 'seasonal workers' and 'casual workers' whose length of contract were less than eight months and six weeks in a three month period respectively, 'contract workers' (paid by negotiated piece-work rates) and 'special workers' (physically or mentally disabled workers), both uncovered by the regulations.

in a Communal Land in the district in which they were registered. This occurred before the 1985 national elections when government officials and Party cadres were granting 'foreigners', particularly on commercial farms, citizenship cards in exchange for one dollar. Although this was an election ploy by ZANU(PF), many farm workers assumed they were now full citizens of Zimbabwe.

There were thus significant government initiatives in these first years of Independence as ZANU(PF) sought to challenge the colonial order it had inherited, including that of the former European farms where white farmers followed a different 'law' than that followed in the rest of the country; a law that was encouraged by the colonial government. Prime Minister Mugabe articulated this very problem: 'The attitude of some farmers was that this land was not part of Zimbabwe. They even say they have their own laws, which the people working for them must obey and that the people's government is a kaffir government.' In reaction to such a situation, to such a space relatively untouched by bureaucratic government, it was reported that, 'A PLAN to set up "decent townships on Zimbabwe's farms, complete with schools, clinics and business centres, to replace slum compounds in which workers are housed," is being considered by the government, says the Prime Minister, Mr. Mugabe.' (*Sunday Mail* February 28, 1982; emphasis in original).

But 'the PLAN', the extension of administrative control over 'social welfare', still had to face the inherited system within the relations of rule. Farm workers continued to lie largely outside formal government channels, although they acquired more administrative representation when the Labour Relations Act replaced the Industrial Conciliation Act in 1985 (see Sachikonye 1986, Woods 1989, Cheater 1991). The new Act required one union per industry. During the early 1980s, labour relations were less formalized on farms as several trade unions competed for members and local Party officials gave themselves a say on some farms. For many workers and farmers, when the unions did arrive on their farm during this period, they were there more for their own personal or political purposes than to represent farm workers in terms of labour relations. In 1986, the General Agricultural and Plantation Workers' Union of Zimbabwe (GAPWUZ), a union that had been competing with others to represent farm workers in the early 1980s, was recognized and began to sit with the ALB on the Employment Board (comparable to Industrial Boards) for the Agricultural Industry.[65]

---

[65] See Rutherford (1996:171, EN 94). Yash Tandon is currently writing a history of GAPWUZ.

The government never carried through with creating, let alone enforcing, 'the PLAN' for extending government responsibility over farm workers' living and working conditions. Farm workers were targeted by early health plan initiatives but, in the absence of any strong government commitment, these were unevenly implemented (Loewenson et al 1983, Herbst 1990, Loewenson 1992). From 1985 to 1988, various proposals to include farm workers within more bureaucratic forms of administration were circulated, often with government interest, but they failed to materialize during this period. As one participant in many of these efforts observed, the 'state has not taken a decisive position and little progress has been made' (Loewenson 1992:72).

In the 1980s, there was growing labour insecurity on commercial farms, with declining employment in the first half of the decade and a growing proportion of non-permanent (mainly women) workers within that workforce (Loewenson 1988). The total number of farm workers dropped from 314,893 in 1977 to 247,400 in 1984 while the percentage of permanent workers in the labour force went from 79 to 68 in the same period.[66] Although the total number of farm workers had increased to nearly 300,000 by the end of the decade, the proportion of permanent workers declined to just above 50 per cent (ILO 1993:26-27).

By the mid-1980s, the government became more sympathetic to commercial farmers' concerns over wages and other issues (see Sachikonye 1986, N. Moyo 1988, Loewenson 1992). The government supported diversification of crops away from maize, while tobacco reasserted its dominance and was grown in more farms as its price rose throughout the 1980s (ZTA 1992:62).

On the farms themselves, the power of workers' and village committees[67] weakened because the government and the Party gave them less support in order to avoid 'disrupting' the farm industry. The emerging bureaucratic relations were also weakened as the Department of Labour lacked funds to properly settle disputes and had no legal responsibility to inspect working conditions on farms. Rather the domestic responsibility of farmers over farm workers was re-emphasized in official discourse. This had remained the

---

[66] Figures come from Reports by the Agricultural Labour Bureau Chairman 1977, 1985.

[67] The power of these committees at this time largely refers to the ability to threaten and/ or to impose their decisions on the farmer, decisions which were not necessarily representative of the thoughts of the farm workers they claimed to represent.

guiding model of governance on commercial farms throughout the 1980s.[68]

This relaxation of state 'controls' is part and parcel of an IMF-informed and World Bank-supported Economic Structural Adjustment Programme (ESAP) and its successor, the Zimbabwe Programme for Economic and Social Transformation (ZIMPREST), which the ZANU(PF) government has nominally followed since 1990 (Zimbabwe 1991b). The aim of ESAP is to decrease the amount of government control over the economy and to 'liberalize' in the classical sense by 'opening up' the economy to global competition through an emphasis on exports and a reduction of barriers to foreign investment and imports. 'Efficiency' and 'productivity' gained currency in official discourses as measurement criteria for policy in most administrative spheres, despite charges by critics that ESAP has led to a rise in unemployment levels, poverty and illness (Kanji and Jazdowska 1993, Sachikonye 1993, Chinemana and Sanders 1993).

In terms of labour relations, the 1992 Amendment to the Labour Relations Act, in keeping with the theme of liberalization, allows for more than one union per industry to encourage 'competition' amongst unions. Employment Councils are also encouraged to negotiate 'employment codes' to govern dismissal, retrenchment and discipline, leaving few powers for Ministry of Labour officials. In fact, individual firms (e.g. commercial farms) may register their own employment codes, which would override that of an Employment Council (Richer 1992).

After initial resistance from the employers, GAPWUZ and the ALB finally organized an Employment Council for the Agricultural Industry in 1991.[69] Annual collective bargaining agreements of the Council now determine minimum wages and conditions of employment. When the industry's Employment Code was finally enacted in 1993, it

---

[68] For example, the ALB Chair articulated this domestic responsibility of farmers to farm workers vis-à-vis government: 'I totally reject the allegations of exploitation. I do, however, agree that the 1.5 million people on our farms could be called the forgotten people of Zimbabwe. They are forgotten by everyone else, but definitely they are not forgotten by the farmer, on whom they are almost totally dependent... Nearly a quarter of the total population of this country lives in these areas, and they and we, their employers, are making a considerable contribution in both direct and indirect taxation.' CFU Annual Congress Report, 1981. In 1983, Minister of Labour Kangai praised commercial farmers for taking care of 'our elder citizens' upon retirement and under-employed workers during the drought. He even floated the idea of encouraging under-employed workers to participate in 'self-reliance' projects such as building latrines or moulding bricks to improve the compounds; an interesting proposal that borders on corvée labour given that this land is not owned by the workers. CFU Annual Congress Report, 1983.

[69] See CFU Annual Congress Report, 1989, 1990, 1991.

47

established formally agreed rules, which now define the disciplinary and grievance procedures, including dismissal of employees. The main mechanism of enforcement is a 'disciplinary committee' of equal members of management and workers on each farm. In practice, this goal of liberalization is formalizing the re-establishment of domestic government on commercial farms.

The emphasis of the Employment Code on individual farms setting up disciplinary committees reinforces the already dominant role farmers take in the administration of labour relations. Indeed, a speech given by Deputy Minister of Labour (later Minister) Chitauro to farm workers on a sugar estate is illustrative of what has been a common official attitude towards farm workers. According to a letter sent to *The Herald* (December 15, 1992), she told them that they must depend on themselves for labour negotiations and intoned that their poverty was their own fault, reportedly telling them, '*Hamuna kudzidza vanhu vokumapurazi, muchafa makadaro*'. ('You farm workers did not study, therefore you will die that way'.) Indeed, from my research in the late 1990s, 'disciplinary committees' either do not exist on farms or typically refer to the farm operator himself or are comprised solely of management workers.

Throughout the 1990s, wages continued to fall as did the percentage of full-time farm workers (see Table 1) as ESAP led to growing unemployment, higher prices, and increasing desperation of more and more Zimbabweans (Sachikonye 1993, 1997). It was an employers' market, augmented in the agricultural industry by the fact that GAPWUZ was beset by a number of breakaway unions (see Kanyenze forthcoming). But in September and October 1997 farm workers carried out wildcat strikes in areas across the country when negotiations stalled during the annual collective bargaining for wages. Thousands blocked highways, stopped work and, in a few areas, destroyed farm property. This unprecedented action caught many – employers, government, workers, and even trade unionists – by surprise, as they did not expect farm workers to assert their rights so boldly.

Rural local government and farm workers

Shortly after Independence, the government promoted a plan that promised to overturn colonial administration, particularly the vestiges of 'traditionalism' of the chiefs and headmen. The theme was to depart from 'colonial models' by shifting away 'from a system of control and trying to use the traditional system (albeit in a

Table 1: Average Earnings (Nominal and Indexed) and Workforce by Full-time Base and by Gender, 1980-1997

Period	Average Earnings (Z$)	Earnings-1980 Prices (Z$)	Full-time/ Total Workforce	Females/ Total Workforce	Female Full time/Full time Total
1980	38.15	38.15	73	26	9
1981	62.04	55.64	75	22	5
1982	76.56	62.39	75	20	3
1983	88.39	59.17	72	21	3
1984	98.05	54.47	—	—	—
1985	103.90	52.95	—	—	—
1986	114.64	52.42	—	—	—
1987	122.18	47.30	63	23	3
1988	138.06	49.75	60	23	3
1989	150.74	48.11	55	26	3
1990	182.87	49.73	58	24	3
1991	203.35	44.85	57	25	4
1992	171.46	26.62	58	26	5
1993	244.23	29.70	53	28	5
1994	286.94	28.55	51	28	6
1995	295.81	24.01	52	29	6
1996	401.39	32.58	49	31	8
1997	527.15	30.12	49	31	8

Source: Kanyenze (forthcoming)

distorted fashion) to a developmental, change-oriented system' (De Valk and Wekwete 1990:91); but such a 'developmental change-oriented system' still had to be taught to 'the people' to enable Communal Land residents to act upon what was declared to be their 'felt needs'.[70]

In Urungwe, the District Commissioner (who was a colonial-era appointee) helped to organize a commission with local ZANU(PF) officials in June 1980 to set up a District Council. Despite claiming allegiance to the new rule that electoral boundaries for councillors were to be set up according to numbers and geographical criteria, they ended up being based on the old tribal boundaries.[71] During meetings with 'the tribesmen' in the Tribal Trust Lands (as documents defined them at the time), officials failed to convince the people about the importance of this new form of local government: 'A large number of tribesmen were not interested in the formation of a Council and indicated as such during the course of the meetings. They were more interested in fresh land and the handouts of fertilizer, etc.'[72] Regardless of this rejection by the 'tribesmen' who identified different 'felt needs', an election for the District Council was held in 1981. The Urungwe District Council consisted of elected councillors, all ZANU(PF) candidates, and a District Administrator (appointed by central government) as Chief Executive Officer.

Control over land in the Communal Lands was still vested in the President after the passing of the Communal Lands Act in 1982. However, land rights were officially no longer contingent on the discretion of chiefs but rather of the District Councils, with the proviso that they must take 'customary' practices into consideration when distributing those rights. ZANU(PF), whose leaders still commonly identified chiefs as supporters of the colonial regime, sought to undercut such a consideration through adding other tiers of administration to solicit 'democratic', not 'traditional', input. In 1984, Prime Minister Mugabe issued a directive to form a nested hierarchy of grassroots structures called Village Development Committees (VIDCOs) and Ward Development Committees

---

[70] This 'development-speak' term (Ferguson 1990a) from the Community Development era of the 1960s is from an April 27, 1981 memo to newly elected councillors called 'A Schedule of What to Do at Ward Meetings'. MLGRUD, Karoi. See also Alexander (1993:329ff.) on similarities between the 'development' initiatives in the 1960s and 1980s.

[71] MLGRUD, Karoi, June 20, 1980.

[72] MLGRUD, Karoi, Memo from District Commissioner, Urungwe, to Provincial Commissioner, Mashonaland North, August 20, 1980.

(WADCOs) to integrate local village needs with government planning goals and implementation of development projects. This administrative hierarchy was based largely on ZANU(PF)'s party structures, but in most areas operated alongside, rather than replacing, them.[73]

Chiefs were not completely excluded from this government. They remained salaried employees and were given advisory roles to the District Council and a prominent position in 'cultural' matters, particularly in motivating the community for 'development' and in respect of 'spiritual matters'.[74] In 1983, 'traditional leaders' were given an official role in land allocation when the Urungwe District Council and the District Administrator decided that applicants for land had to be vetted by Kraal-head, Party, and District Council (see Rutherford 1996 for further discussion and Alexander 1993 for a close examination of these policies in two other districts).[75]

Farm workers were excluded from local government bodies, as commercial farms were under the control of Rural Councils (initially established in the 1960s) which granted franchise only to property-holders. In the name of ending the 'dualistic heritage' of colonial local authorities, the government passed the Rural District Councils Act in 1988 (implemented in 1993). This amalgamated District Councils and Rural Councils. Yet, the franchise of this new act initially depended on the colonial spatial arrangement. Councillors and voting qualifications were divided according to land tenure (communal, commercial, resettlement, and urban). This meant that farm workers, who did not hold property in the commercial farming areas, were still denied the vote in local government elections. Minister Chikowore justified this discrimination on the criterion of

---

[73] One thousand people form a VIDCO and six VIDCOs form a WADCO, which is chaired by the local councillor for the District Council. The 'development needs' are to be negotiated at both VIDCO and WADCO levels before coming to the District Council and District Development Committee comprised of all district heads of central government departments and chaired by the District Administrator. The various District Councils of a Province were co-ordinated into a Provincial Council with a corresponding Provincial Development Committee to co-ordinate provincial heads of central government departments. The underlying philosophy was that this increased 'popular participation' in planning and better co-ordinated central government plans with local authorities (De Valk and Wekwete 1990). Local political ZANU(PF) committees were originally set up during the war in areas occupied by ZANLA (ZANU's armed wing). After 1980, these committees were consolidated and other ones formed with membership and the nested hierarchies of committees based on a combination of demographics and territoriality. (*The Herald*, February 8, 1982).

[74] For example, Hurungwe District Council, Resolution 145 declared 'Chiefs Nematombo and Kazangarare be sent to Rukomeshi to perform spiritual rites as regards killing of elephants'.

[75] Hurungwe District Council, Minutes of Special Interim Committee. September 1, 1983.

class: if farm workers 'were to vote, then 200 workers could vote out their employers or their bosses for whatever reasons et cetera. So these are the considerations that we've had to take into account.' (March 3, 1988, Zimbabwe Parliamentary Debates. Col. 2881). In other words, the Minister declared that the rights of citizenship of those who own the means of production are greater than those who work in commercial farming areas. Only in late 1997 did farm workers get the franchise to vote in local government elections. This made farm workers an important political constituency in the 1998 Rural District Council elections, particularly for ZANU(PF) candidates who largely replaced (white) commercial farmers as councillors for commercial farming wards on many councils.

Farm workers and the 'land question'

Farm workers played a predominant role in the land question during these initial years of Independence. In the late 1970s, Africans began settling vacant state land and abandoned farms, a process which increased dramatically after hostilities ended in 1980. Although commercial farmers protested loudly against these 'squatters', many of the illegal occupants drew support from local ZANU(PF) branches. ZANU(PF) politicians were initially sympathetic to what they saw as black peasants from overcrowded Communal Lands taking 'the land question' into their own hands and often bypassed, or over-ruled, their own resettlement bureaucracy. In many cases, 'squatters' became 'settlers' on government land resettlement schemes *ex post facto* (Herbst 1990:63ff.; see also Alexander 1991, 1993).

'Squatters' were not always depicted as 'peasants' in official discourses. Occasionally they were also seen as 'foreigners', ex-farm workers who had lost contact with their country of origin as well as their jobs on white farms. In many areas, farm workers comprised a high percentage of 'squatters' (Kinsey 1983:172, Herbst 1990:70). The category 'squatters' carried these two identities in official discourses. In the early 1980s, government treated both identities sympathetically, albeit 'foreign' squatters were seen as a responsibility it assumed from white farmers who had abandoned their workers and, more importantly, their *responsibilities* to them. For example, the Minister of Lands, Resettlement and Rural Development told the Commercial Farmers' Union (CFU, the new name for the RNFU) in 1981 that these so-called 'squatters' included 'abandoned farm labourers' of 'Malawian or Mozambican or Zambian extraction. They have absolutely nowhere to go. Nobody can expect government now, with all the other problems, to say that these people should be accommodated elsewhere'.[76]

Commercial farmer groups continued to raise concerns over squatters on unoccupied farms and empty state land. In Hurungwe, farmers in the Karoi North ICA declared that the government had allowed 'a deplorable breakdown in planning when good virgin land could be allowed to be overrun by potential settlers, with no access roads, water supplies, contouring or plans of any sort for the best use and care of the land'.[77] This lack of planning for resettlement farms would lead, they threatened, to a replication of the sites of un-modernity as 'traditional' practices would infiltrate the proposed modern sites of planned development: 'The area would become another denuded TTL [Tribal Trust Land] within a year or two, if government did not exert strict control.'

Government had ambitious plans of settling 161,000 families on land it purchased from white farmers. The targeted settlers were those displaced by the war; war veterans, and peasants from overpopulated Communal Lands (new name for Tribal Trust Lands). Under the guidance of the state (for the schemes were on state land and, as under the Native Land Husbandry Act programme, each settler was given annual permits for residence, cultivation, and pasturing a certain quantity of stock), the government envisioned these resettlement schemes as a means to increase agricultural production in the countryside, and to develop African smallholders and the nation at large (Kinsey 1983, Bratton 1990, Moyo 1995).

However, poor rains, worsening global markets, class ambitions, and limited foreign investment helped to ensure that the new government did not stray too far from the inherited relations of rule. After the early 1980s, rural development pronouncements of government bureaucrats and politicians increasingly followed official articulations of the CFU and major international aid agencies such as the World Bank, which downplayed resettlement and emphasized

---

[76] The next year the Minister of Lands repeated this message: 'Perhaps the families you are mentioning [who lived on a nearby resettlement scheme] must have been the labour force which was found there, *not the problem to government*. Normally this is giving a problem to government. Many farmers have got a labour force and this labour force is mainly from Mozambique and Malawi, they are not Zimbabwe Nationals, and normally when we buy farms we find them there and my Ministry has been accommodating them one way or another.' CFU Annual Congress Reports. 1981, 1982; my emphasis.

[77] Karoi Group of ICA Minutes, November 20, 1980 and August 28, 1982. By 1982, there were two formal resettlement schemes being planned in Hurungwe.

restructuring the Communal Lands. Land redistribution never reached its ambitious targets, although 50,000 families were resettled on 2.7 million hectares by the early 1990s (Bratton 1994, Moyo 1995). The colonial spatialization of power relations resurfaced as official policy – rural areas once again became equated with 'traditional' social relations that needed to be changed by 'modern' commercial and urban relations. Colonial-era policies like villagization, enforced conservation measures and individual tenure were more and more openly floated by bureaucrats and politicians as a way to 'develop' the rural areas (see Alexander 1993, Ranger 1993a for closer examination of the politics and debates concerning this tendency).

The discursive idioms employed by the government to promote ESAP – 'liberalism', 'efficiency' and 'privatization' – have also been used by a more combative CFU against the government's reinvigorated resettlement policy that targets more than five million hectares of commercial farm land for compulsory acquisition. After amending the constitution, the ZANU(PF) government passed the 1992 Land Acquisition Act, which permits the compulsory expropriation of designated farm land (utilized or unutilized). Parliament, not 'the market', sets compensation rates and the judiciary is excluded from reviewing the fairness of compensation (see Naldi 1993).

The government ignored farmers' calls to scrap its legislation and begun to expropriate farms. A number of the initial farms designated under this act in 1992-93 were owned by black farmers, giving the impression that 'economic' utilization and not 'race' is the main criteria for expropriation (*Herald* August 13, 1992, *Sunday Mail* March 7, 1993). However, the government soon rescinded the designation of most of the black-owned farms on the grounds that it should support the 'indigenization' of commercial farming (*Horizon*, October 1993).

For the rest of the 1990s, the government has been tacking back and forth in terms of land designation and identification of settlers, creating uncertainty for everyone. From gazetting over 1,500 farms in late 1997 to de-listing half of them in mid-1998, and from claiming it will follow its own laws in terms of compensation and acquisition to asserting it will ignore the law in order to right a historical wrong, the government has been ambivalent on its plans and policies in the face of pressure from international donors, the CFU, human rights organisations, internal ZANU(PF) disputes, and pressure from land-hungry constituents (Moyo 1998). It has also wavered on who will be selected for resettlement: from land-hungry peasants to indigenous commercial farmers, from well-organized war veterans to people associated with the government and Party. Given the growing scandals about politicians and senior Party members grabbing land, there is concern by many Zimbabweans that this will be mainly a 'land-grab' for the 'chefs' connected to the ruling Party. Of the 4,400 or so commercial farmers, there are a growing number of black commercial farmers, from an estimated 200 in 1990 (Parade, December 1990; *Financial Gazette* March 12, 1992) to almost one thousand in 1999 (*The Insider* February 1999). Many of these are senior politicians, civil servants, and Party members (e.g. Thornycroft 1991, *Financial Gazette*, April 14, 1994).

Even in terms of the process of selecting settlers, there is uncertainty: chiefs and headmen, who have been officially revived as crucial components of rural administration (see Alexander 1993), are given the task of writing down the names of potential candidates for resettlement, yet the District Councils and secular authorities have the final say in making the selections. In short, land has become an even more opaque issue (see Rutherford and Worby 1999).

Up until the uncertainty of the late 1990s, though, farm workers had become identified in official discourses as *persona non grata* in resettlement areas and even in Communal Lands. Their identity is still largely defined by its colonial genealogy, and they continue to be avoided for resettlement. In the colonial period, foreign workers were legally prohibited from settling in the reserves/Tribal Trust Lands. In the early 1980s, that prohibition was lifted and indeed many 'foreign' farm workers in Hurungwe were encouraged by local Party activists to settle in the Communal Lands, as will be discussed in Chapter Seven. They also comprised a notable proportion of the 'illegal settlers' on state and private land. By the mid-1980s onwards, government officials, leaked government reports, various 'experts', and President Mugabe himself have all chastised past resettlement exercises and have recommended, among other things, that selected settlers should have proven agricultural skills rather than being 'squatters' or those without previous farming experience (e.g. *Herald* March 28, 1992, April 13, 1992, April 15, 1992, September 25, 1992). The 'illegal occupants' – those who did not go through the official selection criteria for resettlement – began to be removed.

By the mid-1980s in Hurungwe, resettlement schemes were officially being reserved more and more for black farmers who already had some agricultural implements and experience and hundreds of 'squatters' were forcibly removed.[78] Such 'planning' even began to extend the designation of 'squatters' to those farming in Communal Lands without official recognition.[79]

The 'foreigner' side of 'squatters' was also being stressed as a sign that government has less responsibility for them than the white farmers, their 'previous bosses'. Moreover, the fact that they were (ex-)farm workers was seen by some as a sign that they were incapable of supervising and developing themselves, unable to accept 'order', and thus should not be resettled. As a ZANU(PF) MP, Mr Katsande (Mutoko), declared in support of a motion critical of current resettlement policy,

> 'Again, Mr. Speaker, on the foreigners, I still want to point out that the problem is that they have failed to accept the order... They were left by their previous bosses, the farmers who were there. They were only used to being supervised and they cannot supervise themselves. I think if this is to continue, these people need not just be resettled and be given 12 acres because the meaning of resettlement, since these were commercial farming areas, the intention of the government was to continue on with productivity, to have more production, but this is not happening now because most of these people have no experience whatsoever and they do not have enough implements to use on that land.[80]

Farm workers and 'foreigners' in general were often blamed for the failure of the resettlement policies of the 1980s as officials, donors and commentators began to speculate on redesigning resettlement in the 1990s to make it more 'efficient' and 'productive' (Moyo 1995). As one official reasoned, since past resettlement had not relieved pressure from Communal Lands, government should

[78] On December 2, 1987 the Hurungwe District Council agreed that, among other things, the candidate for resettlement had to have enough agricultural implements 'to facilitate a good take-off in the production process in the new area'. At another meeting, it was suggested that since two resettlement schemes given to landless settlers were not developing, councillors should 'find out 5 master farmers in each ward and those then be considered for allocation'. Hurungwe District Council Minutes, November 24, 1989.

[79] In 1987, a report prepared by six government ministries, the provincial governor, local politicians and CFU members, called 'Squatters in Mashonaland West', identified 49,000 squatters in Communal, Municipal and Resettlement areas and only 1,000 in the commercial farm area. CFU Annual Congress Report, 1987.

[80] February 3, 1988. Zimbabwe Parliamentary Debates. Col. 2710.

pursue a 'reorganisation programme' that included granting title deeds to peasants and selecting only qualified 'settlers' – 'Why should we feel we must give land only to illiterate workers who were formerly working on farms?' (*Weekly Mail*, September 4-10, 1992). The disqualification of farm workers is predominantly articulated in a way that portrayed them as lacking the proper moral constitution for development. As *The Sunday Mail* said in an editorial in 1992,

> *Zimbabweans are normally hardworking given the right conditions to establish homes. But given the labour patterns in the region, there are also those individuals who are unaccustomed to hard work on the land. These are the individuals who traditionally have worked on commercial farms and mines. How will they adjust when resettled in given areas? (November 22).*

To return to the speech made by the ZANU(PF) MP declaring that farm workers 'were only used to being supervised and they cannot supervise themselves' (February 3, 1988): it, like the editorial, portrays farm workers as lacking the self-discipline required for 'development'. Rather, their labour requires the supervision of a boss. The official identity of the farm workers' 'self' was intimately connected with their white 'bosses'. As old colonial plans are dusted off for controlling the 'development' of peasants, farm workers, lacking the disposition for directed self-improvement in these official discourses, become unsuitable candidates for 'development'. Instead, it is assumed that they are more suited to be supervised by a (white) farmer. In other words, the identities forged within the colonial spatialization of development and government, that is of domestic government, still shape policy in post-colonial Zimbabwe (see Moyo, Rutherford, Amanor-Wilks 2000).

Conclusion

Some commentators assume that the natural 'space' of commercial farms, their rural and dispersed nature, is a factor in determining the disempowered position of farm workers (Herbst 1990:179). This view ignores how 'space' is discursively determined in official discourses. This is a crucial factor in terms of the poor resource-access and disempowerment of farm workers. I have suggested that the definition of space on commercial farms as a site of domestic government – as opposed to a site of bureaucratic government, as is the case for Communal Lands and other black workers – has played a key role in the current situation of farm workers; it has created enduring frameworks of interpretation and has constituted particular institutional arrangements.

As I will demonstrate in the following chapters, the access of farm workers to new resettlement schemes has been officially doubted, even if their source of employment, the farm, has been designated for acquisition. Farm workers are stigmatized as morally unfit for 'development', as foreigners who should be looked after by commercial farmers and not by the government. Only a small proportion of farm workers are GAPWUZ members and, with the officially sanctioned on-farm regulation of discipline and grievances, the union's responsibility lies mainly with annual wage negotiations in Harare, leaving it few meaningful ties with existing membership. Farm workers' access to resources on farms – gardens, credit, housing, bonuses – rather depends on the rules established by the farm owners themselves. Yet farm workers, differentiated by gender, age, nationality and job status, negotiate these power relations to challenge, reinforce, and improve their situation.

Colonial spatial distinctions, identities and differences have continued to shape official discourse about farm workers' resource access since Independence. For some, particularly for many commercial farmers, their lack of 'development' is treated largely as a concern for the domestic relations on commercial farms. Alternatively, the conditions of farm workers are interpreted as the result solely of processes of race and class, a sign of super-exploitation, which victimize farm workers and which need to be overthrown. Neither perspective examines how identities of race, class and gender have been part of the forms of government for the site of 'European/commercial farms'. How these official assumptions play out in local discourses of my 'field work' – in responses, replications, resistances, and transgressions that help determine farm workers' access to resources – is examined in the following chapters.

Chapter 3

White farmers in rural Hurungwe

'Race' in the Kariba Room

On a warm March evening during the drought of 1992, the historically sedimented contours of the land debate in Zimbabwe appeared in a Holiday Inn banquet room in downtown Harare. My friends and I joined an overflow crowd of predominantly well-dressed black men and women, along with a small but noticeable number of casually dressed white men and women, gathered to attend and participate in a public debate on 'The Land Question in Zimbabwe' organized by the Southern African Political Economy Series Trust and the African Association of Political Scientists. The impetus for the debate was the Land Acquisition Bill which was speedily making its way through Parliament and, simultaneously, causing much consternation and discussion in local and foreign media and diplomatic channels. The four speakers and/or their organizations – Kempton Makamure, Dean of the Faculty of Law at the University of Zimbabwe; Alan Burl, President of the Commercial Farmers' Union (CFU); Nicholas Mudzengerere, Assistant Secretary General of the Zimbabwean Congress of Trade Unions (ZCTU); and Elizabeth Feltoe, Legal Officer for the Catholic Commission for Justice and Peace – were all known to be critical of the bill for one reason or another.

Although a number of substantive policy, legal and historical issues were raised by each speaker and during the ensuing question period, the evening was defined by the trope of race in both form and content. The style and the dynamics of the debate were very much concerned with racial identities, as the speakers, notably Makamure and Burl who were the dominant presences, elicited laughter, applause, and heckles from members of the audience who identified with the subtle and explicit racial comments and criticisms that were made. For my purposes here, I will concentrate on Burl's use of a 'European identity' in his arguments that night.[1]

---

[1] Direct quotations from Burl's speech come from an edited tape of the debate I copied. For this, I am grateful to the assistance given to me by Ms Penny Lumley. All quotes from the question period come from my own notes.

Burl repeated several times during the debate that it was necessary to overcome the 'us and them mentality' that drives the question of land redistribution, implying 'black versus white' versions used by the government. Yet his whole argument, following the official CFU position on land resettlement (see CFU 1991), was premised on letting 'us', white Zimbabwean farmers, organize 'them', black resettlement farmers. It rested on the 'willing buyer-willing seller' basis, which had conditioned government acquisition of lands since 1980. The proposal was also based on the use of the CFU's district-level farmers' associations and the self-governing Intensive Conservation Area committees (ICAs) to identify possible land for resettlement and to assist Agritex, the government agency which designs individual resettlement schemes, in 'select[ing] the best method of resettlement for each property'. In short, the CFU was arguing for a form of decentralized administration of land resettlement with greater input by what came across as the 'local community'.

Burl began his speech by identifying those whom the CFU represents, those who comprised the 'local community': 'We as much as the *black* Zimbabweans wish to have a law...' (emphasis mine). In other words, the CFU represents *white* Zimbabweans who appeal to the 'law' as a supposedly neutral way to ensure fair treatment. Despite the assumption that all citizens are treated equally before the law, Burl employed sociological distinctions to underpin the CFU's proposal for land resettlement. In this proposal, Burl suggested that local (white) commercial farmers would assist future (black) resettlement farmers. As he put it, these farmers can 'train the resettled people in the operation of cash flow, the procurement of their inputs, and they can see that the goods arrive at the property at the right time'. That is, they would monitor the resettlement programme to ensure that the new resettlement farmers would follow 'commercial' practices and arrest 'the spread of communal land'.

In the CFU's plan, white associations such as ICA committees are vested with the responsibility of providing surveillance of the boundary between modernity (commercial practices) and tradition (subsistence-oriented Communal Lands). As Burl put it, '[l]and use on resettled areas falls under the watchful eye of current ICA committees and it retains the collateral value of land'. Expanding on this point, he claimed that 'communal agriculture' was successful in the 1890s (the decade in which formal colonization began) when the excess of unoccupied land allowed Africans to 'shift around'. But with limited land in the 'modern world', unless people were forced to be 'accountable' (implying private ownership of land) they would try, he contended, to get more and more land without investing responsibility and care in it. Not only was Burl touching upon the hoary 'tragedy of the commons' argument that presumes only private property ensures sustainable and profitable development (e.g. Hardin 1968; see Peters 1994 for a good critique), but he was also assuming that 'shifting cultivation', the colonial designation of 'traditional' African cultivation patterns, and not 'commercial' farming practices, were *still* in use in contemporary Communal Lands and resettlement farms. Once again, Burl was claiming that the CFU should have a greater role in the resettlement schemes partly to ensure that African farmers would be brought into the 'modern', commercial world.

Part and parcel of Burl's modernist argument was a certain form of 'politics'; a politics which James Ferguson (1990a) has called 'anti-politics', a term that describes the translation of political arguments into neutral, technical, so-called 'non-political' rhetoric. Burl invited his audience to recognize the importance of allowing the 'local community', white farmers and their institutions, to play a major role in the future resettlement exercise since they can, through their knowledge and skills, develop the new settlers along modern, commercial lines. To emphasize the non-political nature of the CFU's proposal, Burl contrasted it with the 'political solution' proffered by government which, according to him, selects farms on the basis of race.

Burl, and the CFU, promoted a view that characterizes the administrative (and executive) side of government as 'political', as something that should be external to the decision-making involved in the selection and implementation of land resettlement. Rather the key mechanisms for land resettlement should be clearly laid-out rules, a law, that treats white and black the same, and involves the 'local community'. Race should have nothing to do with it. Yet, Burl's politics in this debate rested very heavily on an 'us and them' contrast, stressing the advantages of a modern 'white identity' to the point that his 'us', the local institutions of white farmers, play a major role in resettlement as a guarantor of its (modern) commercial success. These assumptions of (non)politics, law, (non)race, and modernity carry a lot of contemporary weight in the government of white farms.

Burl's language in the debate is shared by many officials and other commentators, as noted in the previous chapter. It assumes that commercial farmers represent modern practices that should be emulated by resettlement, if not also communal, farmers. Such a view is promoted as a technical, non-political and non-racial solution to the land question. It also presumes that the only local community, the 'public', in commercial farming areas is that of (white) commercial farmers.

The discourse of 'white settler culture'; discourses of 'the modern European'

Alan Burl also used metaphors that inform a discourse of 'European identity' in Zimbabwe. With regard to such an identity, Dane Kennedy (1987) has provided a cultural history of white settlers in Southern Rhodesia (and Kenya) up to the start of World War Two. Surveying a variety of settler practices and assumptions about climate, law and order, white women, disease, language, and conflict resolution, Kennedy suggests that there was an underlying concern in 'white settler culture' to ensure and enforce a hierarchical division and relationship between 'Europeans' and 'Africans'. Although this segregation had definite consequences, it did not, Kennedy persuasively argues, lead to the assumption of racial exclusiveness. Rather this assumption was integral to the identity, part of the 'webs of signification', of 'the white settler culture' that was preoccupied with maintaining its privileged position in the colonial order through distancing itself from 'Africans': 'It was characterized above all by the effort to isolate and institutionalize white settlement within a rigid set of physical, linguistic, social, economic, and political boundaries' (1987:189).

Although Kennedy's explanation is similar to other cultural investigations of white settlers in southern Africa and elsewhere (e.g. Crapanzano 1985, Stoler 1989, Comaroff and Comaroff 1991), he tends to reify 'white culture', giving it an independent and unified agency in and of itself, defining it as a proper noun with a 'the' in front of 'settler culture'. Although I am in agreement with his characterization of some of the major discursive themes employed by white settlers in the past, and will note their continuation into the present, I do not agree with Kennedy's claim that 'the settler culture' is the primary author of these themes, the (functional) source of these narratives and distinctions. I prefer to reverse this assumption and look at how these various discourses sustain, among other things, a notion of a unified 'European culture' or 'race'. Looking at the everyday ways in which a European identity is (re)created, I contend that it is possible to build a sense of how notions, arguments, feelings and attitudes inform and challenge it. The consequences of such discourses on how farm workers access resources will be discussed by locating this identity within the official and local genealogies of government rather than axiomatically equating particular political outcomes with racial and cultural identities.

This latter tendency is common among most commentators on rural Zimbabwe who associate particular political agendas with the peculiar reading of the dualism between tradition and modernity which infuses their explanatory models. Burl articulated the argument which assumes that the practices of white farmers are 'modern' and should, in turn, be the instructive model for edifying 'traditional' Africans: Africans as a 'race' are imagined to be generally an evolutionary step behind Europeans, to be 'traditional' and not 'modern', and thus require guidance. As is dramatically apparent in the events of 2000, others assume that because most commercial farmers are 'white', they all share a common identity of white privilege which is against the interests of 'Zimbabwe': that they are still Rhodesians, of the old order, who have failed to properly adjust to black majority rule. Yet, both assumptions reinforce a reified subject of 'the' European farmer, ignoring the complexities of this 'European identity' and, more importantly for my argument, the particular possibilities it presents and specific barriers it imposes on farm workers. This is not to say that I support, or advocate, race-based identities – indeed, I am trying in this book to challenge these and other essentialist logics (e.g. Appiah 1992). Rather, I suggest that whilst one cannot easily assume such identities to be false and easily changed, they must be taken into account in political critiques. This chapter tries to set out the local knowledges of white farmers in Karoi North ICA, knowledges about which I learned during my research and, more importantly, knowledges that have helped structure the lives of farm workers.

I argue that these contribute to the privileging of the authority of European farm operators as the dominant rule or law on white-owned and -operated commercial farms. It is a law that rests both on a notion of the inviolability of the space of commercial farms against the 'politics' of government and on the assumption that Europeans have a responsibility for edifying their African workers. Both notions coincide and overlap in their assumption of what I call 'domestic government': any conflict or problem that occurs at work or in the compound should be resolved through the authority structures on the farm and not from outside; in turn, the edification, and the lessons for the moral and intellectual improvement of African workers depends on a close relationship between farmer and worker.

Returning to the debate, 'race' was an obvious defining feature in this discourse. Given that Mugabe's government has not been remiss in singling out white farmers for being 'racist', most white farmers I met pragmatically downplayed 'race' (as Alan Burl did). Instead, a sense of 'community' became established by an association of 'Europeans' with 'modernity', a modernity that comprises an iterative historical encounter with the 'traditional' lifestyle of Africans; a modernity, for its speakers, that was above 'politics'. It is an anti-politics in that it indicates a rational and efficient disbursement of resources as exemplified by the 'fact' that rural whites form the bedrock of Zimbabwean commercial agriculture. It is a modernity that is dependent on particular assumptions about individuals, gender, and domestic relations within and between Europeans and Africans; a modernity that made the domestic relation between white farmers and black workers the dominant form of government.

In this chapter on the discursive spaces of white farmers, I concentrate on two overlapping domains that constitute and enforce this 'European identity' in the Karoi area. The first domain is inscribed architecture, the formal and informal spatial boundaries within commercial farms and along their borders. I explore the associations of these spatial distinctions through the difference between 'Europeans' and 'Africans' in terms of authority, the ways in which white farmers value themselves in these spaces as paternal figures in charge of the conduct of 'their' workers. The second domain is 'history', the various articulated traditions and narratives that give a 'past' to these farmers and to 'Africans'. Such histories shape the differing perspectives on the position of 'white farmers' in 'black Zimbabwe'. They help to locate the contrast between 'Europeans' and 'Africans' along the axis of 'modernity' which informs contemporary distinctions between farmers and farm workers, and between both of them and Communal Land farmers. These domains are linked to the issue of 'management', the field of labour relations itself. As I discuss in the next chapter, the ways to supervise, discipline, and reward (differentiated) farm workers draw from the notions of a domestic responsibility produced from these spatial inscriptions and historical genres. I examine these local knowledges and distinctions that contribute to a European identity mainly on Chidhadhadha farm and adjacent commercial farms in Karoi North ICA,[2] and outline the forms of power that shape the access of farm workers to resources. The remaining chapters of this book will expand on some of the points raised in this chapter and examine how different farm workers have responded to these boundaries of authority and control.

Keeping Karoi commercial farms 'European': spatial boundaries

The commercial farms in Hurungwe, as in Zimbabwe as a whole, are predominantly owned and operated by white men. The few black commercial farmers in Hurungwe in the early 1990s farmed on the periphery of the commercial farming areas on land abandoned during the war, or just after 1980, either because of guerrilla attacks or the inadequacy of the soils for tobacco production. Most white farmers maintained an identity as Europeans through formal organizations such as sending their children to private schools (these did not actively discriminate by race but their high tuition fees gave them the reputation amongst local whites and blacks as 'white schools') and through informal get-togethers with other 'whites' for sporting activities (mainly rugby and tennis), bridge nights, parties, fund-raising affairs and holidays. Black commercial farmers made little impact on this identity; commercial farms and farmers were typically associated as 'European' in most conversations with Zimbabweans, in the media, and in academic and policy literature. Yet demographically, whites are a minority, even on commercial farms.

According to a 1982 survey, there were only 260 farm operators, most of them white, in the commercial farming area of Hurungwe, compared to 11,500 permanent and non-permanent workers. The ratio of white to black is even more skewed when one factors in the 44,288 people classified as 'dependants'.[3] The population of the

---

[2] Like all commercial farming areas (see, e.g., Hodder-Williams 1983), Hurungwe more generally and Karoi North in particular is distinct in some of its traditions amongst commercial farmers. For instance, as noted in Chapter Two, this area was frequently targeted by guerrillas during the liberation war. Although there are many similarities between commercial farmers in Karoi North ICA and those elsewhere in Zimbabwe, particularly in their own identification as 'white farmers', it is important to note that there are also distinctive economic, cultural and historical features that help to define the locality of 'Karoi' which are likely reflected in my analysis and argument.

[3] See Government of Zimbabwe (1982b:48-55). The survey did not include 'dependants' of owners/operators. But from my survey of fourteen commercial farmers, which will be discussed in this chapter, the average number of people living with the owners/operators was six – a figure that does not seriously challenge the demographic weight in favour of Africans.

commercial farming area in Hurungwe was 51,270.[4] This marking of commercial farms as 'European areas' was thus not 'natural' but subject to a series of discourses and struggles that explicitly or subtly define them as such.

Most commercial farms have at least four rigidly defined spaces that contributed to their identity: a living area for owners and managers (whom I gloss as 'operators'); the living area for workers called the 'compound' (or for some, particularly those involved in development programmes, the 'farm village'); the actual fields where the crops are grown and animals pastured; and the buildings of the work site. I shall explain these distinctions by providing an ethnographic description and by presenting the results of a survey I carried out among farm operators on fifteen farms in Karoi North ICA.[5] Though I discuss these spaces in more detail later in this chapter, and in subsequent ones, the next section focuses on some of the main demographic and economic attributes of the farm operators and commercial farms in the area. Such attributes are discursive constructs, inscribed by my survey and negotiated during the process of administering and analysing it. I employ these figures to provide a sense of the distribution of resources, forms and genealogies of ownership, categories of workers, and economic uses on these commercial farms.

The home as farm: white residences on commercial farms

When I was looking for a way to carry out my research during my initial trip to Karoi in April 1992, the first white residents and farmers I met told me that finding a place to stay could be difficult. There were not sufficient houses in Karoi for the demand and many people were already renting the few unoccupied houses on commercial farms.

---

4   From 'Total Population by Sex in District and Wards, Total Number of Households and Average Household Size in District and Wards, Mashonaland West Province, Hurungwe District', kindly sent to me by the District Administrator, Hurungwe District, Mr B. Chahuruva.

5   I administered a survey to fourteen of the nineteen operators on fourteen farms in Karoi North ICA in March 1993. I had previously carried out a survey of farm workers on fifteen farms, but I was unable to arrange a time to survey the operator of one of the fifteen farms. On Chidhadhadha, I tried to carry out a census of most of the permanent and seasonal farm worker households and some of the contract workers from September 1992 to January 1993. Then I carried out a survey asking similar questions to twenty randomly selected farm workers' households on each of the other fourteen farms. In my survey of the farm workers, I treat every member of the household who was currently working as a farm worker. I employed four local secondary school students in addition to Rinse Nyamuda to assist in conducting the survey.

Not finding a place to stay, I raised the possibility with a few people I met of living in the workers' compound. Their response was a look of incredulity followed by a polite comment that this was not an option. As one white farm manager explained, a white person could not live in conditions similar to Africans because 'white men are not used to living on the bare minimum like they are'. Living spaces were marked not just by class but by a racialized essence.

I eventually met Geoff and Dan, owner-operators of Chidhadhadha farm, who not only had a place to rent but also allowed me and Rinse, my research assistant whom I met in Harare, to have a more or less free run of their farm; a privilege, I soon discovered, that strongly distinguished us within the local field of power and discourse. My living arrangements confirmed my *murungu*, my white, status to farm workers – not only did I have recognizably better accommodation, but by virtue of living on the *murungu* side, the entire farm was open to me. It was, in a very real sense, an extension of my home, a privilege given to *varungu*, whites.

In my experience, the living area for owners and managers was the most rigidly separated space, with each house surrounded by a three to four metre-high fence, occasionally with a security guard posted at the gate, characteristics which owed much to the insecurity felt during the liberation war. But their maintenance during a time of putative peace in postcolonial Zimbabwe was telling: white farmers have still been very much a 'target', though at that time it was in the form of government nationalist rhetoric, pro-land reform promises during elections, and the actions of thieves rather than in terms of guerrilla attacks. In many ways, they were mini-compounds in and of themselves. 'Home' was a privilege that had to be defended.

On Chidhadhadha there were four such mini-compounds. Each of the two farm owners and their wives and children lived in a large house with adjacent gardens and surrounded by tall fences and walls. The father of one of the owners lived in a smaller house, though it also had its own garden and had a large chain-link fence along its perimeter. Sharing one of its fences was the mini-compound for a thatch-roofed cottage. Though it was the smallest house, it still had four spacious rooms, electricity and running water, a small flower garden and a few fruit trees. It too was surrounded by a fence, but its gate did not have a lock. I rented this cottage.

A few days after arriving on the farm, I discovered the restrictions and permissibility of these spaces. Although feeling a bit uncomfortable entering a strange place, Rinse and I entered the compound without much hesitation to introduce ourselves to the men of authority amongst the farm workers. When I told the village chairman that he could come to my place any time if he had further questions he sheepishly informed me that this would be impermissible. Only foremen and those workers who worked in or nearby the houses of the whites could approach my house, he told me. By living on the white side of the fence, and with permission of the owners, Rinse and I were able to have access to all the spaces of Chidhadhadha. It clearly placed Rinse and I on the farmer side of the forms of authority, leaving many workers suspicious of our intentions. According to the conventions of the farm, it was 'natural' for me as a *murungu* to live in a mini-compound, but it was odd for me to spend a lot of time with the farm workers; it was 'natural' for Rinse as an African to work for me, a 'white man', but it was odd for him to live with me. Rinse initially feared some form of retribution such as witchcraft, particularly from senior workers, for having access to such a privilege. My living arrangements also aroused discomfort in some of the white farmers I knew; by having Rinse live with me in my cottage, the separation of white and black was broken. Farmers' domestic servants, typically the only black workers allowed into their houses, all lived in the compound with the other workers. Although I heard that some white farmers were offended by my arrangement with Rinse, we had no problems with any of them, given our acceptance by Geoff and Dan.

In my survey, twelve of fourteen farms were run by European men, the other two by African men. All of the men were married. Twelve were owner-operators, one was a manager for the owner of four adjoining farms and the other leased his farm from a widow who still lived on the farm (but whose own adult children had no interest in farming).

On average there were six people living with the operators in their residences, of whom two were children. This relatively high number was due to the fact that four of the farms had more than one operator; on all but one of these, the additional operators came from within the immediate family. The other adults were retired parents, managers, and tenants.

The majority of the respondents came from farming backgrounds – three were farming on what had been their parents' farm; nine of the respondents' parents had owned their own farms. Half of their spouses came from farming backgrounds. All but one respondent had previous farm experience. All were currently full-time farmers with no other occupation, excepting one who was also a director of a Karoi company. Legally, twelve of the farms were incorporated as limited liability companies. Almost all of the directors were family members.

These indicators seem to confirm the stereotype of Zimbabwean commercial farm operators (used, for instance, by the CFU and media) that they are married white men, come from farming backgrounds, are full-time farmers, and, though knowledgeable about business practices (as signified by the high number of incorporated farms), are supported largely by their own family. They are both 'modern' and 'rugged individuals' (see von Blanckenburg 1994). Yet, all these 'indicators' are subject to cultural definition and contest in historical arenas of power and political interest.

The 'farm village', or compound life

Whenever I made a first visit to any of the farms near Chidhadhadha, the operator usually gave me a tour of the place. Most took me to the farm's compound, knowing that I was interested in the lives of farm workers. Passing through the barbed-wire fence that inevitably separated the compound from the work site and his own house, the operator always impressed upon me the work he had done, or was going to do, to improve the living conditions of the workers. Indeed almost any talk of edification of farm workers by these Karoi North farmers, and the CFU itself, centred exclusively on the compound. The domestic comforts of the farm workers took priority over their work conditions.

On Chidhadhadha, the link between the compound and the work site was a gate in the four-metre high barbed wire fence, manned by a security guard twenty-four hours a day (see Map 4). Where the compound touched the main road there was no gate. Unlike the operators, the workers were never completely fenced in; they were less physically rooted to the farm than the operators. Most of the fences, originally installed during the war[6], were kept after 1980 as a security measure. This was necessary, I was told by farmers, to prevent workers from stealing property. The compound was marked not just as a place of workers, a site of Africans, but also as an area of possible danger.

---

[6] The Zimbabwe war of Independence 1967-80.

Table 2: Work-force by Contract and by Gender on Hurungwe Commercial Farms Surveyed

Farm surveyed	PERMANENT WORKERS Number (and % of Total Workforce)			SEASONAL WORKERS Number (and % of Total Workforce)			TOTAL WORKFORCE Number (and % of Total Workforce)		
	Male	Female	Combined	Male	Female	Combined	Male	Female	Combined
1.	237 (98)	5 (2)	242	40 (33)	80 (67)	120	277 (77)	85 (23)	362
2.	90 (100)	0 (0)	90	19 (37)	33 (63)	52	109 (77)	33 (23)	142
3.	35 (100)	0 (0)	35	17 (41)	25 (59)	42	52 (68)	25 (32)	77
4.	40 (100)	0 (0)	40	16 (52)	15 (48)	31	56 (79)	15 (21)	71
5.	40 (100)	0 (0)	50	27 (52)	25 (48)	52	67 (73)	25 (27)	92
6.	51 (100)	0 (0)	51	27 (45)	33 (55)	60	78 (70)	33 (30)	111
7.	70 (93)	5 (7)	75	15 (25)	45 (75)	60	85 (63)	50 (37)	135
8.	40 (98)	1 (2)	41	15 (60)	10 (40)	25	55 (92)	11 (8)	66
9.	62 (95)	3 (5)	65	32 (53)	29 (47)	61	94 (75)	32 (25)	126
10.	65 (100)	0 (0)	65	35 (44)	45 (56)	80	100 (69)	45 (31)	145
11.	45 (70)	19 (30)	64	8 (53)	7 (47)	15	53 (67)	26 (33)	79
12.	90 (98)	2 (2)	92	32 (43)	42 (57)	74	122 (74)	44 (26)	166
13.	60 (100)	0 (0)	60	20 (40)	30 (60)	50	80 (73)	30 (27)	110
14.	48 (96)	2 (4)	50	19 (61)	12 (39)	31	67 (83)	14 (17)	81
Total	973 (95)	37 (5)	1,020	322 (43)	431 (57)	753	1,295 (74)	468 (26)	1,763
Average	70 (96)	3 (4)	73	23 (43)	31 (57)	54	93 (74)	33 (26)	126

In terms of the workforce, my survey shows that there was a considerable variation in its size but common trends in terms of the gender division of labour by contract (Table 2). On average, there were 126 permanent and non-permanent workers on each farm, with the actual numbers ranging from 66 to 362.

The term 'permanent workers' refers to those who were hired full-time and paid according to a particular grade as set out in the collective bargaining agreement between GAPWUZ and the ALB and who were contractually entitled to sick leave, vacation periods, industrial holidays and termination benefits. On average there were 73 permanent workers per farm, though the figures range between 35 to 242. Permanent workers were almost always men (70 of the 73, on average). If the one farm, which employed 19 women as permanent workers, is removed as an anomaly, then the average would be 71 men to one woman permanent worker. Aside from this farm, women were hired as permanent workers solely for domestic jobs or as village health workers. On average, men and women permanent workers comprised 59 per cent of the total work force.

'Non-permanent workers' were defined by industry regulations as either seasonal or contract. 'Seasonal workers' received the same wages as permanent ones, but they received no benefits and could be dismissed on a day's or a week's notice. If employed for more than eight consecutive months, they became permanent workers. 'Contract workers' were hired for specific tasks with wages 'negotiated' by contract. Most operators hired contractors only to construct buildings and for brick-making and left it up to each contractor to find his (all those I met or heard about were men) workforce.[7]

There was a high number of contract workers on some farms surveyed which indicated the blurring of the distinction between contract and seasonal workers by the operators. Legally, the contractor, whether an independent person or the farm operator himself, was supposed to pay the minimum wages, but in my experience that rarely happened (see also Loewenson 1988). The two categories are combined into one here because most farmers I met confused them when it came to women workers. They classified all women workers as contract workers even if they did not negotiate separate contracts with them, and paid them the same daily rate as

[7] Also included in the figures are five 'special workers'. These were employees who, because of a physical or mental disability, were capable of doing only part of the work required of an able-bodied employee. These were usually old men who had worked for a long time with a farmer and were kept on for certain light jobs as 'retainers'.

permanent or seasonal workers when they were employed in 'permanent' jobs like grading tobacco. On average, there were more women than men seasonal workers and most of the women (31 of 33) were hired in this category. The percentage of seasonal workers for each farm ranged from 19 to 55. It is important to note that the survey was carried out in March, a period of high demand for seasonal workers in tobacco grading but a period of low demand for contract workers like builders and brick-makers.

On average there were 93 male and 33 female workers on the surveyed farms. By convention, the women tended to be relatives of the permanent workers, although as I will discuss later this was not always the case. Nevertheless, operators saw them almost entirely as wives or daughters of their (male) employees. As one operator put it, he hired only married men with families as permanent workers so that he had a 'casual labour-force' in the compound. Another told me that the best way to solve labour bottlenecks was to hire twenty permanent workers, which gave you eighty workers – the men, their wives and two children. This practice not only cut down the need to build more houses, most operators argued, but it also helped out 'their boys' by giving them two incomes. As I discuss in Chapter Five, single women were hired less frequently on most surveyed farms, save for Chidhadhadha. The politics of 'marriage' had important implications for the access of women to jobs.

In terms of the physical features, the average compound size was 7.4 hectares, giving an average population density of 17 workers per hectare. Most respondents were not sure of the exact size of their farm's compound and some included in it the maize fields and gardens given to workers. Nevertheless, this gives an idea of the confined living area reserved for workers. The figure slightly overestimates the number of workers living in the compound because some permanent workers lived in the adjacent Communal Land and thus should not be included as compound residents. More importantly, it severely underestimates the total number of people living in the compound by not including non-working dependants residing with workers.

On all the farms I saw, brick houses were considered to be the best houses available for workers, but the standard was quite varied. On some farms the brick houses had one small room. On others they were divided into two units of three or more rooms each, with two workers and their families living in them. The survey showed that on average each farm had 33 brick houses, with five of them built in 1992. On many of the farms, operators had only recently begun to build these houses. On Chidhadhadha, aside from a few houses reserved for senior workers, the past owner, whom I call Mr Schmidt, only started building brick houses – for one or two families – in the late 1980s. The new owners were trying to build more, which the survey showed was a common practice on other farms as well. Of the houses surveyed, an average of 26 per cent had electricity, though that figure comes mainly from three farms, which had fifty per cent or more of their houses electrified. On five farms none of the workers' houses had electricity.

There was also some variation in terms of services offered on a farm. Five of the fourteen farms had a store and/or a butchery. These were actual commercial stores on the farm, open to the public, as opposed to the 'tuck shops' some operators ran from their houses to sell basic food and household items to their own workers. Operators paid an annual license fee to the Rural Council to run a store or a butchery, whereas tuck shops are technically illegal. Both operations usually offered some form of credit to workers on the farm.

There were six schools on the surveyed farms. According to government officials at the time, farm schools were more numerous than public (government) schools in Hurungwe's commercial farming areas. The Ministry of Education does not require registration of farm schools, though more and more are being registered. Decisions over employment of teachers and enrolment (for example, whether children from other farms will be accepted) was ultimately up to the farm owner, but some operators followed the practice in public schools of having 'parent committees' to advise them on these matters. For the farmers who did register their schools, the government provided a small grant, paid the salary of the teachers, and set the school fees according to countrywide standards. The farmer remained the local authority.

There were four crèches on the surveyed farms. 'Crèches' refer to a form of day-care operating in the farm compound, usually under the guidance of the village health worker. This person, frequently a wife of a permanent worker, was designated by the farm operator to take a course with the Ministry of Health in Karoi on preventive and basic health care and pre-school training. The programme was started to compensate for the few public health clinics in the commercial farming areas – Karoi Rural Council had six health clinics which charged a $3 fee per visit (see Loewenson et al 1983, Laing 1986, Herbst 1990). The purpose of a crèche was to look after pre-school children during work hours to ensure that mothers did not have to bring small children to possibly dangerous work-sites. However, as the survey results show, less than a third of the farms had one.

There were six operating beerhalls on the surveyed farms; a number of farmers had closed theirs because of fights and because, in their view, the workers 'wasted' their money in them. 'Beerhalls' are establishments which buy sorghum/maize beer from the country's monopoly brewery, Chibhuku Breweries, and sell it under license from the Rural District Council. They were not commercially registered under the relevant by-laws, and all profits had to go to a social welfare fund. However, the ways in which these 'social welfare decisions' were made depended on the operator. Some let their workers decide, through a self-selected committee, on how the money was to be spent. Others determined themselves which 'social welfare' events to fund, without necessarily making it clear that the money came from the beerhall itself. Others permitted individual permanent workers to operate the beerhall for a week on a rotating basis and to collect any profits.

Schools, crèches and beerhalls were the main physical institutions on the compounds in Karoi North, although some farms also had church buildings and government clinics. All were run by blacks, either farm workers or their relatives, or other employees such as teachers. But aside from the clinic, these institutions were all created and governed by the farm operators or their spouses. The compound and its features were associated with farm workers and their dependants, but these spaces were recognized as an integral part of the farm and controlled as such. This will be discussed in Chapter Six.

The 'lands'

The bulk of the commercial farm was comprised of 'lands', which were categorized according to their suitability for crops, pasture or scrub in terms of soil, drainage, vegetation and history. Managers and most long-term workers knew the recent cropping and fallow history of areas marked as arable fields. Non-arable land was reserved for the grazing of domestic animals and any wildlife present on the farms.

Table 3: Farm Size, Cropping Mixtures, Livestock and Wild Game of Hurungwe Commercial Farms Surveyed

Farm surv- eyed	Year arri- ved	Arable land (ha)	Total land (ha)	Tobacco planted (ha) 1st year	92/93	Maize planted (ha) 1st year	92/93	Other crops planted (ha) 1st year	92/93	Total planted 92/93	% planted /arable	CATTLE (number) 1st year	92/93	Other livestock /game (number) 1st year	92/93
1.	1991	810	1,215	166	155	14	54	70	80	289	35.7	0	0	315	377
2.	1983	800	1,380	24	27	20	70	0	0	97	12.1	12	500	0	0
3.	1982	957	1,157	0	41	41	81	0	0	122	12.8	25	350	0	35
4.	1986	810	1,013	12	41	0	41	0	0	82	10.1	500	500	70	120
5.	1958	567	891	16	31	4	50	0	0	81	14.3	0	400	0	0
6.	1964	600	959	20	60	0	30	0	7	97	16.2	0	172	0	0
7.	1981	800	1,155	50	58	101	70	0	0	128	16.0	226	450	0	0
8.	1988	242	828	36	42	20	35	0	0	77	31.8	0	0	0	24
9.	1980	2,405	4,780	20	60	81	48	0	0	108	4.5	200	630	5	430
10.	1986	368	1,215	41	73	12	69	0	0	250	67.9	270	550	0	0
11.	1984	587	734	32	44	0	44	0	0	88	15.0	0	0	0	0
12.	1980	810	1,215	40	40	160	100	0	8	148	18.3	0	600	0	0
13.	1991	400	1,013	28	37	0	0	0	0	37	9.3	0	2	0	0
14.	1988	505	1,250	36	47	36	50	0	0	97	19.2	200	400	0	0
Total		10,661	18,805	521	756	489	742	70	95	1,701	n/a	1,433	4,554	390	986
Average		762	1343	37	54	35	53	5	7	122	16	102	325	28	70

Unlike the operators' mini-compounds, the fields were more accessible to farm workers. There were many paths crossing the fields to the compound and to neighbouring farms, avoiding the main gateway between the compound and the barns. Many workers, particularly women and children, both working and non-working, used this access to collect wild plants like *bonongwe* and *kanzota* to cook as relish or pick wild fruit like *hacha* and *tohwe* to eat or chew. They were not, however, supposed to collect wood without permission from management and if a farm had dams stocked with fish, there were strict rules governing their access and use.

The survey gave an indication of the size and commercial usage of the commercial farms in the research area (Table 3). The size of the farms was fairly uniform, around 1,300 hectares.[8] On average, 57 per cent of lands were arable, although on a few farms this was as low as 30 per cent. To give an idea of the cropping mixture and changes over the years, the table also shows the operators' responses regarding the type and amount of crops planted in two periods: in their first year on the farm and during the year of the survey, 1992/93. Tobacco and maize had always been predominant. Only a few farmers planted other crops, but a number of them expressed interest in diversifying into flowers, fruits or spices as some of their neighbours had done.

There had been a significant increase in the amount of tobacco planted since the operator's first year on the farm, largely as a result of high prices during the 1980s and early 1990s.[9] The average area planted to maize more than doubled. In 1992, the maize price increased significantly to support the building up of the country's grain reserves after the drought. According to the respondents, the low percentage of land under crops – on average 16 per cent in 1992/93 – was the result of the need to rotate crops to allow the soil to build up nutrients in fallow fields. As my survey did not include questions concerning the percentage of fallow land, it unintentionally minimizes the amount of land in the farm's production cycle. The high cost of the planting practices on commercial farms – on Chidhadhadha, Dan said that it cost $22,000 to plant a hectare of tobacco – was also a factor in the low percentage of fields under cultivation.

---

8   The one farm, which is exceptionally large, was actually comprised of two farms which were run as one.

9   According to tables provided by the Zimbabwe Tobacco Association, the average return per hectare (in current dollars) for Zimbabwean flue-cured tobacco growers jumped from $1,515 in 1980 to $3,182 in 1981 and, except for 1987, it had been increasing every year to 1991 when it was $29,989 per hectare (ZTA 1992:63).

Another factor was the livestock and wild game population on the farms. Cattle were by far the most popular livestock, and average numbers rose significantly from the first year the operators arrived. On the other hand, the number of other livestock and game, especially sheep and goats but also ostriches, increased. Although many operators had talked to me about increasing their wild game population to attract hunters or tourists, only a few utilized wild game in their operations at the time.[10] An important factor for a successful farm operation is the availability of water. Although these farms are in a good rainfall area, averaging between 700 and 900 millimetres a year, the seasonal nature of the rainfall restricts the timing and number of plantings. On average, each operator had four dams holding 966 million litres of water. These were mainly rain-catchment dams or dammed-up seasonal rivers on or bordering their farms. They helped to ensure sufficient water during the dry season to start the tobacco seed-beds in June, provided water for livestock and, if sufficient, permitted one or two plantings of irrigated crops before the rains.

The barns

The last significant space on commercial farms was known in the vernacular as 'the barns' because of the looming presence of the coal- or wood-burning curing barns that distinguished most farms growing flue-cured tobacco. During the time of curing, these soot-stained buildings belched out black smoke while the churning mechanical coal-feeders offered a constant grinding hum to the work-yard, lending it an industrial atmosphere.

Curing barns were crucial to the farm's operation. The amount of tobacco that can be harvested depends largely on the availability of barn space to cure the reaped crop. The average number of barns increased from 21 to 25 between the time the respondents first arrived and operated the farm to the time of the survey in March 1993 (Table 4). The varying number of barns per farm (from 13 to 42) indicates the range of capital investment of different owners and is often a

---

[10] Wildlife was emerging as an industry in Hurungwe commercial farms for both consumptive and non-consumptive tourism. Wildlife is legally *res nullis*, or open-access, meaning a wild animal is not owned until a person exercises control over it (Farquharson 1993). A few farmers I knew had been putting up tall game fences along the perimeters of their property to keep wildlife on their farms for this very reason. These farmers tried to maintain a particular population of wildlife, supplementing such animals as entered their farms on their own (like sable, waterbuck, duikers) through buying and exchanging wild animals with other farmers (see also von Blackenburg 1994:65-66).

Table 4: Means of Production of Hurungwe Commercial Farms Surveyed

Farm surveyed	Year arrived	Number of curing barns		Number of tractors		Number of lorries
		1st year	1993	1st year	1993	1993
1.	1986	38	42	14	16	1
2.	1983	20	22	3	6	0
3.	1982	12	13	4	4	0
4.	1986	24	24	4	6	0
5.	1958	10	18	2	6	0
6.	1964	0	23	0	7	0
7.	1981	14	14	5	11	1
8.	1988	21	21	4	5	0
9.	1980	28	32	3	4	0
10.	1986	22	28	14	20	1
11.	1984	14	18	5	3	1
12.	1980	38	38	4	7	0
13.	1991	21	21	2	3	0
14.	1988	27	29	3	5	1
Total	n/a	289	343	67	103	5
Average	n/a	20.6	24.5	4.8	7.4	0.36

good indicator of the productivity of the farm in terms of hectarage of tobacco planted and tonnage harvested. For instance, the farm that planted the most tobacco in 1992/93 also had the most barns. Tobacco is a labour-intensive crop in Zimbabwe. The main machine on the tobacco farms in my research area was the tractor. It was used largely for preparing fields and transporting crops, workers, water-carts for dry-planting crops, fertilizer and other agricultural inputs. The average number of tractors increased from five to seven between first occupancy and the time of the survey. Only five farms had their own lorries to transport their crops to the tobacco auction floors in Harare or to marketing depots in Karoi and elsewhere. Farmers without lorries paid for private transportation. The work space also contained workshops to fix and store tractors, sheds to store and grade tobacco, and offices to carry out the administration of the farm.

Operators tried to restrict the entrance of farm workers into the work site to working hours. On Chidhadhadha, if workers had requests to make of the farm operators outside of work time, they had to line up at the office reserved for the clerks and foremen where they spoke through a window. More rarely they waited outside the operator's office. Usually the only workers who approached that office, and with deference, were senior workers in more managerial or unique posts, such as foremen, clerks, and lorry drivers. Senior workers approached an operator's house only if there was a major problem that needed Dan's or Geoff's immediate attention.

These different spaces were not only physical distinctions with economic purposes, but they were also crucial in establishing and sustaining boundaries and their distinctions. The number of tractors, barns, lorries, dams, brick houses, stores, crèches, and the types of crops grown all have economic importance for the operation of farms. As owned property, these means of production formed the difference between operators and their workers. Through unequal relations of access, these means of production assisted in the creation of hierarchies amongst farm workers. But as 'objects', they were also culturally formed and forming, having semiotic and political value and producing social and cultural distinctions, in historically sedimented and pragmatically realized situations (e.g. Appadurai 1986, Ferguson 1988, Burke 1996). The location of these various objects in the four predominant 'spaces' of the commercial farm, with rules governing their accessibility and narratives about their meaning, contributed to, produced and regulated, salient divisions between European and African, men and women, management and workers, on commercial farms and between the farms and Communal Lands. They supported and produced lines of authority, lines that converged on a principal subject, the authority of the 'European farmer'.

Sowing the seeds of modernity in the wild

Being modern. Such an identity takes on many different entailments for various groups and positions depending on historical and social circumstances (e.g. Friedman 1990, Appadurai 1990). Amongst the white farmers I knew 'being modern' consisted of consumption strategies and discourses that helped to define a subject position of (Western) 'possessive individuals' as discussed in social science literature (e.g. Macpherson 1962, Handler 1988). They celebrated their possessions, property, and the desire to have more consumer goods as signs of their modernity. They saw themselves as global citizens. By keeping abreast of current market trends for tobacco, coffee, and other agricultural commodities, using and understanding contemporary technological devices, and maintaining an interest in international sporting and political events, they had a sense of a 'single global culture' in which they and I shared (Featherstone 1990). From plant chemistry to American baseball, ultra-light aeroplanes to Gorbachev, the discussions I heard and engaged in were very familiar to me, echoes of the different milieus I know in North America. The operators' furnishings and decor, their home spaces, reinforced this familiarity. On most occasions I felt quite comfortable, 'at home' one could say. Their interiors were arranged to express not only their 'tastes', but, as in an ideal of middle-class domesticity with which I am familiar, also their personal, gendered identity: of 'the man' with his bar and collections of aeroplane pictures and pennants in his den; and throughout other parts of the house open to guests, pictures, china, statuettes and other items of 'the wife' (see, for example, Stewart 1984, Comaroff and Comaroff 1992, Burke 1996).

But a difference of this discourse of modernity amongst white farmers compared to what I knew in Canada was that it carried an *immediate* sense of mission, an undercurrent that served as a support to the frontier milieu it assisted in creating (e.g. Kopytoff 1987). The target of this edification was always Africans. Although these discourses 'othered' along the lines of race, created stereotypes of 'Africans' in opposition to 'Europeans' in similar ways to late nineteenth- and twentieth-century colonial discourses (e.g. Fanon 1967, Said 1978, Bhabha 1994, Spurr 1993), they did not create an unchanging sense of 'self' and 'other', of European and African. 'Africans', for example, were differentiated by spatial category (those who lived in the reserves and those who worked on the farms), by gender, and by work position. And, most importantly, all were subject to pragmatic contexts, negotiations, and subversions.

Despite the importance of understanding the pragmatics of discourse and my wariness of creating a stereotype of 'the European farmer' by conflating my experiences of Karoi North farm operators with an essential characterization of white Zimbabwean farmers, it is difficult not to underline the role of racial identities on these farms. These identities are how commercial farms are typically known in official discourses. They also shaped daily incidents and decisions on Chidhadhadha and operated on my own sense of identities.

This section develops a 'strong' sense of the authority of the white farm operator, arguing that the discursive assumptions of a 'European identity' have had a determining role in shaping power relations and in (re)producing the lines of domestic governance on commercial farms. The remaining chapters investigate how these assumptions more directly affected farm workers' lives.

Pioneer stories

Although some of the oldest active commercial farms in Hurungwe district were located in my study area, most of the farms there were first cultivated by whites only in the 1950s, after the initial 'K' Block farms were settled. A few began operating as such in the mid-1960s and were some of the last commercial farms to be 'opened up' in Hurungwe.

Many of the current farmers whom I got to know became primary operators after 1980. Some bought farms on the market, a few through assistance programmes of the Agricultural Finance Corporation (the government agricultural bank), and others bought or inherited from relatives. In my survey, the current farmers, on average, first took ownership or began operations, in 1982. However, 'history' was still a relevant topic to these farmers, despite the relatively young age of many of them.

'History' here refers to the forms of knowledge that provide a sense of a past, the ways and conventions of remembering and narrating past events. While carrying out my research, I carried a more 'objective' notion of 'history', of trying to solicit the 'solid, empirical facts of the past' for my project, to reconstruct the significant local history of Karoi's farms. However, my numerous attempts to engage farmers in this latter sense of 'history' continually ran up against the former sense of 'history'. Their sense of 'history' – what was significant in the past for present purposes of recollection – rarely included the particulars I was seeking, lending weight to the current, critical notion of 'history' which examines the power involved in deciding the terms and procedures of making and legitimizing 'history' in various contexts.[11]

Whenever I pushed white operators for more historical 'details', I was repeatedly told to consult *The Legend of Lomagundi* (Black 1976), a book concerning the 'persons and places' of the European farming settlements in what once was a united 'Lomagundi District' (but is now composed of Hurungwe and Makonde Districts). It was put together in the middle of the liberation war by an association of local government bodies (rural councils and town councils) for the white residents. This book embodied 'history' for these farm operators.

These farmers would likely find my application of the term 'history' to their narratives concerning the 'past' inappropriate since they lack the wealth of empirical detail that, among other things, helps sustain a notion of 'history' as an objective recounting of past events. That convention of 'history' even daunted the woman who wrote the foreword to *The Legend of Lomagundi*. She placed the compilation of materials that comprised this book in a very different category from 'history':

> *We have tried to tell a story – certainly not a history – of Lomagundi over the years. To my mind, this book is a tribute to the pioneers of the vast area, who endured heavy hardships yet left behind a store of valiant and humorous anecdotes to soften and link together their disappointments and achievements. (B. Laver in Black 1976:3)*

Her (implied) category, 'pioneer stories', was the genre of history orally employed by many white farm operators in the area; it situated the story-teller and the farm on an advancing border of civilization,

---

[11] Conventional academic history, at least in most of the twentieth century, has tended to value the (uncritical) use of documents and/or oral histories as positivist evidence of either the (causal) links between past events and present conditions or the origins, or traces, of particular identities of current humanistic subjectivities such as the 'individual', 'woman', 'class', and so on. Such a viewpoint has been strongly challenged (see, e.g., Foucault 1972, Hirst 1985, Young 1990, J. Scott 1992).

bringing modern order to the bush (e.g. Pratt 1985), while at the same time it nostalgically invoked a simpler time compared to the hustle and bustle of 'modern times'. These stories thus tended to signify the modernity of white farmers compared to, and incorporating, workers and, simultaneously, the difference between white farmers and 'modern life' in cities.

'It was absolutely wild. As I said, there was nothing here. Nothing, except this road here [which] was just a mine's track. That's all there was.'[12] These were the words of an older white farm operator I interviewed, one of the few remaining of the original ex-soldiers who settled after 1945. He was describing what it was like starting his farm: the 'wild' from which it developed was signalled by his own self-declared 'primitive' housing, constructed like the local African houses out of poles and dagga (mud), the lack of roads and well-maintained stores – the 'butcher' in Miami (now Mwami), he chuckled, 'was a pole and dagga thing there, the flies pushed you out when you walked in' – and plenty of wildlife like hyena, lion, elephants and leopards roaming the lands. In the 'pioneer' narrative of this older farmer, there was an emphasis on self-sufficiency, of making do with what one had, of being a master of many skills. The beauty and danger of 'the untamed' set the stage, as it were, for the frontier on to which the 'pioneer' came.

Pioneer stories emphasised the 'individual'. Such an individual was gendered as male. These stories I heard and solicited came solely from the white male farmers and were predominantly about them and other white men. They were the ones who hunted, who supervised the workers, who innovated with scraps, who 'opened up' the farm and 'made do'. When they talked about neighbouring white farmers, about the 'community' that developed between them in the face of common adversaries – like when the tractor got stuck in the mud, or marauding wild animals had to be shot – they were always men. They were named and given personality characteristics and generally invoked in a feeling of camaraderie, even though there were occasionally different forms of gossip tied to several of these figures.

'John George was a good farmer and helped out a lot, but you had to be careful around him. He was a real businessman. He always took advantage of any personal dealings. Everything was a 'deal' to

---

12 Taped interview, Karoi North Commercial Farmer, April 2, 1993. All further references come from this interview.

him.' So opined one white farmer as we sat on his patio for a 'sundowner', a cold beer at the end of the day. But he only ventured that somewhat critical opinion of a neighbouring white farmer after we had known each other for more than a half year. Otherwise, most recollections were positive.

'When I arrived here all this was bush. And that was only 30 years ago. It was me and my young family and parents. We lived in mud and pole houses for several years. All around you...' the white farmer motioned with his brown arm to the barns, several houses, and other farm buildings, '...was built with my hands. I went out in the fields with my chaps and we ploughed up the first tobacco seed-beds and I mixed the tobacco seeds in the watering-can myself and poured it over the soil. Since then, it has been hard work and determined and disciplined perseverance that has made the farm, made me and my family, what we are today.'

The lands and the barns figured prominently in such narratives. These were the farm spaces that mattered in pioneer stories, the sites of productive change, that marked out 'progress' by expanding fields, erecting barns and digging out dams. Women figured peripherally in these stories, mainly as the representative of the farmer's family life. They looked after the homes, managed the domestic servants and gardens, making sure all was neat, tidy, and respectable (e.g. Kirkwood 1984b). Rather, it was white men who were the neighbours, and who opened up the farms, while the structures of the emerging landscape of Karoi – the garage, the post office, the hotel, the Club – were the progeny of the 'pioneers'.

I use 'progeny' to give a sense of how these pioneer stories stressed the generative capacities of white men, bearing testimony to the products of their activities. Many times while sitting in a farmer's living room hearing about the 'old days', I found these stories slightly narcissistic as they dwelled for an inordinate amount of time on the 'I' of the narrator overcoming obstacles and difficulties in adversarial encounters. In the interview noted above, the operator spoke for a long time about his death-defying experiences in World War Two and his hunting trips in the Zambezi Valley. More commonly, operators I knew talked about their experience fighting, defending their farms, during the 'past war' in the 1970s. These experiences were not recounted with sadness or rage, but often with a wistfulness, almost a nostalgia, for lost times (e.g. Crapanzano 1994).

It would be easy to explain these stories as part of what one white expatriate who had lived amongst white farmers in Karoi for years found to be the 'incredible arrogance' of southern African whites. But I found them to have various purposes; boasting was only an occasional one. A more common reason for these stories, I think, was to confirm the farmers' proprietorship and their sense of a self to me and, perhaps, to themselves. It was a subjectivity ineluctably connected to Africans.

Although Africans were differentiated by their location in relation to the farmer's spatial categorization, they were figuratively frozen into stock characters whose purpose in these narratives was to act as instruments of the farmer in 'opening up' the bush, to be part of the wild, an element of nature that had to be tamed.

An older farmer discussed how curing was done back in the 1950s. As he was describing how cured tobacco was moistened by removing it from the barns and laying it out in the night air for dew to cover it, his thoughts seamlessly moved into reflections on his labour force. 'Soon as you feel it [the cured tobacco] getting soft at the top there, you turn it around until it softens so you can handle it. And I had a lot of little piccanins in those days, the little [African] children never went to school.' He continued discussing the work of the children in a way that suggested their eagerness to assist him on his upward path, both literally and figuratively:

> Sometimes those little youngsters, they loved it, they started singing when they started working, they would sing through until one, two o'clock and then they had it. They would sit there untying [tobacco from the curing barns] but they were fast asleep. They still got to go to bed for a little while, then get up in the morning and go reap again. Ah, we started up the hard way. But, hey, I moved from the bottom where I lived and I came up here and I built a pole and dagga here.

This story-line was told repeatedly by farmers. Older men talked about the presence of 'Africans' in a way that confined their agency and activities to assisting the settler, eagerly and without complaint, in developing the 'virgin' land. Even when recounting present-day events, younger white farmers employed the attributes of this pioneer genre.

'Hey, that lioness was a crafty beast!' declared Mike, a young farmer who grew up in Hurungwe. He was addressing myself and several neighbouring white farmers. We had gathered together for a *braai*, a barbecue, at Mike's place. He was talking about an old lioness which had been stalking and killing cattle on a number of the commercial farms.

'But Will was a hunter, learned those skills from his old man and from the war [of Independence, fighting for the Rhodesian army]. And no lion was going to get the better of him. Nor any of us, for that matter. He called out a number of his neighbours and they set up a trap with the help of his blokes. Sure enough the old lioness fell into it and ptoooee! Will shot it in the head. If he hadn't got it then, who knows when it would have turned on us, on our small children. It was old and had to be put away...'

As Mike's voice trailed away, one of the men emphasised Will's hunting skills. Soon, another had a story about how they found a eight-foot python on their farm, eating stray dogs and who knows what else.

I heard many tales from white farmers about wild animal scares and about ways of being self-sufficient by adapting materials on the farm, getting help from neighbours, and having the support from their 'chaps' in their various endeavours. The stories were not told in a purely matter-of-fact way; they were distinctive rhetorical markers of location, a way of identifying the narrator as being on the frontier of modernity. 'Hey Blair, you're out in the bush here!' I was often reminded by white farmers, who saw themselves as the bearers of modernity to this frontier, a 'frontier' and a 'modernity' which was generated by the discourses of the white farm operators themselves.

Differential edification

Rural white Zimbabweans that I met consistently contrasted themselves with Africans. They continually explained how this difference required, and conferred, a certain responsibility to edify Africans. The form of the edification, however, depended on whether 'the Africans' in question were located in 'reserves' or on farms. Either way, these narratives confirmed a 'modern' identity of 'European farmers' – a subject position that also drew on a historical narrative of government and development.

Most white operators tended to comment favourably upon the past policies of the colonial government towards the reserves. 'We were developing them along proper lines through a variety of government programmes,' one insisted to me, 'but then in the 1960s, some Africans, the present leaders, began a campaign of destabilization that prevented the reforms from working. Yet, at Independence, the new government re-introduced all these institutions that they had discarded – like the District Administrator instead of the District Commissioner.' This argument did not lead to a call to improve the efficiency of these institutions; instead, it concluded with a declaration of the need for the government to 'commercialize' the reserves. The farmer quoted above explained that the present system permits Africans to remain 'idle'. 'The African is at heart an idle person,' he opined, 'only the commercialization of the reserves, the conversion of land tenure into a freehold system, would make Africans responsible for their own livelihood.'

'African culture', another informed me, 'was suitable for traditional times but it's a dead weight in the commercialized world: old African men drain money off the innovative young men through *roora* (bridewealth) and the chiefs control land tenure in a way that prevents sound conservation practices from developing.' He too proposed a break-up of this 'traditional culture' by 'giving title deeds to those poor farmers in the reserves. Force them to take responsibility for conservation of their land. It's time they are brought into the commercial world we have been living. That's what development is all about, hey?'

The pervasive theme – from AIDS to conservation, from sex to firewood – was that Africans did not recognize their responsibility for future consequences since their 'value system' promoted endless consumption in the present. For these white men, responsibility and deferred gratification were key markers of cultural and evolutionary difference.

This pioneer genre of history informed a sense of paternalistic duty towards those in the Communal Lands. Several farmers on the border with Mukwichi Communal Land carried out projects there. They told me how they had tried to assist 'Afs' through agronomy advice, lending inputs, building a rain-fed dam and so forth. They had also offered to come to Agritex meetings in Mukwichi, provide credit, advice, extra tobacco seedlings, cheap maize milling services, water, and other such attributes of their 'modern' knowledge to those in need. Most often the denouement was one of tragedy, of advice not heeded, offers not accepted, and the proof came from

87

pointing to the hilly and sparsely forested land in Mukwichi as a sign of backward and destructive agricultural methods.

This is not to say that the intent of 'goodwill' was not there, nor to denigrate possible benefits that have (and did then) come from such advice and assistance. But it is important to draw the link between the sense of history held by these operators and some of their actions towards their neighbours. Their actions were also informed by an instrumental politics of 'good neighbourliness', by which they tried to increase their value to as many of the neighbouring Communal Land farmers as possible in an effort to avert problems such as poaching and fence-cutting. During my research, there was also a growing awareness amongst farmers that such 'assistance' to peasants had overt political importance, as a way of currying favour with local Party officials in the hope of staving off government designation of their farm; of showing that they, the white farmers, are an integral part of the community of Zimbabwe. Other farmers refused to engage in these activities. They claimed they were 'burnt' before, having had loans reneged on, advice not heeded, and seeing the Communal Lands turn into a 'mess' which was not their responsibility.

But this ambiguity about the form of edification due to those in the Communal Lands – perhaps provide assistance, perhaps avoid helping – was more muted when it came to the operators' use of the pioneer genre in discussions of their own workers. If 'commercialization' was the dominant idiom used in discussions about modernizing 'the reserves', the return to more farmer control was the predominant theme for 'improving' conditions for farm workers.

The permissible measures of controlling farm workers in the colonial period were often looked upon fondly by white farmers. Providing rations to workers ensured, many argued, that farm workers and their families received proper and sufficient food. The new government, I was told, declared rations to be a 'patronizing' practice and hence legislated minimum wages. Many of these operators bemoaned the results of mistakenly making farm workers 'responsible', of giving all of their remuneration in money, of permitting workers to decide how to use their wages. The operators associated their loss of control with worsening conditions for farm workers. I heard many tales about how 'workers waste their money on beer and women', ignoring the priority of food. The aphorism heard constantly was that 'workers cannot budget'. Although such assertions may be used by many employers unwilling to pay higher wages, on Zimbabwean commercial farms they were explicitly tied to an imperative of intervention to assist and edify. Many white farmers not only openly wished for a return to mandatory rations and lower wages but also wanted to formally resume a more active, dominating role in the lives of their workers in order to 'assist the welfare' of the workers and their families.

The necessity of intervention to edify Africans was present in their narratives about Communal Land peasants in the colonial period, but with a change of government from white to black, colonial to post-colonial, the means of edification became 'the market'. The new government, I was told, did not have the proper discipline within the 'reserves' to ensure that policies were carried out; officials were too soft, because everyone was a '*bhururu*' (relative, friend). The implied comparison was with the colonial administration, which had the (paternal) interest of the Africans in mind and the strength to carry out the proper policies (see McClintock 1995). Now, with an African administration (marked as undisciplined), the 'market' became the exclusive means of achieving 'development' in 'the reserves'. Yet, for farm operators, the colonial political project was still the preferred model since workers were under the farmers' control, their own domestic authority as opposed to government regulations. Farm workers, betwixt and between the site of un-modernity of the reserves and the modernity of European living and morals, remain the responsibility of those who owned and operated the space on which they lived.

An example of the type of control farmers exerted or hoped for in the colonial period is given by an experience recounted by an older white farmer. He explained how, many years before, he once used his 'boss-boy' (now called foreman) to recruit a 'MuDoma', an ethnic marker for very 'primitive', six-toed 'tribesmen' living in the Zambezi Valley (e.g. White 1971; see Lan 1985:17). This 'bloke', being a MuDoma, the operator informed me, was afraid of the farmer himself – 'they were so scared of the white man because they lived in the bush all the time. All the kids were born in the bush and they stayed in the bush'. He only took orders from the boss-boy who had recruited him. 'The boss boy gives him his work. He does his work. He finishes his work. He's off to the bush and you never see him again. He comes back at night. The food is in his house and he eats. Eventually he becomes tamer, tamer, tamer.' Through contact with modern life on the farm, the farmer implied, the MuDoma was losing his bush instinct. One day, while looking after the cattle, the MuDoma was mauled by a leopard. 'And that bloke', the farmer said, drawing in his breath in a quieter voice, 'I said he's not going to live. He's done in.' Then the farmer began to speak more rapidly:

> *Three or four times I had to send people to go and look for him. They'd catch him right down here about five, six, seven k's [kilometres] away. He and his wife. He's so sick. He can't walk. She's dragging him. He wants to get back to the bush. He wanted to die there. He does not want to die here. I said, now listen, come back. Come here and we'll go see a doctor and put stuff in your ears. I went back to Harare and I came back and he was dead. He's buried here on the farm. But he didn't want to die here. Three or four times he ran away. No, no, he reckoned he wanted to die there, where he comes from, up in Doma there, by those* gomos *[hills] there.*

I did not pursue why he insisted that the MuDoma worker die on his farm. I was embarrassed that I was an active part in a repetition of such an open display of colonial 'care'. The allegorical implication I drew from his narrative then, and now, was that even though he recognized the man's desire to die at 'home', the farmer wanted to ensure that he was buried on the white man's land away from the bush, close to a site of modernity, as a way to show that the MuDoma was 'tamed' at the end of his life. In the colonial period, it was up to the farmer to decide what was important for his workers. His authority, recognized by government, legitimately governed almost all the actions of his workers, even when they were dead. That assumption of domestic government was still a guiding one for white operators, though it has been challenged by the changes which came with Independence.

Domestic and textual authority

The telling of such histories, and others in this type of pioneer genre I heard, helped to consolidate a sense of the white farm operator as a political actor, albeit one whose actions had become circumscribed when Rhodesia became Zimbabwe. This genre contributed a sense of past, common tenets, and a purpose beyond immediate economic goals for others of the same identity. White operators often talked of other white farmers in Hurungwe and Zimbabwe as belonging to the same group, producing the impression that they were a small 'community'. Organizations like the CFU and ZTA not only helped to facilitate the purchasing of imports and other supplies and silently lobbied and worked with the government on behalf of farmers, but also assisted in forging a sense of unity amongst white farm operators. They're 'our voice', was how Dan put it.

In Karoi North, the members of this 'white community' called upon each other for a range of economic assistance, from lending lorries at nominal cost, to delivering tobacco to the auctions in Harare, to permitting a neighbour to use part of one's land for crops or grazing.

The emphasis on 'white community' was also expressed in terms of the sale of commercial farms in the area. It was expected that a son, if there was one, would take over the farm. A common practice amongst the farm owners I knew was for the son to return to his father's farm after gaining experience elsewhere (at another farm, agricultural school, tobacco training centre, or even in a non-agricultural occupation).

The financial assistance of neighbours and family was important for many white operators as the costs of farms and farming, which put them completely out of reach for most black Zimbabweans, also had become onerous for many white Zimbabweans. Many stated that opportunities for their sons to get farms on their own (outside of inheritance) are almost non-existent. Farms were extremely expensive and the Agricultural Finance Corporation reputedly would not help whites to purchase them. Moreover, the government has, since 1985, the right of first refusal on all farms for sale and will buy them, particularly if they are inexpensive. Unless a white man has a lot of money, collateral, or inheritance, I was told by many whites, he could not buy a farm.

However, as should be clear from the above discussion, not all members of 'the family' were treated identically in respect of property and wealth. Daughters were not typically seen as possible inheritors of the farm. Rather, as one commented about his teenage daughter, they were expected to be married off. Sons were the ones who mattered in terms of property inheritance. If the government makes it impossible for my son to make a living in Zimbabwe, Dan told me matter-of-factly, we will leave for another African country, perhaps Zambia or Tanzania, where they seem to be interested in developing their economy. The ability to patrilineally pass on the family inheritance, to control succession, emerged as a theme amongst white farm operators on several occasions during my research.

If there was more than one son who had an interest in farming, the farm owner might give equal company shares to all, or perhaps pass his farm to one son and try to assist the other to buy a nearby property. Two farmers I knew were trying to do the latter when I was there. They had sons already helping them manage their farms and wanted extra farms for other sons. The first was trying to convince a neighbour to subdivide his land and sell a portion to him for his son; a suggestion resented by the neighbour since he had two sons of his own helping him run the farm and did not want to make it smaller for the benefit of someone else's lineage. The second was hoping to convince a widow to sell her farm to him for one of his sons. The importance of family in managing the farm was also apparent in the survey, which showed almost all the directors of farm-owning companies to be family members.

Family members did not contribute equally to the farm operation, however. Children tended to help their parents in the farm business, at least in my experience, only after they had left school. Teenage children went to boarding schools and returned home only on holidays when they would relax with their family. On the other hand, wives of the farmers I knew helped out in many ways in this domestic economy. They not only supervised domestic workers who daily laboured in their houses and yards but they also assisted their husbands by, for example, doing the accounts, running the farm store and butchery and supervising the farm school and health clinic (e.g. Kirkwood 1984b). As mentioned above, however, women were not part of the white men's pioneer stories. They were excised from the commentary, except as part of the background, as private figures in relation to the more public efforts and accomplishments of their husbands.

Yet in addition to their important economic roles, women contributed a significant part to the poetics of the white farmer's portrayal of himself as the paternal head of the domestic economy of his home and farm.[13] More importantly, white women had their own tactics, forms of authority and resistance with regard to farm

---

[13] Margaret Strobel's comments on the role of white women in the British Empire this century resonates with current assumptions held by many white farm operators I knew: 'If running a government department or a commercial establishment constituted men's work, women's work was to maintain the status of the family and preserve social boundaries between Europeans and indigenous peoples' (1991:13).

workers as well as to their husbands and family members and other farm operators and their spouses.[14]

These poetics of the white farmer, this construction of the subject position of the 'European farmer', to which these pioneer stories contribute, were not unassailable, unbending, or untainted by pragmatic contexts. The pioneer stories were often presented to me for a number of reasons. One concerned the national debate surrounding the Land Acquisition Act. Some operators, even those with whom I built up friendship, were uncertain about the purpose of my research. Although I assured them that I was not working for the government, nor was I out to prove that white farms should be divvied up among black peasants, many explicitly or implicitly assumed that this was the driving motivation of my research. They tended to regard white expatriates who enjoyed 'African' company as being sympathetic to the cause of massive land redistribution (see Thornton 1995). By aligning themselves with the larger force of modernity *against* the traditions of Africans, they assumed that the obvious stupidity of such a redistribution would be conveyed to me. Many looked at their workers and asked, with a chuckle, 'would I want to see *them* get this farm?' One operator with whom I conducted the survey played with the stereotype of the 'racist white farmer' by initially answering some questions within an exaggerated version of that stereotype. In response to how he disciplined workers, he replied straight-faced, 'I beat the hell out of them', before smiling and going on to explain the informal procedure he used. By playing with the stereotype, I understood him to be conveying the poverty of such an understanding of white farmers and showing that he knew the dominant image of white Zimbabwean farmers in certain transnational discourses.

This difference between European and African, between modernity and tradition, also produced the sense of mission which was stressed in many interviews. Some farmers weighed their words carefully to ensure that I noted the time and energy they spent trying to assist their workers and 'Africans' in general. 'I forgot to tell you,' one mentioned to me several weeks after I finished my survey of farm operators, 'that I also loan money to several fellows in the reserve growing tobacco. Make sure you write that down, hey!'

---

[14] Doris Lessing's novels and short stories from the 1950s offer insight into these dynamics during this period.

Most of the men seemed confidently certain of their perspective on their workers when discussing them with me, even though I was assigned a 'liberal' bent given my interest in the lives of 'the Afs'. They were likely trying to demonstrate that they were concerned employers, an identity which not only refers to their uncertain situation under the ZANU(PF) government (i.e. they did not want to risk having their farm expropriated because the government heard that they were harsh employers), but also to my own obscure identity and interests.

They wanted to ensure that I understood that they always thought of the best interests of their workers, despite what 'the government' said. The 'chaps' and I get along wonderfully, if only the politicians would leave us alone, was a common refrain. 'Politics', as it was for Burl, was a curse-word for most white farmers I knew. It implied unwanted and unnecessary outside (government) intervention into their domestic lives, into a sense of domesticity which included obligations to 'their' Africans. Their public persona included a concern for and responsibility towards farm workers.

It is in this interlocutory context that I heard their pioneer stories. They wanted to convey the weight of their responsibilities to the workers by giving a sense of what they and their forefathers had carried out on the frontier of modernity, and how this underwrote their current authority on the farm beyond the reach of government. By being accepted by the farm operators, I participated in the forms of authority predicated on race, gender, class, and modernity within the confines of the commercial farm's boundaries; boundaries, which such predicates helped to form. As a 'white man' living on the farmer's side of the fence, and with permission to travel the farm and ask any workers if they wanted to talk, I too was part of these forms of domestic authority.

Conclusion

Domesticity has been linked with the civilizing mission of colonialism, a crucial area of colonial intervention as a way to properly shape the conduct of 'natives' (Comaroff and Comaroff 1992, Burke 1996, Stoler 1997), as well as with the importance of home to bourgeois social practices, of a private life geared towards social prestige (Davidoff 1973). In this chapter, these two meanings of domesticity have been merged in my characterization of the forms of authority on white-operated farms in Karoi North ICA. The four spatial divisions of farms not only indicate differential economic capacities and functions, but entail differential ability of travel and use along the lines of race, gender, and labour form. Combined with discourses of modernity, supported by pioneer stories which established the presence of white (male) farmers as the paternal authority of their families and their workers, the authority of their 'homes' extend into the rest of their property, shaping 'labour relations' and, less significantly, my study of this topic.

Moreover, the spatial boundaries of 'domesticity', of 'domestic government', were also inscribed with what Johannes Fabian (1983) has called 'spatialized Time', a predominant evolutionary narrative in the 'West' where '[d]ispersal in space reflects directly... sequence in Time' (1983:12). The homes of the operators, with their decor of bourgeois domesticity and technological apparatus, duly surrounded by barbed wire fences, serve as the exemplars of modernity on commercial farms for both operators and workers. The distance between the 'mini-compounds' of the operators and the compound for the workers was inscribed with an evolutionary trope. It becomes a difference of 'modern' living and 'non-modern' living, or what farm operators commonly called the 'conditions of the Africans'. From the perspective of many white farmers I met, I should say 'semi-modern' living. By living on the commercial farms, under the domestic authority of a 'modern', European farmer and his family, farm workers were a step above the 'traditional' lifestyle of Africans living in the 'reserves' (e.g. Du Toit 1977). From this perspective the importance of edification, of morally improving the lifestyle and conditions of Africans, contributed to shaping the domestic government of commercial farms in a way that distinguished farm workers from farmers in the Communal Lands. The latter were on the other side of the frontier created by the boundary of commercial farms. As I shall discuss, workers saw themselves living a non-modern life compared to the operators, but the path of improvement often led towards, not away from, the 'reserves'.

In this chapter, I have provided examples of some of the discourses contributing to the 'European identity' in Hurungwe's commercial farms and explained how they inform the authority of government over farm workers. It is an authority which was legitimated as the form of colonial governance, with the combined aims of control and edification, and that has continued in post-colonial Zimbabwe, despite being challenged and modified by changes since 1980. To understand how this identity informs (differential) access of farm workers to resources, it is necessary to closely examine the power relations of domestic government which have shaped the different sites of farm workers and, in turn, the responses of those workers. I have represented authority on farms as being stable. I now discuss how this authority is put into motion within the contexts of farm work.

Chapter 4

Working on the margins

The 'Lesson' in the beerhall

One evening in April 1993 while walking in the compound, I came across a meeting in the compound beerhall. I was told that the workers' committee called a sudden meeting about the rules of credit and the increasing numbers of people leaving work. I made my way through the thick crowd and positioned myself at the edge of the doorway. To my surprise, it was not Luke, the chairman of the workers' committee, speaking, but George, the senior foreman, and Daniel, a new foreman on the farm who had previously been a teacher at the nearby primary school.

George was seated on a chair in the middle of the end of the beerhall close to me. There was an empty chair next to him, and Daniel was pacing back and forth. Both were speaking very loudly, gesturing with their arms to make their points. They were speaking to the workers sitting side by side on the benches running along the length of the walls and seated on the floor at the far end. After a few minutes, Daniel caught sight of me in the shadows of the doorway and invited me to sit down next to George. I initially felt uncomfortable being centre-stage. I felt even more so after hearing what Daniel and George were saying.

They were passing along two messages from the farmers, otherwise known as the '*varungu*', the whites. The first concerned credit. Indicating that last month the farm had given out the 'high amount' of $12,000 in credit, they told the assembled workers that the farm was going to put a ceiling on credit of $6,000 a month for the entire workforce. Once the farm had given out that amount, no more would be dispersed no matter what 'need' was given or on what day of the month the limit was reached. To make sure this limit was respected, the farmers planned to restrict the available credit to workers. Any new (thus seasonal) worker would only receive *upfu* (maize meal) and $50 at the store per month. They would not receive any farm credit for school fees or health expenses until they had stayed on the farm for several months and demonstrated their trustworthiness. Workers who had been with the farm longer would still receive the extra credit, but not as much as before. They could only get credit for school fees at the start of the three terms (when the schools required them) and they could only get up to $50 for funeral expenses. A higher amount of credit, up to $300, was available to them only if the village chairman or the workers' committee chairman vouched for them. This amount would be mainly reserved for *roora*, bridewealth payments. As for purchasing fertilizer and/or seeds on credit, the farm would now require them to make a down-payment of 40 per cent of the cost.

The second message related to the organization of the farm, which was described as operating as a 'family'. George said that like any family, if you besmirch one member, you besmirch all the members. He then made his analogy more direct by saying that if one bad-mouthed one of the farmers, one is bad-mouthing both of the farmers. If one claimed that one is a 'good *murungu*', and the other a 'bad' one, one forgot that they are a 'family' and are one and the same. Moreover, he implied that this was actually the farmers' management strategy. One acted nice, the other acted tough. But at the end of the day they shared stories about the workers and laughed about them. 'Do you ever see them yell at each other?' George asked rhetorically. 'No,' he continued, 'because they work together against you.'

Whereas George defined Geoff and Dan as members of a family distinct from the workers, he did emphasize that as senior foreman he and other foremen were with the workers. Like a family, the foremen were with the workers and not above them. One might get yelled at by the foreman, but that also happens within a family. One does not sever one's links with a family because of it. 'Thus,' Daniel elaborated, 'if one gets yelled at, one should not take it personally and, like someone with *manyoka* (diarrhoea), let it all out on management and give notice to leave work.' 'Instead of leaving,' George reiterated, 'one should sit down and think about it. Hand in a three-month notice, not a one-month one, and the farm would look after them, which may lead them to re-evaluate and stay on the farm.'

George and Daniel talked for about 45 minutes after I had arrived. The sense that the 'floor' was the foremen's was confirmed during question period and afterwards. George only permitted three questions after their presentation. The questions were asked with great deference and were dismissively answered in a single sentence. George then disingenuously added that if people had questions they should ask now, as he did not want to hear grumbling afterwards.

Luke, the workers' committee chairman, then asked to speak. With permission from George, he stood up, raised his right hand in the air several times, and hoarsely cried, '*Pamberi nevashandi! Pamberi nekubatana! Pasi nenzara!*' (Forward with workers! Forward with unity! Down with hunger!). These calls were common at many meetings since Independence as they were part of the sloganeering of ZANU(PF) and thus they commonly elicit responses from the crowd gathered. But the assembled workers that night only feebly responded with their scripted chorus of *Pamberi! Pamberi! Pasi nayo!* (Forward! Forward! Down with it!). Disregarding this lack of support, Luke launched into a passionate discourse about the 'true' reason why people were leaving. In reality, he averred, workers were only leaving from the section of one of the farmers. 'The workers of this *murungu* have no credit at the store,' Luke pointed out, 'and on approaching him for credit, the *murungu* would yell at him *Futseki!*' (chiLapalapa for 'go away').

Although I had heard complaints about this one farmer many times from a number of workers and foremen, only one worker in the back of the hall clapped. Instead, one of the older workers heckled Luke during his speech, claiming that he was just telling stories. After he stopped, George heatedly denied that this was the main cause of 'problems' on the farm. The cause, he stressed, was that workers were unable to budget properly which leads to heavy debts to the farm and the closing of their credit accounts.

Ezia, the village chairman, stood up next and repeated George's message. He said that the previous owner, Mr Schmidt, made the workers 'stupid' by freely giving out credit. Now the one farmer about whom Luke was complaining was actually making people think wisely about their money, teaching them how to budget. But after this flattery of George, he continued with a *chichemo chidiki* (small request) concerning overtime. With Mr Schmidt, Ezia claimed, when workers worked overtime, they were given the money right away and had the money in their pockets. 'Now, when we make a request to a foreman for overtime, nothing happens.'

George curtly said that 'their letter' (of complaint) was being attended to and he scolded Ezia for raising the issue in this forum.

Furthermore, he continued, people did not realize that they often worked less hours than necessary, finishing their *mugwazo* (task-work) at noon, for instance, and still getting paid for a full day. Overtime had to be seen within this wider monthly equation. One worked fewer hours one day, more the next, but they evened out to nine hours a day at the end of the month. 'No one works for free!' he added before declaring that the meeting was over.

After the meeting finished just past nine o'clock, I talked with a few workers. Most were rather pensive, thinking about what was said. As Ezia explained, the beerhall meeting was their 'school' for the night. That was an apt metaphor for the meeting in several ways. Not only did George and Daniel lecture the workers on what the new rules were going to be on the farm, but they also stressed the edifying elements of these new guidelines, the measures that would lead to the moral improvement of workers. Their message was that if workers learned how to budget properly and understood the demands of the two distinct moral communities of management – one of which comprised both workers and foremen – workers could improve their lot on the farm, as well as learn to become more responsible, possibly more like the farmers. It was a lesson about what I call 'domestic government', the form of power relations on commercial farms since the colonial period. But its pedagogical content was clearly marked by changes that have occurred since Independence.

In this chapter, I detail what this 'domestic government' entails, juxtaposing it with the modernist identity of capitalism which is so closely associated with commercial farms in Zimbabwe in official discourses. 'Capitalism', for both its proponents and its detractors, is not just a powerful social force shaping people's lives, it is also a powerful identity throughout the world. Analyses commonly discuss attributes of this identity of capitalism as evidence of an all-encompassing, essential capitalism, rather than as examples of 'contemporary discourses of capitalist hegemony' (Gibson-Graham 1995). In holding to a strict definition of capitalism, what I call 'official capitalism', analysts not only miss other constitutive practices but also the constitutive effects of their own definitions.

As the 'lesson in the beerhall' suggests, the modification of official capitalism includes an unusual calculation of time and wages: the importance of money in non-wage forms such as credit, the intricate connection between the compound and the work-place, and the pivotal role played by senior foremen in mediating between the 'family' of operators and the 'family' of workers within the space of the commercial farm. At the same time, I argue that this 'domestic government' has undergone substantial changes since 1980. The lines of power have spread out from their colonial concentration in the figures of the white farmer and his 'boss-boy', and they have rested less on the threat of physical force and more on the ability to respond to monetary demands, both for consumption and production, through the entitlement of credit. Both shifts have taken place, however, within the rhetoric and power relations of domestic government and have occurred partially as a reaction to the creation of new, alternative sources of power on and off the farms after Independence.

This chapter principally looks at the effects of domestic government on male farm workers in terms of their paid farm work. The next chapter concentrates on female farm workers at work. However, I begin with a brief sketch of wage work in tobacco farming to note some of the activities for which farm workers receive payment.

'Fodya-Fodya': work on a tobacco farm in Hurungwe

On almost all commercial farms in Hurungwe District, 'work' means tobacco production. Although the operators on Chidhadhadha also grew coffee and maize and raised sheep and ostriches, *fodya* (tobacco) is the main emphasis of their operation. It earns most of the income and is the source of most of the expenses.

After Brazil, Zimbabwe and the U.S.A. compete to be the world's second largest exporter of flue-cured tobacco. Tobacco is the highest earner of foreign exchange in Zimbabwe. If one includes production, processing and selling, tobacco is also the largest employer in the economy, accounting for a quarter of the agricultural workforce and 12 per cent of the industrial workforce. Good agricultural conditions, a growing world market, and strong support from the Zimbabwe Tobacco Association (ZTA) had led to rising tobacco prices during the 1980s and early 1990s. Tobacco volume increased more or less steadily throughout the 1980s and into the 1990s, leading to the record sale in 1991 of over 170 million kilograms at an average price of 1,157.29 cents per kilogram, almost double the previous year's average price of 648.54 cents (ZTA 1992:63).

The severe drought of 1991/92 destroyed most food crops in the country, but its effects on tobacco appeared to be minimal. However, when the auction floors opened at the end of March, the prices were significantly lower than those of the previous year. By the end of the auctions in November, a record amount of tobacco had been sold, but the average price had dropped below the 1990 level to 810.37 cents a kilogram (*Business Herald*, March 25, 1993).

Nevertheless, despite a severe foreign currency shortage, double-digit interest rates, and significant water scarcity for the upcoming season, industry leaders forecast that tobacco would rebound during the 1992/93 growing season.

These were the official indicators for the 1992/93 tobacco-planting season and were some of the understandings which the Chidhadhadha operators took into consideration. Dan and Geoff were keen on making as much money as possible from tobacco as they had gone heavily in debt to purchase the farm a few years earlier. They had paid over $7 million to the original owner, Mr Schmidt (who himself had bought the farm from the government in 1953 after it opened up the farms surveyed for the ex-soldier resettlement schemes to the general, i.e. European, public). In addition to paying the bank loan for purchasing the farm, Dan and Geoff had also taken out loans for planting their crop, which worked out at around $3 million, or $22,000 per hectare cropped. Interest payments were over $1 million. Yet, as Dan said with a chuckle, farming is a gamble, and they grossed about $5 million in their first year. 'We could have made a few more million,' he noted, 'but the drought acted as a convenient excuse for the buyers to pay inappropriately low prices.'

There are several distinct stages in tobacco production. Below is a brief overview of them on Chidhadhadha farm in 1992 (see Rutherford 1996:241-261 for a more thorough description).

In June, the tobacco seeds were sown in specially prepared seed-beds. After attentive care over a number of weeks by a select few workers, the tobacco seedlings were strong enough to transplant. There were three transplantings on Chidhadhadha in 1992: two were done with irrigation and the third occurred with the onset of the rains in November. Once transplanted, the tobacco plants were weeded, topped, suckered and received several applications of pesticide. After eight to ten weeks, reaping started. Leaves were usually picked when they began to turn from green to yellow, a process that begins with the bottom leaves and works its way upwards. Each field was completely reaped in about four to six weeks.

The reaped tobacco was transported to the curing barns where workers hung it to be dried. After a week of curing, the tobacco leaves were brought to a storage building were they were pressed into bales by slate-packers. The bales were stored until they were graded. At the grading sheds, three different groups of graders differentiated the tobacco leaves into separate categories according to their colour, texture, and leaf quality. The leaves in each grade were then tied into bundles, or 'dhukes', by women and pressed into hessian-covered bales by two young men. A few older men sewed the hessian shut and the bales were transported twice a month to Harare to be sold on the auction floor.

Each stage involved distinctive work processes by workers differentiated by gender, age, skills, and relationship to the farmers and the foremen. Each activity was supervised by a foreman or a senior male worker, with occasional visits of varying duration by the two farm owners who were at the apex of the management structure of the farm.

Liberalizing labour and the entailments of domestic government

Many commentators have outlined how different forms of discursive control have been part and parcel of 'capitalist practices', from notions of a quantifiable time to disciplinary regimes of the body and populations – tendencies and predispositions produced through institutional arrangements and discursive understandings which workers internalize in a form of self-discipline, or, more appropriately, in a disciplining of the 'self' (e.g. Foucault 1965, T. Mitchell 1988, Comaroff and Comaroff 1991). But these elements of the 'culture of capitalism', so to speak, are not directly transferable to, or identical with, labour practices on Zimbabwean commercial farms. Rather they are strongly shaped by the power relations entailed in domestic government; power relations that lead to a different form of disciplining of the 'self' by both operators and workers. Commercial farms are on the 'margins' of the identity of capitalism.

On Zimbabwean commercial farms, management is part of domestic government, which presumes an intimate, paternalistic dependence of workers on operators. Such an understanding informed many of the management practices on the farms, so that the constituted work differed substantially from the usual notion of work in official discourses of capitalism. Within the arrangement of practices on commercial farms, there were three major modulations of the elements of the 'culture of capitalism'. To begin, money is not just the universal medium of value for buying and selling commodities, including labour-power, but it is also a marker of modernity itself, tied to an arrangement of awards and forms of control to edify farm workers. Connected to this practice, 'time' also has a different emphasis from the stereotypical western order of 'rational bourgeois routines and a universal calendar' that has been connected to the emergence of industrialism and colonialism (e.g. Comaroff and Comaroff 1992:56). Rather than just acting as a quantifiable entity and as a secularized division between 'work' and 'leisure', 'time' also holds value in light of domestic government, acting both as a negotiated reward and as an obligation within the historical weight of the relationship between farmer and workers. Lastly, the spatial division between domestic and work sites, between 'home' and 'work', upon which a standard of modern life, economics and labour law rest, is blurred in the commercial farm context. Both the farmers and workers assumed, and daily practices treated, the setting of the entire commercial farm as belonging under an authority more or less independent of wider forms of government, particularly those that emerged from the central government.

The paths of money

In the economic discourse of 'modern capitalist systems', money tends to be the constant, immutable symbol that acts as a base-line for understanding and living in these societies. For both neo-classical and Marxist economic theories, money acts as the register and symbol of capitalism.[1] In neo-classical theories, money symbolizes the forces of supply and demand, which ultimately derive from individual human preferences and needs. For Marxian analyses, money, as the ultimate commodity, is fetishized in capitalism to disguise underlying relations of production and its antagonistic class conflict within the mode of production.

In this rudimentary account of the approaches to capitalist economies by two major theoretical schools, my point is that both are analyses which reify money as an indicator of underlying forces. Neither focus on money as a cultural register, whose value comes not (just) from economic 'laws' but (also) from politically contested and meaning-laden regimes within an institutional arrangement (Appadurai 1986, Hutchinson 1992, Burke 1996, and especially,

---

[1]   The use of the term 'money economy' to dub the 'modern' side of the putative 'dual economies' in the 'developing world' is an apt case in point for neoclassical theorists, whereas the critique against the colonization of 'life-worlds' throughout the globe by money for some Marxists is another example. See Wolff and Resnick (1987) for a discussion of the discursive attributes of these two theories.

Simmel 1978). It is with such an approach in mind that I will examine the issue of 'money' and 'time' on Chidhadhadha.

Since 1991, GAPWUZ and the ALB negotiate within the Employment Council for the Agricultural Industry to set minimum wages for different grades of workers. The wage increase for each grade during my research period was ostensibly significant since the collective bargaining took into account the high rate of inflation, although the increases only covered, at most, half the inflation rate (Table 5).[2] These figures do not include the stipulated monthly allowances the operator had to pay if housing, transport, cooking fuel, and lighting were not provided. Although some farmers paid long-serving workers a bit more, and foremen considerably more, a common practice (in Hurungwe at least) was to pay all other general workers, the vast majority, the minimum wage of Grade 1.

'Minimum as maximum' was the refrain most farmers recounted concerning factors they considered in setting wages. A few commented that they did not want to pay more as it could distinguish them from neighbouring farms, and they needed to maintain a common front. As one recollected from his war-time experiences as a farm manager, 'if I raised my wages unilaterally my neighbour would come over and beat me up' (see also von Blanckenburg 1994:90). In my survey of farm operators, approximately 90 per cent of the farm workers were paid the minimum wage of the lowest grade.

The legislated minimum wage for the lowest grade of farm workers has climbed steadily since Independence. Farm workers, along with domestic servants, have had the lowest minimum wages of all formal sector employees, but their wage increases remained above the level of inflation for most of the 1980s unlike most other employees (Herbst 1990:203). By 1992, real minimum wages had returned to pre-1982 levels. Relative to the price of maize meal, the staple of the workers' diet, they declined to pre-1981 levels (see ILO 1993:58).

Money acted as more than just a wage. Bonuses, the payment of wages, and credit all acted as points of leverage on commercial farms, just as they had since the colonial period, and as an index of farmers' modernity and workers' non-modernity. They helped to reinforce

---

[2]   The Central Statistical Office stated that the average rate of inflation for 1992 was 47.6 per cent and it forecast a higher rate of inflation for 1993 (*Sunday Mail* May 2, 1993). However, the official inflation rate was considered to be lower than the real inflation rate, at least in the commentary in the pages of the business-oriented *Financial Gazette*.

Table 5: Minimum Monthly Wages and Percentage Increases for Different Grades of Agricultural Workers, 1991-1993

	1 July 1991 to 31 August 1992 Minimum monthly wage (% change from previous wage)	1 September 1992 to 30 April 1993 Minimum monthly wage (% change from previous wage)	1 May 1993 to 31 August 1993 Minimum monthly wage (% change from previous wage)
Grade 1 General Worker	$157.41 (up 18.0 %)	$170.00 (up 8.0 %)	$185.00 (up 8.8 %)
Grade 2 Unqualified Mechanic	$169.22 (up 20.8 %)	$183.00 (up 8.0 %)	$199.00 (up 8.7 %)
Grade 3 Mechanic, Junior Clerk	$181.02 (up 29.2 %)	$196.00 (up 8.0 %)	$213.00 (up 8.7 %)
Grade 4 Senior Clerk, Crop Scout, Junior Foreman, Tractor Driver	$190.07 (up 28.4 %)	$205.00 (up 8.0 %)	$223.00 (up 8.8 %)
Grade 5 Senior Foreman	$199.12 (up 20.4%)	$215.00 (up 8.0%)	$234.00 (up 8.4 %)

Source: SI 17/92, SI 327/92, Collective Bargaining Agreement: Agricultural Industry.
NB: There are two other grades of workers (6 and 7). They are generally not applicable to farms in my research area. The Collective Bargaining Agreement does not cover managers' salaries.

the notion that the farmer was a paternal figure to his workers, who were rewarded with different forms of remuneration if they acted within the guidelines of the *mitemo yepurazi*, the rules of the farm.

I was talking to one of the Chidhadhadha sheep-herders on a Sunday afternoon in early January, 1993, in the compound. Bernard was usually in good spirits when I talked to him, but that afternoon he was glum. When asked why, he said quietly that he was currently the only 'sheep-boy', his assistant having been transferred to a reaping span. The other day three of the 250 sheep went missing. As punishment for this oversight the operators decided not to give him his wages; they would pay him only when he found the lost sheep. When I blurted out, 'the laws of the country do not permit this!' Bernard shrugged his shoulders and replied, '*pane mitemo yepurazi*', it is the laws of the farm.

Like other businesses in Harare, farm operators also used money as an incentive to reward workers. For example, they gave a range of annual Christmas bonuses depending on their view of a person's 'work'. But, at the same time, the contractual rights of workers to various forms of pay were often interpreted by operators more as a personal dispensation to their 'chaps'. This attribute manifested itself in the actual payment of wages, credit, and overtime.

In the colonial period, farmers occasionally delayed paying their workers. When I queried a worker who had been working on farms for 30 years about this practice, he replied, 'These whites of the past had "by-and-by" [*mbaimbai*, delays] certainly'. I asked what people would do then and he responded, 'Nothing, because they were able to get all the things to eat.'[3] When I asked him if workers ever demanded their money, he answered negatively, 'Back then, a white man was fierce, the whites were beating [workers]. No person was demanding anything from a white man.' I probed further, asking if workers ever refused to work because they did not receive wages, since I knew from archival reports that this had happened occasionally. He laughed incredulously at my question, 'No, no one. Refusing to go to work? You would be mad!'[4]

The timing of the payment of wages in the colonial period was definitely the prerogative of the white farmer, whose authority was not challenged due to the fear of his temper and the backing of

---

[3] Taped interview with retired man farm worker. Mukwichi Communal Land. March 2, 1993.
[4] *Ibid*. See also Rubert (1990: 252ff.).

authorities. Yet, workers could continue to work if they received their food. If they were dissatisfied, they fled the farm.

This was corroborated by a white farmer who told me about a deceased friend who during the war refused to pay his workers for several months as a way to encourage them to run away so he could forego paying them at all. He knew that in practice farm workers had no real recourse to getting their money.

Farmers today, I was told, rarely delayed paying their workers for several months. Most of the workers' remuneration was in money. Mandatory provisioning of rations ended at Independence. Although, as I shall soon discuss, it was not as straightforward as that, workers were to rely now on their monthly pay to purchase various goods and services. Some operators still paid workers at irregular intervals, but not as infrequently as during the colonial period. On Chidhadhadha, pay-day was frequently pushed back several times. Friends would tell me of their plans to go to Karoi, or even Harare, on Saturday after they received their pay only to have their plans cancelled when they found out that that pay-day would be delayed. It was even worse when workers needed to buy maize meal and ran out of credit. For the operators, these did not seem to be big concerns. Usually they could not pay on time because either they had not finished calculating the pay for their workers or they had not made arrangements with the bank to get money that day.

When they did arrive, pay-days were both happy and sombre occasions for workers. The joy came from having cash. The sorrow, however, was connected with getting very little of their monthly pay after deductions for their purchases on credit at the store, butcher, or from the farm itself. Many workers expressed to me how good it was to receive $50 of their $173 monthly pay-check. 'Credit was small this time,' they would say sincerely. Many bought items at the store and butcher on credit and took loans from the farm for extraordinary expenses. It is largely as credit, as I discuss below, that money took on a different role in the management forms that emerged after 1980.

The farmers rarely saw low wages as the cause for this need for credit or as causing poor nutrition. Lack of 'budgeting' was the explicit sign of this non-modernity. Farm operators constantly talked about the poor money-sense of farm workers. 'Hardly any had bank accounts!' I was told. 'You give them a big bonus and before you know it all the money is gone, spent on beer and women.' Some believed that their workers, just as in colonial times, only needed a bit of pocket change. Although occasionally they noted that the pittance given for minimum wage in these inflationary times could create a 'need' to drink and womanize to get some 'enjoyment' from their 'miserable lives'. The bottom-line, however, was that workers squandered the wages they earned and so the fault ultimately lay with the workers themselves.

Although their justification for paying low wages may be similar to that of other employers ('workers waste what salaries we give them'), such discourses were always figured through notions of the non-modernity of workers and the modernity of farmers looking out for the best interests of their 'backward' employees. As Karl, a white farmer in the area, put it, 'Raising minimum wages at Independence was a mistake. These chaps aren't ready for so much money. It'd be much better, I'm afraid to say, if we went back to the ration system. The workers would prefer it.' Such talk cast the operators as the modern citizens trying to help their non-modern workers. And yet, when it came to the question of payment by time, farmers often took a position contrary to their 'modern' inscription. Domestic government, with its emphasis on the modern European farmer as the source of control and edification of the non-modern farm workers, strongly modified the official assumptions about the role of money in a capitalist enterprise like a commercial farm.

Quantifiable time or domestic time?

In my survey, I asked farm workers for their suggestions about how to improve conditions on the farm. Although many of them focused on ways of improving the compound, the most frequently heard suggestion in terms of work conditions concerned time: 'The *varungu* [white men] start us too early in the morning and let us go at odd hours!' 'We will be finished our jobs and then be called back out of the compound to help load up the lorry with tobacco bales!' 'We've been working for over ten hours each day and not getting any overtime!' In short, the schedule was not only subject to daily decisions of the operators with little say by the workers or their representatives, but, in addition, the payment of overtime was seen as an (informal) gift to workers rather than as a (formal) entitlement.

According to the collective bargaining agreement in force at that time, the work day was nine hours, excluding lunch and including one fifteen minute break. Overtime was to be paid at pay at time and a half or, if agreeable to the worker and employer, by time off in lieu. However, on many farms I knew, overtime was part of a larger equation. Dan pointed out to me what George had said at the beerhall: 'Many times the workers worked less than nine hours a day, especially when they have *mugwazo* [task-work] and yet still get paid for a full day's work.' It was thus viewed as an exchange: some days workers worked more than nine hours and got paid for nine, on others they worked fewer hours and still got paid for a full day. Many farmers considered overtime as part of their largesse to workers. To get overtime pay, Robert, Chidhadhadha's senior clerk, told me, workers first had to get their foreman to tell Robert that they had worked beyond the normal hours. Then, Robert would approach the operators, who might grant the overtime pay or not. As Ezia's question in the beerhall meeting showed, workers were not hesitant to display their frustration, to the foremen at least. Despite their legal obligation, farmers viewed overtime pay as a matter of their discretion. As one operator earnestly responded when asked if he had any incentives for the workers on his farm: 'I pay overtime.'

The other question regarding the farm's definition of time and pay was *mugwazo*, task-work. Assigning a daily task was a common way for operators to set a work-schedule. Apart from transplanting and topping, most jobs could be made into *mugwazo*. The operator or the foreman would set what work the individual worker or group of workers needed to do to finish their day. In theory, the tasks came from a guide prepared by the ZTA or Conex (the colonial precursor to Agritex, the government agricultural extension service) that stipulated what an average worker could do in six hours. But in practice the *mugwazo* was set according to how much work the operators wanted done or, in their opinion, what the ripening of the crops required. A fine example came when the slate-packers' *mugwazo* was pushed up from nine bales a day, which they usually finished in just over nine hours if they did not take their full one and half hour lunch break, to twelve a day since Geoff needed more clips for the reaping. To meet that target, the slate-packers started work before 4 a.m. and finished after sundown (around 6 p.m.). And, in that case, the foreman refused to ask Robert to request overtime payment from the operators. Ezia was a slate-packer, which partially explains why he raised the question in the beerhall.

Sometimes workers were able to finish their work early with *mugwazo*, perhaps even before lunch, sometimes the *mugwazo* was quite onerous and took the entire day or longer. On occasions, workers would be docked a day of pay or only be paid half a day's wages if they had not finished their task, even if they had worked ten hours or more. GAPWUZ periodically confronted operators or their representatives about this practice, noting that *mugwazo* often meant workers had to bring in others such as their children to help them finish their task and those people were not paid wages. But farmers typically responded by claiming that it was the parent's responsibility and not the farmer's. Although workers could go to GAPWUZ or the Labour Relations Officer to lodge a complaint, workers I knew usually completed the *mugwazo*, accepted the lost pay, and complained to each other afterwards. *Mugwazo* and the practice of paying not according to time but by task, workers told me, was simply part of the *mitemo yepurazi*, the rules of the farm, which they were powerless to change.

As in the official cultural repertoire of capitalism, 'time' on commercial farms was a quantifiable item, which broke the days and weeks into discrete parts, linked to a work 'schedule'. However, the time distinctions associated with an industrial environment and upon which the collective bargaining agreement for the agricultural industry is based were modified by the discretion of the farmer, who, in terms of the *mitemo yepurazi* (but not the collective bargaining agreement) was authorized as the ultimate decision maker over the time of work and the remuneration by time spent working. Overtime, task-work, and other issues concerning time were negotiated and struggled over ultimately within the power relations on the individual commercial farm. Indeed, the boundary between 'work' and 'non-work' was itself not very well defined.

The blur between work and non-work

The compound was a vital part of the farm's operations. What should have been, according to the common distinction in official discourses, an area used solely for the leisure and domestic life of the workers was subject to direct intervention from management, not only in its physical layout but also in terms of control over the time schedule. Although I shall discuss these attributes of the compound within the domestic government in Chapter Six, I will briefly note some of them now.

Dan told me that operators use housing, and not wages, as the primary way to reward workers. There was a wide range of housing quality and management used it as a way to compensate those workers who were useful to them. Since farm operations are dependent on the weather and prone to sudden emergencies because of, for instance, hail or grass-fires, the operators needed to be able to find their foremen and workers when needed. On such occasions, the operators had a guard or a foreman to sound the bell which, every worker knew, meant they had to go to the assembly point by the barns. The bell, located at one foreman's house, was typically rung in the morning to get people to rise for work.

Having workers live on the compound helped to reinforce the notion that workers were at operators' beck and call. They were there solely to assist the bosses, and their own lives and 'leisure time' were subordinate to that. The biggest difference between Communal Land farmers and commercial farmers, Dan told me, was the ability of the latter to mobilize great numbers of people for jobs, while the former could only round up, at most, family members. 'Commercial farmers can even mobilize the family members of their regular workforce!' he exclaimed. 'Otherwise,' he added, 'there is really nothing else that separates us, we're both operating according to the whims of the market.' Conversely, one could say that both commercial farm operators and peasant farmers rely heavily on a 'domestic' authority to secure their labour supply.

This very play between 'being modern' – involved in capitalist markets as well as exemplifying the practice and ethos of edifying 'non-modern' peoples – and 'being un-modern' – living on the frontier of modernity, emphasizing paternalistic ties rather than rationalized, corporate structures – results from the modulation of the official cultural attributes of capitalist enterprises by the relations of domestic government. The modified rules concerning money, time, and the separation of work from non-work with respect to (what are taken as) conventional practices of capitalism derive from the assumption that the entire commercial farm, including the workers, is under the domestic authority of the farm operator.

I do not want to give the impression that this 'domestic government' has remained unchanged and un-negotiated in its colonial form for more than a decade after Independence; I now turn to some of the changes that have occurred within the domestic government, what may be called features of 'management', since Independence.

Management as inflated surveillance

Violence and mealie-meal: colonial forms of management

'Eee, that ol' *murungu* still hits hard! He will kick off his shoes and start running after you and then bam, he'll slug you...' I was listening to this tale about a neighbouring commercial farmer as I sat outside a *musha* in Mukwichi Communal Land. I was at the four-hectare farm of Chimpeto, an old Chidhadhadha worker, listening to his son-in-law speak. Nodding in agreement, Chimpeto pitched in by noting that *varungu* these days are more selective in their hitting. They tend to hit the small and timid, someone who would not hit back or would not report them to 'the Labour' (Relations Officer) or to the Police in Karoi. Before Independence, he reflected, it was a different story. 'One would never dare strike back at a *murungu* for then the farmer would really beat you. Complaining to the Police was also futile.' Chimpeto took on a pained and worried look as he said in a halting voice, '*Bwana Porisa, bhasi vakandirova*'. (Sir Police, my boss beat me). 'But,' he continued, in his normal voice, 'the boss would have phoned ahead to the police with his story.' Puffing himself out, he then said in a low voice, 'You *mambara* you, *shupikai* boss, hey? *Mambara* you, *Futseki*!' (You trash you, you were bothering the boss? You trash, go away!), while he was making the motions of beating someone. We all laughed at his act. His parody of the 'Rhodie', the white Rhodesian, accent coupled with the futility of trying to stand up for one's rights as a worker conveyed a sense of ironic acceptance and disruption of what was commonly called by farm workers, *upenyu hwemaboyi*, 'life of the boys'. Acceptance, because, as he and others said so often, they obey without choice the 'laws of the farm(er)'. Disruption, because unlike the common notion held by operators that they were 'helping' their 'chaps', Chimpeto was challenging that notion by laying bare the unequal relations through his mocking tone.

However, all workers with whom I talked about it agreed that violence and the 'colour bar', their idiom for cruelty, declined after 1980. Operators and foremen still occasionally hit people, but they tended to be more discrete about it. That was not the case during the colonial period. As one older man recalled work on the farms in that period, 'When a black person [*munhu*] spoiled work [in the old days], he was just told "you must work well". When a person made a big mistake, he was beaten. This is the same with children whom we look after. For the child who makes a big mistake, you beat him. For the one who makes a small mistake, you do not beat him. This is what the *varungu* [white people] did [to us].'[5]

This was a modification of the family analogy employed by George and Daniel at the 'lesson' in the beerhall. The farmer was now treated as a parent and the workers as children. Moreover, rather than the

---

[5]   Taped interview with man farm worker. Karoi North farm. April 25, 1993.

foremen and workers being part of the same 'family', as George put it, these workers depicted foremen as part of the farm operators' 'family', and as deriving their power from this moral proximity.

Foremen were interstitial figures. It was possible to fight a foreman since he too was a black person and lived in the compound. But in doing so a worker was also challenging the authority of the farmer, with whom the foremen were associated. As one worker explained, a foreman who disliked a worker could lie about him to the farmer, getting him beaten or fired no matter what the wronged person said. 'The *murungu* could not agree to what was being said by the person because he, the *murungu*, knew that the foreman was "my son".'[6] On Chidhadhadha, the 'son' of the farmer in the colonial period was a man whom I call Maoko.

> The [workers] were not fighting back in the old days because the boss-boy who was there, who was called Maoko, was beating people a lot. So when the murungu was about to beat a person that boss-boy would be close to him because Maoko would have first told him that I want so-and-so beaten. So workers feared that this person [Maoko] had more power than the murungu since he could have the murungu cause you harm. People never fought back.[7]

I was constantly told that Maoko was feared. 'Schmidt kept him,' one foreman said, 'because he had harshness and hatred towards the workers.' This is why he played such a pivotal role in the regulation of life on the farm for so long. Not only did he carry out Mr Schmidt's tasks in the fields; like other boss-boys during this time, he was the main enforcer of the rules in the compound as well. The 'rules' were not from the government: 'On the farm, laws were of the *murungu*, the owner of the farm. He was the one who was telling the foreman that "I want that here. I want that there." I was seeing that the *murungu* was the one who was giving people laws on his farm.'[8] If the owner was the 'government' who made the rules of the farm, then the boss-boy was the policeman enforcing the rules and the initial judge of transgressions. Or, to use the more popular pairing, one was chief, the other *sabhuku* (kraal-head).

---

6 Taped interview with retired man farm worker. Mukwichi Communal Land. March 2, 1993.
7 Taped interview with retired woman farm worker. Karoi North farm. April 22, 1993.
8 Taped interview with retired farm worker. Mukwichi Communal Land. March 2, 1993.

> *The problems of the people in the compound were solved by the foreman. The foreman was the one who was like a* sabhuku *on a farm and he was the one solving the problems of all the people like fighting of young children. Or when a wife and her husband bothered each other, they would go to the foreman. The foreman was the one who solved these cases. But when he failed to solve them he would go with these people to the* murungu. *The* murungu *was like a chief. Many* varungu *back then did not want to be called 'bosses', they wanted to be called* nkosi *[Nguni for God, little God, Lord or King, used also to describe the colonial District Commissioner].*[9]

Like the colonial official, white farmers in the colonial period did not deal directly with their subjects but had underlings who were paid intermediaries, a single 'boss-boy' in the farmers' case rather than 'chiefs' or other 'traditional authorities'. Unlike the latter, however, the boss-boy did not have any other potential source of legitimation outside of the farmer. Boss-boys then and foremen today may have tried to claim a unity with workers as a single 'family', but workers tended to see them, and still do, as aligned more with the farmers.

On Chidhadhadha, Maoko was responsible for enforcing the *murungu's* rules on the farm and its compound. He was helped by a few foremen underneath him – over whose promotion he had a major say – and a number of spies in the compound: 'People were surprised to hear the foreman saying "You! You! You have been saying this and that!" When there was a person who was planning to run away from the farm, the foreman's informers would tell him and he would then tell the *murungu.*'[10]

From several accounts I heard, Maoko had become very paranoid by the early 1980s. He was illiterate and not fluent in English. He talked to Schmidt in chiNyanja and chiLapalapa. Bornwell had been a clerk for several years and was gaining respect from Schmidt. George had just started as a driver and there were rumours that he was looking to become the senior foreman. There were other junior foreman who were literate in English and Maoko was trying his best to keep them out of Schmidt's confidence. In short, there was a change occurring in the role of the 'boss-boy'

---

[9] Taped interview with retired foreman from a Karoi farm. Mukwichi Communal Land. April 12, 1993.

[10] Taped interview with man farm worker. Karoi North farm. April 25, 1993.

and Maoko did not fit the new model. Sensing his marginalization, it seems that Maoko directed his frustrations against the general workers and other senior workers, including buying magic from a *n'anga* (Shona healer) to use against them. Workers and foremen began leaving because of Maoko and the atmosphere was tense. Finally, Mr Schmidt had his son fire Maoko.

If violence, or the threat of it, was a common form of coercion on farms in the colonial period, the provision of rations and a little money was the reward. As I discussed above, wages were not always paid regularly and even when they were, they were paltry. The irregularity of pay also acted as a way of bonding workers to the farm. For any purchases in the periods between the payment of wages, they received credit from the operator because, as one worker recollected, the '*murungu* would just give you [credit] and he just knew that this is my person now, even if I give him money there is nowhere he could go.'[11] When I asked him what this credit was used for, he replied, 'Some [workers] were paying school fees, some were buying clothes, some were taking credit to marry wives, and some were sending the money to their parents in Malawi. Food was not a bother because we used to receive food.'[12] The male workers received weekly rations of maize meal, oil, salt, fish and occasionally meat; extra of each if they had wives and children. Although workers disagreed when asked whether the food was sufficient or not, they all said that in general the *murungu* looked after them. The power relations of domestic government contributed to the workers' associating farm operators with the role of provider.

Credit was not ubiquitous in the colonial period, however. As one worker reflected, 'When I came to Rhodesia [in 1951], there was no credit. There was no credit because there was nothing that a man failed to get... Back then, all the things we were given them [by the *murungu*].'[13]

An old worker, who was watching a boiler in one of the curing barns, sighed about the state of life for the *mudhara*, old men like him, who worked on farms and took 'shit' from the boss:

> *If a boss or a foreman gave an order we [old men] will do it without talking back as we are afraid of going against an order. We do not want to be sworn at. Since we lived on farms*

[11] Taped interview with man farm worker (2). Karoi North farm. January 10, 1993.
[12] *Ibid.*
[13] Taped interview with retired man farm worker. Karoi North farm. April 25, 1993.

in the old days, we know how hard a murungu *could hit a black person who made a mistake. We black people just eat. We do not move, nor invest money. It is the responsibility of the owner to give us money to survive. We do not get any more than that. Geoff is responsible for the chickens [to sell] and the butchery. Dan has the maize meal and the store. They each have their things to make money for them. I remain here and work at their command. I can begin work at midnight and work right up to nine at night the next day if they are loading barns and they need me to look after the boiler. I am like a* simbi, *a piece of metal. I saw this anvil [pointing to a rusted anvil] when I came here in 1969. Like the anvil, I stay here and rust.*

'Isaac 1' (the operators attached a distinguishing number to each of the many 'Isaacs' on the farm) evoked the paternalistic attributes of 'domestic government' which emerged in the colonial period. The *murungu* provided everything for his workers who, in turn, worked for their *murungu* and rarely openly challenged his authority. Workers rarely resisted the control of white farm operators in the colonial period, I was told, for the government was clearly on the side of the owners. When I asked how workers related to governmental bodies during the colonial period, the conventional answer was that the *varungu* worked together. If one dared to go to the 'Labour', the farmer would phone ahead with his story and then the official would either just laugh at you or beat you. As one woman noted, 'When people were having problems with their *murungu*, black people used to say that, if they were angry, they would just leave work. The whites had no spirit of judging [*mweya wokutonga*] whites who were ill-treating black people because they were the ones who were ruling.'[14] Running away was the usual method of dealing with bad *varungu* or boss-boys. Workers would run away to other farms or back to their *musha*.

'One was fed and had money for clothing. You never got rich working on a farm back then – money was for existence, not advancing.' These words were uttered by a retired foreman who had worked for almost 25 years on a Karoi commercial farm. He now was a successful tobacco farmer in Mukwichi Communal Land. But such investment into productive activities by a farm worker,

---

14   Taped interview with retired woman farm worker. Karoi North farm. April 22, 1994. See also my previous discussion in Chapter Two.

even a senior one, occurred predominantly after Independence, not before. In the late colonial period, farm workers' wages went mainly into consumption items and paying taxes, not for 'advancing'.

The introduction of 'politics' on the farms

Since Independence, there have been a number of changes in the government of commercial farms. There are more foremen, the position of the clerk has become more popular, and literacy has become an important element for those workers who have taken on more administrative duties. These were some of the changes that led to the firing of Maoko. But the biggest change had to do with a direct challenge to the domestic regime of the white farmers.

This change can be discerned in what is likely a report about Maoko. Although I could not confirm if the foreman referred to in the event described below was actually him, it does fit the accounts I heard of his travels after he left Chidhadhadha. The report is from the Karoi labour officer in 1985. The event became a 'case' after a white farm operator in the district fired a foreman, hired a new one from a nearby 'reserve' and all 48 workers on the farm refused to work. According to the operator, he fired the foreman because he was too friendly with the workers. He wanted a foreman who could 'give commands'. But the official heard a different story when he talked with the workers.

> *When the workers were addressed by our Karoi officer about three-quarters of them said they had run away from a neighbouring farm, where the newly imposed foreman was once [the head] foreman, because he was too inclined to whites and he harassed people at work, even going to the extent of beating workers. The officer told the workers that the new foreman would be told to reform and if he did not, then his case would be reconsidered. He gave the workers' committee the task to observe the new foreman closely and to report the progress after two weeks. When this was presented to the incoming foreman, he said he was no longer prepared to take up the new post. The workers felt relieved and happily returned to work at 2:00 p.m.[15]*

---

[15] The officer continued his report by stating that the operator 'seemed to have the "sjambok [whip] at work" days in mind, hence his search for a foreman whom he knew had the reputation of driving and harassing people at work in the hope of getting better results'. February, 1985. Monthly Report of the Regional Industrial Relations Officer, Mashonaland Region. MLGRUD. Karoi.

For a government official to tell workers, and a farmer, that a foreman would essentially be put on probation because he had the *reputation* of being harsh, would have been impossible during the colonial period; as would a request that the workers do the monitoring themselves. Independence has had its effects: the workers' committee, village committee, and a *huremende hwevanhu* (literally government of the [African] people), have not been inconsequential to the domestic government on commercial farms.

Workers' committees and village committees have provided forums for workers to raise grievances with farmers, demand overtime payments, and, especially, temper the violence that figured so predominantly in the colonial period. It was no coincidence that Luke, the workers' chairman, and Ezia, the village chairman, asked the tough questions at the meeting in the beerhall. When these committees first emerged in the early 1980s, they not only stood for workers' rights but also openly challenged the authority of farm operators on many issues. At that time, these committees were closely associated with ZANU(PF) which had the power and authority to impose these structures on recalcitrant farmers and workers. The interests and activities of the committees were thus not purely labour-related and they often made far-reaching demands on management in terms of access to resources, making decisions on production and management, and on political loyalties (the latter were also made on farm workers).

Most operators I talked to remember those latter actions and dismissed the first years of Independence as 'the time of politics'. 'Politics' was the word used by operators to talk about challenges to their authority. Dan said, 'if workers are working poorly, I know that someone must be causing problems in the compound. Sure enough, in a few days, I find the person and get rid of him. It's one thing I can't stand,' he said adamantly, 'having someone bringing "politics" into my compound!' The preposition is telling. 'Politics' was something that came from outside the farm, outside the domestic space of the paternalistic farmer and his workers, entered from beyond the proper sphere of regulation of daily life. The oft-repeated phrase I heard from operators concerning the ZANU(PF) government was that if they just leave us alone, we, the workers and I, get along real fine. As one nearby farmer, Al, put it, 'government mis-understands the relationship between the farmer and his workers. Paternalism is necessary,' he concluded.

119

For instance, Jake, a white farmer in his early forties, was telling me that in the 1980s his farm's village chairmen were 'hot-heads' who tried to force things on farmers. They constantly had meetings and would tell the farmer not to fire certain people. He said inevitably within a year he and the Chair had a 'major disagreement' and 'parted ways', his euphemism for firing. Jake started a sentence by saying, 'They tried to flex their muscle against us, but...' He paused and I filled in the silence with, '...but they hit the barrier of the farmer...?' 'No,' he said, 'that's not it. We had to change our ways.' To understand that change, I will start with changes in the type and numbers of workers whom operators tend to call management personnel.

Changing managerial personnel: *maziso emurungu* (eyes of the white person)

According to the farm operators I surveyed, the number of management workers had risen between the time they first arrived on the farm, and the time of the survey. When the operators first arrived, only a third of them had managers, compared to more than half in 1992. The manager's job was to organize a daily work schedule, ensure that foremen monitored its implementation, and assist the operator in his administrative duties such as hiring and firing workers. Of the nine managers in the survey, seven were black and only two were white. Farmers told me that this was indicative of a process of 'Africanization' of farm managers that began just before Independence, but increased dramatically afterwards.[16]

The number of foremen more than doubled during this period. This was connected to the growing number of workers on their farms, and the increased hectarage of tobacco which led to several operations occurring at once (reaping, planting, curing, etc.). In the discourse of domestic government farm worker supervision was linked to the operators, and not to, for instance, the worker's own moral conscience or 'work-ethic'.

Operators also noted an increase in the number of clerks. When the respondents first arrived on the farm, only two of them had a clerk. In 1992, seven out of fourteen had one. This position was relatively new in the area. Chidhadhadha had its first clerk in 1981.[17] The clerks represented this change towards more 'modern'

---

[16] In the mid-1970s, Duncan Clarke (1977:158-159) commented that there was already a partial 'Africanization' of farm managers.

[17] In Duncan Clarke's (1977) thorough study of the labour system of Rhodesian commercial farms in the mid-1970s, there is no mention of the position of 'clerks'.

management, especially in the mediating role, as discussed below, between operator and workers in terms of credit, a key element of the paternalistic relationship. Operators without a clerk kept track of the records themselves, had their spouses do it, or hired accountants.

Two main groups represented workers' interests to management: the workers' committee and village committee. They were not 'management workers' *per se*, but they have played a role in the domestic government of commercial farms since the 1980s. In the survey, there were on average six members of the two committees per farm.

The duty of the workers' committee, in theory, consisted of taking work grievances to management and passing on concerns of management to workers. They were elected by workers during meetings organized by the GAPWUZ representatives or the Labour Relations officer from Karoi. The village committee was initially a creation of ZANU(PF) activists in the early 1980s. It was to deal with problems and concerns relating to the compound and act as a government presence on commercial farms. But the Party ties of the Karoi North village committees were quite weak by 1992/93, and it had only a limited presence amongst farm workers I knew. Instead, it was the commercial farmers who knew most of the local Party leaders, who contributed to their celebrations and assisted them in their own agricultural activities. Although I was unable to learn the perspectives of the local ZANU(PF) leaders on this change, most workers I met attributed this declining relevance of the Party on the farms to the government's growing interest in 'money' rather than *vanhu*, the people.

The other 'big workers' (*vanhu vakuru*) in the compound did not have managerial duties. Security guards mainly monitored the barns, crops and animals to prevent theft, but occasionally they were called upon to inspect the compound for stolen or prohibited goods. Some operators gave security guards explicit 'spying' duties, keeping their eyes on the workforce to look for thieves and 'disturbers'. The tractor and lorry drivers and the mechanics received higher wages than the general workers but their responsibilities were mainly consigned to the workshop and the tractors. The gardeners and, especially, the domestic servants of the operators had both higher prestige and higher pay. As I discuss in Chapter Six, by being physically close to the operator's home these workers had access to greater resources and opportunities than others.

During the period of my research, Chidhadhadha had between seven and nine foremen. George and Bornwell were the senior foremen, although Bornwell left the farm at the end of 1992. Farmers either hired foremen from outside the farm, based on recommendations, or selected them from within the workforce.

When farmers selected foremen from the outside, they did so because they were looking for qualified foremen, men with experience and training at one of the agricultural or tobacco training centres. They might also be trying to upset the balance of power within their workforce by bringing in someone new. Dan and Geoff knew that George and Bornwell had a lot of power within the farm, that they favoured their friends and lovers and persecuted their enemies. When farmers selected a worker from the 'gang' to be a foreman, they usually listened to the advice of the senior foremen and hence a number of their friends or relatives were promoted. But operators also remarked that they looked for a special quality of worker to promote to foreman. Farmers defined such qualities as 'authority', 'ability to handle labour', 'leadership', 'initiative', 'cheeky and intelligent'. Like the 'boss-boys' in colonial period, foremen were still valued for their ability to control labour.

Although George was the most senior of the foremen, Bornwell assumed that they were co-equals. George was 'almost a manager', according to Dan, but Geoff constantly referred to him as 'just a foreman'. As senior foreman, George ensured that the various tasks for the day were assigned and carried out. He also took responsibility for the farm if both operators were absent. But at other times of the season, during planting and grading, both he and Bornwell, like the other six foremen, were assigned a specific task with a group of workers.

George's prominence did not rest on his moral characteristics. The farmers of Chidhadhadha had caught him a number of times either stealing or extorting money from workers. Nevertheless, he was retained, Dan said, because he was not afraid of the workers and the workers feared him.

One day when I was with the tobacco planters, one of the farmers was furious because a worker was late leaving the compound and missed the tractor-ride to the fields. This man was constantly late, I was told by the farmer. When he finally arrived, about fifteen minutes later, the farmer told George to go and 'see him'. When the worker was no more than ten metres away from us, George approached him and calmly asked why he was late. The middle-aged man said that he was taking a child to the clinic (he lived with his three children in one of the dorm rooms). George called him a liar and asked to see the clinic card. The worker said he would produce it for him later. George matter-of-factly replied that he had to punish him. The man's shoulders visibly drooped as he pleaded 'No, Mista foromani, no.' George was about to take him behind a large ant-hill when another foreman handed him a small hand-hoe and said something. George then said within my hearing that I will punish you by making you do the hard work of patching up the gullies.

It seemed obvious that if I had not been there that worker would have been beaten. He was a relatively timid and slight man, and so would probably not have complained to the Police or to GAPWUZ.

In all these senses – controlling labour, spying on workers, punishing workers – foremen were very 'close' to the operators. Workers called the foremen *maziso emurungu*, the eyes of the white boss (just as *masabhuku* are called the 'eyes' of the chief). Their duties were not focused on motivating workers but on monitoring them. Despite my emphasis on the important surveillance role of foremen, there have been changes since Independence. Violence, or the threat of violence, has lessened and other means of control have increased.

Foremen are not the only people who carry out managerial duties on the farm. As senior clerk, Robert was responsible for keeping track of all the records of supplies and pay-sheets, including absences and holidays. Robert also helped in the management of workers' requests concerning loans, and the distribution of subsidized maize meal. The farmers had him deal with these requests in order to lessen the number coming directly to them. In fact, the senior clerk took on increasing responsibility during my time there, with his stature rising commensurably.

Robert, who graduated from Form Four in Harare, assumed that he was 'above' the other, 'uneducated', workers and foremen. In turn, the workers tended to despise him. 'He takes himself to be the *murungu*!' was a common criticism. He thought of himself as the boss, when he was only a clerk. The owners, though, preferred it this way as he screened workers' complaints and demands for them. Workers had to submit their requests to him for credit and Robert would make up his own mind if the requests were to be fulfilled. Some workers did not like Robert having such powers and often bypassed him and went straight to the operators.

Both Robert and the senior foremen were seen to be close to the operators. They were at the top of the hierarchy of workers, and gained favours such as commissions, high bonuses, access to the lorry, and brick contracts on the farm. But they were still 'workers'. The foremen were still hesitant to approach an operator without the latter's permission. Even Robert, who occasionally worked in the operators' office, approached their desks with downcast eyes and deference. Although the operators often joked with them and treated them as 'staff', as opposed to 'labourers', they still would yell at them if they made a mistake and ensure that they were aware of the differences in power between them. The operators and their wives maintained this distance by referring to each other as 'Boss Geoff' and 'Madam Karen'. Only infrequently could senior workers address the operators and their wives by their first names; for other workers, it never happened.

The surveyed farms exhibited several styles of management. From the perspective of the operators of Chidhadhadha, management centred on Dan and Geoff and spread outwards in descending order through senior foremen, foremen, clerks, and security guards, depending on the task. Neither Dan nor Geoff were fluent in chiShona or any other language spoken by workers in the compound. Rather they communicated to workers through chiLapalapa, a command language created on South African farms and mines mainly from siZulu and Afrikaans nouns and imperatives to communicate with a polyglot workforce. They and their wives tended to use chiLapalapa even with English-speaking workers because they felt any worker who spoke English had an 'attitude', feeling superior to other workers and being on the same level as the bosses and madams. That, in their eyes, was a sign of pride and being 'uppity'.

The farmers relied heavily on their senior staff, most of whom were at least functional in English, to act as interpreters when they required information which was too complicated to be communicated in chiLapalapa and when they wanted information from and about the workers. But if the farmer did not request their assistance, foremen and clerks would rarely translate the commands of the operator, even though many workers, particularly the younger ones, claimed that they did not understand chiLapalapa sufficiently well. The resulting poor communication between operator and workers was caused by the foreman abiding by their subservient position and obeying the formal 'chain of command'.

But whereas the operators assumed a pyramidal structure of management, workers saw a more fluid form of power operating, with different nodes of influence to the operators. Any of the '*vanhu vakuru*' (big workers), from village chairman to senior mechanic, from gardener to foreman, could potentially exert influence on someone's behalf. One such node was constituted through ethnicity.

On 'ethnicity'

A significant number of 'VaNdaus' worked on the farm. They came from south-eastern Zimbabwe, or southern Mozambique, and although they did not necessarily claim it themselves, most workers and the operators assumed they all came from Mozambique, having fled the war between the FRELIMO government and the Renamo 'bandits' supported by the apartheid government. Many of them had found work on the tea estates in eastern Zimbabwe. Their presence on Chidhadhadha was precipitated by the actions of the original farm operator. In 1985, Mr Schmidt sent George with a lorry to a tea estate in Manica Province, over five hundred kilometres away. George's brother-in-law was a farm manager there and the two *varungu*, the operators of the Manica estate and of Chidhadhadha, had arranged a deal which brought twenty workers and their wives back to Karoi North. Chidhadhadha was just starting to grow coffee and Mr Schmidt wanted 'experienced' pickers for this relatively new crop.

Ezia, the village chairman, was one of three men and one women remaining of that original group. He said that he and the others left the eastern tea estates since they were only working on contract there. In October, when George came, their seasonal contracts were ended. George had offered them – whom he specified as only 'married men and their wives' – full-time work. Ezia said that most of his co-travellers from the tea estates had 'run away' from Chidhadhadha shortly after arriving because the work was too hard. I also heard that a few years after the 'Ndaus' had arrived, the Police raided Chidhadhadha and neighbouring farms looking for illegal workers and took a number of refugees away.

No more VaNdau had arrived until 1991 when Ezia told me that he approached the new co-owner, Dan, and suggested that he could call for some friends from that area who would be 'hard workers'. Dan agreed. A week after their arrival on Chidhadhadha, Dan, pleased with their work, came to Ezia with a command to 'bring more!' Ezia spread the word to his relatives by mail. Even during my research, there were more arriving to join the sizeable contingent of 'VaNdau', who comprised about a tenth of the labour force by 1993.

Dan and his senior foremen had told me several times how well the 'Ndaus' worked as they did not have the 'distractions' of being close to their 'home' in the reserves. Unlike in Manicaland, they received the same pay as other workers and did not act as a source of cheap labour for the operators. However, some of these workers told me about their fear of being caught by the authorities and sent back to Mozambique; a fear which no doubt motivated them to complain less and to work harder than others.

Yet the description of them as 'Ndaus' spoke more to the classificatory system of the farm than to their own individual identities. It was with regard to these workers that 'ethnicity' as a system of identity distinction was most noticeable. Aside from marriage practices which occasionally were discussed in terms of ethnicity or citizenship (as discussed in later chapters), 'ethnicity' as a shaper of social relations on Chidhadhadha mainly concerned the 'Ndaus'; they were the ethnic 'other' for the farm workers who considered themselves to have a more legitimate claim to living on the farm, and to be more respectable.

The 'Ndaus' were a non-traditional source of workers for Hurungwe farms. Most of the foreign workers during the colonial period had come from less far away places: the chiNyanja-speaking areas of eastern Zambia; the chiTonga-speaking Lake Kariba region; the Zambezi Valley in Mozambique (chiNsenga- and chiChikunda-speaking areas); and central and southern Malawi (chiChewa- and chiYao-speaking areas). Many of the workers from or descended from such areas saw the 'Ndaus' as strangers, and as supporters of Ezia. For example, the few refugees working on Karoi North farms whom I met who had fled from the Zambezi River parts of war-torn Mozambique were not, in contrast to the 'VaNdau', distinguished as 'refugees' or outsiders.

During my research, the 'Ndaus' tended to stick together, living in one area of the compound. The men, aside from Ezia and a few others who had more prestigious jobs, mainly worked together in spans while the women tended to work in the coffee fields. Most were easily identified as a distinct group: they tended to have lighter skin; they spoke chiShona with different words from the local Korekore dialect or the more common standardized (chiZezuru) dialect taught in the schools and spoken by most of the younger farm workers; and the women often had cicatrices on their cheeks. They clearly saw Ezia as their 'Baba', father; even if they had no formal kinship or affinal relationship with him, he intervened on their behalf with management and with other workers.

Not everyone so designated saw themselves as 'Ndau'. Some held other ethnic identities such as Tonga. Others had the more localized identities of the chiefs of the parts of Mozambique they came from. Then there were those who did see themselves as Ndau but resented the label. 'Ethnicity' on the farm, as elsewhere in the country (see Worby 1994, 1998, Alexander and McGregor 1997, Ranger 1999, Alexander, McGregor, and Ranger 2000), carried with it hierarchical distinctions based on notions of modernity. The 'Ndaus' were assigned the status of 'primitive' in terms of their scars, their language, and their clothing.

For example, while I was picking coffee one day, I heard a woman talking loudly about the 'primitive' Ndaus. 'These VaNdau came to the farm wearing no clothes, waiting until they get $20 from picking coffee and then they rush to Karoi to buy clothes from the Zambians. But, even then, they don't know how to dress as they wear their clothes sloppily!' A quieter voice from another row told the woman to shut up as everyone was here to earn money. But the woman continued for a few more minutes until a MuNdau woman came over and confronted her. They began to argue and soon about a dozen or so women joined together. One shouted, 'Come on Chidhadhadha, let's go against these strangers!' More non-Ndau women came. 'This is Korekore country and we don't want these VaNdau from Mozambique here!' continued the woman who began the taunting. Many women shouted their approval, even those whose descent was from countries to the north. The arguing continued and a fight seemed to be about to break out when the foreman came and chastised the non-Ndau women for starting the trouble. The original instigators related the story of a MuNdau woman who arrived naked to work on a farm in Mhangura. 'They are all primitive!' The foreman responded, 'Should all Korekore be categorized a certain way because of the actions of one of them?' With the presence of the foreman, the debate subsided and the women went back to work. But the equation of the VaNdau with 'primitive', and non-Ndau with 'Chidhadhadha' was held by many workers.

The farm acted as a collective identity to which non-Ndau belonged, occasionally shading into a Korekore identity which many of the seasonal women workers assumed. Clothing – or the lack of it – has been a salient marker of fashioning ethnicity-*cum*–modernity in the region since the arrival of missionaries in the nineteenth century (e.g. Comaroff and Comaroff 1997, Alexander and McGregor 1997). The recent hiring of the Ndau, the slight difference in body practices some of them had, and especially their identification as a distinct group by management and by the leadership of Ezia contributed to their distinction as the ethnic 'other'.

Workers' organizations and the increasing surveillance

Shortly after I first arrived on Chidhadhadha, I introduced myself to the then chairman of the workers' committee. When asked about his duties, the first example he gave was passing the farmers' warnings to workers. He probably answered in this way because he saw me as a friend of the *varungu* and wanted to give an answer which showed that he was aligned with them. But, at the same time, and as I began to learn only later, he and his fellow committee members were widely considered to be weak, and vulnerable to the whims of the operators. He was closely tied to the management system since his first wife, who had died the year before, was the sister of Bornwell. He was promoted to a position of grading clerk, with an increase in wages, after he became the chairman. There was a trend of what workers viewed as co-optation on Chidhadhadha. The two previous chairmen also were promoted while in office.

Several months after I arrived, that chairman stepped down when the local GAPWUZ officers arrived. An election was held. Three of the seven members of the new committee were from the workshop. The new chairman, Luke, was a senior tractor driver.

For the workers, the fact that most members came from the workshop was a sign of the strength of the new committee. The owners could not co-opt them by promoting them since it was unusual for foremen to come from the workshop, and, if they got fired, they could easily find other jobs. In practice, Luke was successful in raising some issues with the operators. But the committee's powers had definitely been curtailed since the early to mid-1980s.

For instance, Luke called a meeting to tell the workers about the new labour code that had been negotiated at the Employment Council, and to answer questions concerning changes in the access to maize meal. However, as George did not show up to represent management, Luke on his own could not answer workers' questions on the latter topic. The meeting fizzled out and a number of workers openly complained about it being a waste of time. The fact is, that George played a far more important role than did the workers' committee in the government of Chidhadhadha.

The most important function of the workers' committee was to ensure that fired permanent workers received their proper termination benefits. Farmers occasionally terminated employees without giving them their leave or holiday pay. If the worker wanted to contest it, he had to go see Luke who then asked to have an audience with the operators. If they could not resolve it, the worker might go to the GAPWUZ office in Karoi, although from the middle of 1992 he would have to be a member of the union in order to get free assistance from them.

Not many workers were members of GAPWUZ in Hurungwe. Out of a permanent workforce of around 50,000 only 2,240 workers, less than five per cent, were members in January 1992. The union had severe staffing problems, with only two officers in the district to deal with all the farm workers in addition to the thousands employed in the fishing industry on Lake Kariba. Moreover, they did not have their own means of transportation.

On Chidhadhadha, the weakness of the union was reflected in opinion held by most workers that GAPWUZ was too distant and rarely came to their farm. When they did come, workers said GAPWUZ only lectured rather than helping with the problems they were facing. Their arrival on Chidhadhadha in 1992 to elect the new workers' committee was, I was told, their first appearance on the farm for many years.

Another cultural factor working against GAPWUZ was the common equation on Chidhadhadha of 'politics' with the trade union. 'Politics', as noted above, was by definition a transgression of the laws of the farm.

One day I was in the workshop on the farm talking to Luke and the senior lorry driver. The driver casually mentioned that he got no extra time for lunch breaks when he was driving. Luke became very serious and said that he should get time off, and should talk to GAPWUZ to see if one of their officials would come down to talk to the farmers with him. The driver became tense and said it was not a big problem, that perhaps his co-driver did not want to stop for lunch, and he quickly changed the topic. After Luke left several minutes later, the senior mechanic who was working nearby warned the driver to keep away from GAPWUZ. 'The *murungu* does not like people bringing "politics" onto the farm!' he exclaimed. The driver nodded grimly.

Innuendo, rumour, fear, and the ability to curry favour were the ways workers and management manoeuvred in the 'political field' of Chidhadhadha. An ex-chairman of the workers' committee said that since the *murungu* 'won' the struggle on farms in the mid-1980s, workers have been dispirited and the spies have increased. If someone began complaining in the compound, he would quickly be punished. To punish a worker for his ideas or, for example, petty theft, foremen informed me, they would just give the person a really hard task such as stumping lands. If they wanted the worker to leave, they would keep giving that worker hard tasks and would continually harass him until he decided to leave 'on his own'.

Rinse and I were incorporated into these discourses, especially as the workers were unsure of our motives and alliances. When I was carrying out a census of farm workers in the compound and asked if they had any suggestions for improvements of the farm, several workers told me that they could not tell me since they had been warned by senior workers not to talk about their problems to anyone – a comment I took to mean me. Rinse and I had also been warned when we first arrived on the farm; Dan cautioned us, particularly Rinse, about George, saying that he might feel threatened by our presence and try to make life difficult for us. The warning was sincere, I believe, and its effect, deliberate or not, was to make us quite careful about our forms of questioning and how we went about our tasks of research. The seed of fear was planted in us, more so for Rinse than me. Being a *murungu* and a foreigner I was outside some of the circuits of retribution, such as witchcraft, of which Rinse was a part. However, I soon entered another type of circuit, which has emerged as the major distinction of the post-Independence form of management on the farms I knew.

Credit, consumption, production: revamped domestic government

While carrying out research on Chidhadhadha, I returned periodically to Harare to pursue research there. As I had a car, and because certain items were considerably cheaper in Harare than in Karoi, let alone on the farm, I thought I could help workers out by buying things for them. Soon, I had to plan to spend a considerable time during my trips to Harare seeking cheap blankets, pots, towels, plastic buckets, record needles, English-Shona dictionaries, microphones and, most of all, radios and '*makaseti*', portable cassette-players.

Getting payment for expensive items such as the cassette-players was often difficult. On a few occasions I had to go to Robert, the clerk, to arrange a pay-back schedule or, with the agreement of the man who owed me money, to get it from the farmers, who then deducted a monthly amount from the worker's pay-check.

And so I participated in a problem which faced most of the farm operators: the repayment of credit. At first I thought this was just a side-issue of 'doing field-work', which given the disciplinary tendency to study marginalized populations anthropologists typically encounter – the demands made upon their greater access to travel and to commoditized resources than that of the people with whom they work. However, as more and more workers approached me with their '*kachichemo kadiki-diki*' (tiny, tiny requests) and as I spent more time purchasing items in Harare and pursuing people who owed me money, I started to rethink this 'side-issue'. Putting it into a historical context, I argue that farm workers' need for money has increased since Independence along with the demands for commoditized consumption and production. The inflated importance of money heightened the tension surrounding access to it.

On Chidhadhadha, for instance, most permanent workers received up to $50 monthly credit at the farm store, $20 at the farm butcher, $8 for a chicken, and tins of subsidized maize meal depending on their family size. If they took this credit, the money was deducted from their salaries which, in late 1992, was $173 a month. If a worker fell behind with the payments, his credit at the farm store was restricted to $35 for 'necessities' such as maize-meal, salt, and cooking oil, and to $7 at the butcher shop. This, Dan informed me, was to ensure that these workers did not 'waste' their money on blankets and other 'luxuries'. If the worker was still not paying back his loan, the farmers would set up a schedule of automatic deductions from his monthly pay. Although Dan told me that workers would always get at least $30 in cash, a number of workers who were heavily in debt barely got any money at month's end.

Credit was used for a variety of items. During the drought, many workers used it to buy extra food to send to relatives in the

Communal Lands or to feed those relatives who were sent to live with them because there was no food in the *musha*. Some had to pay school fees not only for their children but for other relatives as well. Contributing to a relative's funerals was a common expense. Many also bought maize seed and fertilizer for their crops in the *musha*. These demands for access to agricultural inputs on credit will be explored in Chapter Seven. But I want to stress here that the demand for and the provision of agricultural means of production began primarily after Independence.

> *The* murungu *used to give credit to a person whom he trusted with this money [in the colonial period], but not to help in terms of giving people seeds or fertilizer on credit. People were not able to grow crops for selling because there was nowhere they could sell these crops... People did not even have the G.M.B [Grain Marketing Board] membership cards back then [which one needed to sell maize legally outside Communal Lands].*[18]

The provision of credit for agricultural inputs became a part of the obligations of domestic government, a condition extended by the farmers to show that they 'helped' those workers who assisted them on the farm. Credit in the colonial period was used mainly for buying food and clothes, and for weddings, funerals and travel. Most people declared that credit was relatively limited back then.[19] Credit was still largely used for these purposes during my research as well, although it extended to other areas such as school fees and personal farming expenses. As in the colonial period, wages barely covered the costs of feeding a family and meeting other financial demands. But both purposes of credit – to meet daily financial needs and the demands of one's own farming – became an expectation associated with working on farms.

Farmers had greater access to loans in the 1980s than they did before (Loewenson 1992:46ff.). Many I talked with also recognized that workers had correspondingly greater monetary needs, often driven by attempts to be 'modern', especially through education and

---

[18] Taped interview with retired foreman of a Karoi North farm. Mukwichi Communal Land. April 12, 1993.

[19] It was difficult to find corroboration for this assertion. The data from Clarke's study (1977:197ff.) of one farm near Salisbury suggest that credit was minimal. The workers, Clarke reported, found the farmer to be stingy and instead borrowed heavily from friends (1977:204-205). In his research on farm workers in pre-1940s Rhodesia, Rubert (1990: 253ff.), however, found that farmers extended credit to workers for food, household items, bicycles, bridewealth, and taxes.

farming for themselves. This was also tied to a notion of more opportunities arising with Independence, with the '*hurumende hwevanhu*' (government of the [black] people) enabling (some) black people to make money from their *musha* in the 'reserves', get a house in Karoi, or get a higher paying job on the farm as a mechanic, a clerk, or even a manager.

A common refrain I heard on Chidhadhadha was that 'they work us hard here for little money, but we won't complain if they give us good credit.' It was similar to the colonial period when, I was told, farmers who frequently beat workers paid higher wages to attract workers.[20] Greater violence in the colonial period often meant higher wages. Harder work in the first decade and a half of Independence often meant greater access to credit.

But I do not want to overstate this access to credit, or give the impression that every worker received generous credit or used it for the *musha*. Credit had become a valuable part of the operation of domestic government since 1980, and as such it was under the paternal control of the operators.

One clear example of how some goods provided on credit were part of a paternalistic relationship and not, say, an exchange between two autonomous individuals, comes from the sale of maize meal. All surveyed operators provided maize meal on credit, almost always at a subsidized price, but only two permitted their workers to sell it. Cheap maize meal was a gift to *their* workers and, especially in the time of maize shortages, the operators did not want their workers to go and sell it to others. On Chidhadhadha, this prohibition even extended to their farm store. Although it was open to the public, the operators got alarmed when people from the nearby Communal Land bought up the supply of packaged (i.e. non-subsidized) maize meal, as they were selling it at a cheaper price (actually the official price) than in the Communal Land stores. They forbade their storekeepers to sell maize meal to anyone but their workers. Yet, still they lamented to me, 'every time we drive down the road, we see strangers walking away from our farm with bags of maize meal on their shoulders. Our own workers are selling their maize to people from the reserve!'

Although farmers saw credit as a perk for workers, a way to attract workers, many also discussed with me the need for credit as

---

[20] Taped interview with retired man farm worker. Mukwichi Communal Land. March 2, 1993.

an indication of the different 'values' held by Europeans and Africans, between 'us' and 'them', and a reason why 'we' should (re-)assume more control over 'them': workers were irresponsible because of their non-modern culture. This difference was a major sign for white operators of how farm workers were dependent on them.

Al, a nearby farmer, stopped giving credit except in special circumstances after a month in which he issued $17,000 in credit out of a wage-bill of $24,000. He said he realized that his workers are not making much money, but they are doing a lot better than 'most other Africans!' The message here was less that workers were poor 'budgeters', though he had described them as such on other occasions, but more that *as Africans* their cash needs should not be so great. Whereas many workers saw access to credit as a necessity and as a way to increase their income through investing in their own *musha* or through buying and selling goods, many farmers in contrast saw the demands for credit, and the resultant high debts, as a sign of their workers' 'backwardness'. It was not surprising, then, that when Geoff and Dan decided to restrict credit, there was a lot of anger. The 'lesson' in the beerhall was a reaction to dissatisfaction that had been brewing since at least Christmas 1992.

When I returned to Chidhadhadha on December 27th from a trip to Harare, every worker I met was extremely bitter. Their 'Christmas box', their annual bonus, had been significantly lower than they had expected. The operators told the workers this was because they were still paying off their debt from purchasing the farm and because tobacco prices were low, but the workers I talked to did not believe it. 'We had irrigation', one exclaimed, 'how could they not have made good money!' Another older worker told me, 'it would be no different if we spent our time in jail rather than on the farm since we get no respect here.' Aside from a few tractor drivers, only the foremen did well. 'They received thousands of dollars for just standing around and giving orders,' the worker complained, 'while we worked hard.' 'The foremen,' said another, 'are friends of the *murungu.*' When I asked what people would do, they said they would complain, and possibly leave work.

Combined with other transgressions by the farmers of presumed attributes of domestic government, many workers were fed up with the new owners. By mid-January, a number of them began to leave, or threatened to leave, the farm. Most of them came from the section of one farmer in particular. They complained to the other farmer that they were going to leave. In turn, he often offered to place them in his section. Many workers were angry at the other farmer because he did not know how 'to treat Africans right'. What they meant was not that he made his workers work hard, but that he did not provide sufficient credit.

'He does not listen to our complaints!' said one worker to me. 'You approach him and you get yelled at.' Another compared the approaches of the two operators in the following way. 'One makes you work hard and long, making you board a tractor at 4:30 a.m. and leave work after 3:30 p.m. without a break. He steals time. But he has a good heart. He listens to our complaints and requests.' As for the other boss, 'he does not work workers that hard. He is fair about breaks and the length of the work day. But he thinks that black people do not need any more money and he does not listen to their requests. He does not have a good heart.' Rumours circulated about the harshness of the latter farmer towards blacks and Chidhadhadha's reputation began to decline amongst its workers and, I imagine, among other farm workers in the area. As George lamented in January, 'if more workers keep leaving, soon the farm will only have bad workers who cannot keep a job elsewhere!'

His prophecy did not come true, at least not while I was there. As far as I could assess, no more than twenty or so workers left during this time, some of whom were fired. Nevertheless, the farmer who was attributed with having a 'good heart', did raise the subject with me. He was worried that workers were leaving and those that remained did not have a 'good attitude', but were just putting in time. 'But,' he continued, 'the other owner has his ideas about credit and workers and, though we have talked about the matter in private, as his partner I have to agree with him in public.' To use George's words from the 'lesson' in the beerhall, they were 'like a family' and had to maintain an appearance of unity to outsiders.

A few days later, on a Sunday, I was walking out of the compound and noticed several workers who usually looked after the curing barns casually talking to each other. I asked what was happening and they replied that there was a power shortage and so there was no electricity to feed the curing barns. Neither operator was on the farm, so they took the period as a break. A few minutes later, we heard the roar of the fans start up and the workers sauntered back to their posts. The guard who remained behind at the gate laughed and shouted sarcastically after them, '*Mhanya, mhanya bhoyi!*

Purazi rakakosha! (Run, run, boy! The farm is important!). The others turned and smiled. They had just been talking about credit and how little the farm does for them now. Violations by farmers of the assumed arrangements of domestic government had resulted in less than enthusiastic work by farm workers.

Conclusion

'Helping the boys,' helping them learn about 'modern life', that was the task, at times the burden, of the white farmer. Or so they told me. Farmers defined themselves as modern in relation to farm workers and by that very attribute took it upon themselves to control workers' lives, both on the job and in the compound. This identity was extended to commercial farms as a whole in most official discourses, so much so that there has been more emphasis on this seemingly apparent 'fact' than on how this notion has been constituted. And yet, part of their 'modern' practices have included an emphasis on an operator-centric version of 'keeping (and paying for) time', of blurring the distinction between work and leisure, of using money for reinforcing paternalistic ties, and of emphasizing the ability of foremen to control workers, partially through fear. All of these practices would go against the common equation of modernity and commercial farming in Zimbabwe. Yet even the chairman of the Agricultural Labour Bureau observed the tension between 'modern' and 'traditional' management practices. In a speech given to the CFU congress in 1999 on the motivation and productivity of farm workers, he noted that even though the ALB has been championing current management theories of labour relations, many farmers find the 'traditional theory' has great success in motivating workers; a 'theory' which includes close supervision, doing the thinking for them, and providing them with detailed instructions.

In many ways, the colonial era power relations of domestic government have modulated crucial elements of the official repertoire of the 'culture of capitalism', enabling farm operators to make farm workers labour for them. The power relations within the space of 'labour relations' on farms shape, and are shaped by, class relations and state policies. Labour relations on commercial farms in Hurungwe in 1992-93 were similar to those in the 'traditional' times of the colonial period, upon which some farmers reflected with nostalgia.

I put quotation marks around 'traditional' to indicate the poverty of employing the 'modern/traditional' contrast to understand commercial farms in southern Africa (cf. Marcus 1989). Given the importance of 'family' in managing farms, the lack of proper administrative procedure in respect of labour relations, and the operators' attitude towards controlling workers, it is easy to call commercial farms and farmers 'traditional' as opposed to being 'modern' enterprises. However, the solution would then be to 'modernize' commercial farms, ensuring better management techniques and proper grievance procedures. The problem with this 'solution' is that it ignores how the trope of 'modernity' has for decades been closely related to 'European' identity, how whites have been 'modernizing' farm workers since the colonial period.

The other problem is that such a dichotomy ignores how this 'traditional/ modern' form of governance has changed since Independence: how there has been an extension of the operator's 'domestic' control through an increasing number of foremen and clerks; how village committees and worker committees have had an impact, albeit in various ways at that time and in a declining fashion since the mid-1980s, on these forms of control; and how credit, for both consumer and productive goods, has become an integral element of the relation between operators and workers. For most workers, the insults of the farmers and their 'management' personnel, the swearing and the shaming, the potential for physical violence, and the hard work may be tolerated if farmers are generous in listening to and meeting their requests. Many of the requests were similar to those made during the colonial period, but others, such as getting agricultural inputs and paying school fees, are more ambitious.

This chapter has tried to show the problems of employing one side of the dichotomies modern/traditional, capitalist/non-capitalist to explain the situation on commercial farms. Without doubt, the class relations, the division between the owners of means of production and the sellers of labour power, and the larger political economy of which they are a part are capitalist. However, being 'capitalist' does not necessitate already scripted identities and forms of consciousness. Rather, the shape of local struggles and identities within capitalist relations always depends on the particular knowledges and power relations, which situate capitalist enterprises in historically sedimented sites (Watts 1992). Assuming a pre-scripted notion of capitalism, scholars have often discounted the local forms of power relations and sites of struggle built around domestic government on commercial farms as, at best, irrelevant and, at worst, as examples of 'backward', 'feudal' or pre-capitalist forms of struggle that need to be modernized to become authentic class conflict. It is an assumption that is caught up in the trope of modernity.

Farm workers have been caught up in this trope of modernity, and it informs their lives in several ways. Most assumed that it was the farmer's responsibility to assist them as not only '*vanhu*' ('black people') but also as '*mabhoyi epurazi*' ('boys of the farm'). Such an assumption was built into the primacy and legitimacy of the *mitemo yepurazi*, the rules of the farm, which gave farm operators that responsibility of assisting and edifying them in exchange for their obedience. At the same time, many workers wanted to 'become modern', be it through buying consumer goods or through investing in their own agricultural production, which depended on farmers meeting their requests. When that did not happen, when an operator had been attributed with a bad heart in meeting these expectations, discontent and conflict were sure to follow.

This discontent and conflict must, for those who seek to improve the situation of farm workers, be understood within the intersection of local and wider forms of meaning and power and not dismissed as inauthentic, un-modern forms of struggle. Many farm workers know the channels through which their situation can be improved; they should not be condemned by too strict a notion of 'politics' – one wedded to an official identity of capitalism – if progressive 'change' is imagined.

These arrangements may also be discerned in the strategies of women farm workers, workers who as a group have been marginalized from the routes and routines leading to credit and wages, and who have differentially relied on other paths and identities to gain access to resources.

Chapter 5

The margins of the margins: women's work

The work of women farm workers

Mai Chido had arrived on Chidhadhadha from a neighbouring commercial farm almost five years before I arrived. She left the latter after she and two other women working in the grading shed were blamed for discarding tobacco scraps instead of grading them, even though she alleged that it was the clerk who had instructed them to remove the scraps, so he could use them as manure on his garden. The manager there had not asked them to explain themselves but rather fired them on the spot, she noted while we sat outside her room in the dorms beyond the compound.

About fifteen minutes into the interview, I began to ask her about her work cycle since coming to Chidhadhadha where, as she phrased it, 'work never ends'.

'I arrived here in April. I first worked in the coffee [fields]... In June, I was then taken and sent into the grading shed.' When asked what type of work, she replied, 'I was tying some dhukes.' That work had finished in August. Her next job started in September: 'We started to put soil in plastic bags for coffee plants.' The questioning continued like this, as she traced her work from one task to the next. After preparing coffee seedlings, she worked as a coverer in the planting of tobacco. Then, she and other women did 'every job now. Sometimes we went weeding, sometimes we went to apply fertilizer, any work which was wanted to be done by the *murungu*,' until the grading season started. That had been her routine on Chidhadhadha until last year when she refused to work in the grading shed and returned to work in the coffee fields. When I inquired why, her previously pithy answers extended into a more engaged response. She said she was 'not having a good relationship' with Bornwell, the foreman of the grading shed at that time:

> *What used to happen here was that when you were short-changed on your wages, you were not allowed to ask why. But I complained anyway. I used to go to his table, and ask him "with what?" I showed him the money I had received, saying, "Now, I shall send what to school? I shall eat what? And the money for buying soap, where will I get it?" He saw me as a bad influence on other workers. After others saw me refuse my wages when the clerk short-changed me, others followed suit. The clerk [Bornwell] was the one who was preventing people from asking him why their wages were short.*

I asked Mai Chido to elaborate on the conflict.

> *That clerk used to ask you, "How do you know that your money is short?" So I used to ask him as well, "Tell me, on a day how much money am I working for?" Or on* mugwazo *[task-work], "How much are we supposed to receive, so that we earn wages which are similar to others?" This clerk then said to me, "I no longer want to see you in this grading shed. You go and work outside!"*

Sensing that she did not wish to discuss the matter further, I steered the interview back to her annual work schedule, asking if she was ever stopped from working on Chidhadhadha. She replied that for those women who do not work in the grading shed, work is slow for several weeks in March and April. 'Even in the middle of the year work can be short. Men would be the ones who would be working only... So the days when men will be doing the work of women, we would be having no work.' I asked whether women are treated in the same way as men. 'This will never be the same,' Mai Chido replied solemnly, 'A woman is kept solely as a contract worker.' She then elaborated:

> *It is different. We see it at bonus time when men are being given bonuses. A man who would have started work yesterday, you see him being given a bonus while you, the woman who would have had many years being on this farm, you are not given any bonus or anything else. That is why I am saying it is different. When there are holidays, men who are on a ticket [permanent workers] do not go to work but women keep going to work.*

'Who decides this is the case?' I inquired. 'I think that this rule comes from the owner of the farm. This is the government [*huremende*] of the owner of the farm.' Taking my line of questioning to its conclusion I asked her, if women were allowed to be permanent workers, would she want to be one. Mai Chido answered in her dry monotone, 'I should be a permanent worker, yes. Here, I have five years now. Starting in April this year, I will be starting my sixth year.'

I, like others on the farm, found Mai Chido a remarkable personality. She worked on the farm, as a single woman, for over five years. She was putting her three eldest children through secondary school and was raising her nine-year-old daughter. She had also managed to get a piece of land in Kazangarare, which, as discussed below, was not without its problems. She also confirmed the gender inequities among farm workers noted by others (e.g. Loewenson 1988). She exposed the fabrication that women were just 'seasonal workers', working 'no more than eight months a year'. She made it clear that actually she and other women were working more or less all year round. Moreover, Mai Chido stood up to a dominating foreman for fair wages. She spoke out against being short-changed as well as insisting that *mugwazo* workers must get the same daily minimum as others. She stressed that she was a permanent worker in terms of the length of time she had worked, but not in the way she and other women were treated by the government of the farmer.

Mai Chido confirmed many of the suspicions I brought to my research, as well as those I developed during my year on Chidhadhadha. She represented a woman who, despite adverse conditions, was able to provide for herself and her three children, relying, more or less, on her own strength and resources, and not those of a man. But her story, though important, is not the complete story of women workers on Chidhadhadha. Her identity was not simply that of a black woman oppressed by black and white men. There were other divisions, differences, 'subject positions', that she took during that interview and others, which challenged my desire to make her a representative 'African woman worker' who stood up to patriarchy and exploitation (see Sylvester 1995b). To better understand the possibilities and tensions amongst 'women workers', and contrast these with the various projections of the 'African woman worker' (in the singular), which have furnished the assumptions of management and male workers to constrain, regulate, and define the lives of women workers, I need first to elaborate on the life of Mai Chido.

Mai Chido was born in a mining area in central Zimbabwe. Her father acquired a farm in the Vhuti African Purchase Area (in north-western Hurungwe District) in 1962 where she worked for him. She married a 'foreigner', a man from Mozambique, in 1969 and worked with her husband between the Karoi commercial farms and her father's farm at Vhuti. Her first husband died in the late 1970s, and since he had no relatives, she kept the children and returned to her father's farm. She married again in 1982 and had another child. They moved to a resettlement farm close to Vhuti, since her brothers did not want her husband to stay permanently on their father's farm, in case he thought he could inherit it. However, her new husband did not want to look after her other children so she left him in 1987. She returned to Vhuti. For a year, she worked on her father's farm and on neighbouring farms at weekends to earn some money to pay for school fees and clothes. Since she was having difficulty making enough money, she found work on commercial farms.

In 1990, she went to a local *sabhuku* (kraal-head) and Village Development Committee (VIDCO) in Chief Kazangarare's area of Mukwichi Communal Land and received a piece of land. She took her eldest son, then in his early twenties, with her, and put the land in his name. As he works full-time for her father in Vhuti, he was not (yet) prepared to spend any time on this land in Kazangarare. When I asked why she had put the plot in his name, she said matter-of-factly that he was the man in her family and men should be the owners of the *musha*.

However, she had not farmed the land. A neighbour would not allow her to grow anything on it, claiming that it belonged to him. Neither the VIDCO, the *sabhuku*, nor Chief Kazangarare had attempted to settle this dispute. In 1992, she borrowed a small piece of land from a man who was also originally from the same mining area. There she and her eldest daughter, Chido, (who lived with her in the dorms) planted and tended two acres of maize during the weekends. But she told me that she will persevere; and when she finally gets the land that is firmly 'hers' (through her son), 'I shall no longer be working here; what gives me the drive to keep on working on this farm is that even if I go back to my father's, there is nothing which would help me [there].'

In the interview, Mai Chido had a number of subject positions which challenge simple sociological categories: as a 'worker', her main goal was to get a rural home, a *musha*, to live full-time as a farmer; as a 'woman', she had to rely on her son in his early twenties to be able to get access to land (and it did not bother her); and, as I shall now discuss, as a 'woman worker without a man', she also remarked on a major division amongst 'women workers' themselves.

I asked Mai Chido to talk about the differences between living in 'the dorms' and living in the compound. In terms of who decides who lives in the dorm, she observed that the 'law of the farm' says every person who comes here, who is a woman without a man, must stay in the 'dorms'. But, she continued, 'men without women must stay in the compound.' She then went into a lengthy explanation of this difference:

> This was done so that there would be no 'quarrels' [mhere-mhere; literally 'noise']. It is said if women without men stay in the compound there would be a lot of quarrels because married men would now be leaving their wives and going into houses of women without men. At these dorms [beyond the main compound] there once was a fence, but it later fell down. A man was not allowed to enter inside the fence. Men used to arrive waiting outside the fence for a woman they would be wanting. If a man entered here and was known, he could be reported to the murungu and he would then have to pay a fine. Equally, if a woman from the compound came in here to make 'noise', it also was a case [mhosva; a 'court' case].

But the 'solution' did not help much. Pointing at some scraps of wire fencing in the nearby bushes, she said the fence fell down last year (1992) 'because men used to come here and lean against the fence until the poles which supported the fence slowly bent bit by bit.' When I asked whether the prohibition against compound women entering existed because they felt the 'dorm' women were stealing their husbands, she agreed. When I queried if there was a way to stop the 'quarrels' between the women of the compound and dorms, she answered, 'There is none... Problems of prostitution [*chihure*; from English, 'whore'] have been here for a long time.'

Mai Chido was very much against *chihure*. Although she lived with many women in the dorms, she had not built up a strong relationship with any of them. She also forbade Chido, her eighteen-year-old daughter, from befriending them. Chido later told me that since most of the women in the dorms are prostitutes, if she befriended any of them her mother would call her a 'whore'. So Chido kept largely to herself: helping her mother with the cooking, looking after her younger half-sister, working on their piece of land in Kazangarare and as a casual worker in various tobacco jobs on Chidhadhadha, attending Apostolic services in the compound, and studying to re-write three of her O-level (Form 4) exams.

Mai Chido expressed many of the tensions, desires, representations, and possibilities that defined 'women farm workers': the differential status of women and men workers with respect to labour security and remuneration; the importance of access to a *musha*; the contrast and underlying antagonism between women of the dorms and those of the compound – between, that is, single women and married women; the need for money; the constant presence of men looking for sex; and the difference between marriage and prostitution. I will try to convey my sense of these differences and how they played out in the 'government' on commercial farms in Hurungwe. In the next chapter dealing with 'the compound', I discuss the issue of prostitution. As I argue in this chapter, to understand the various forms of work that women perform on the farm and the changes that Independence brought, it is important to examine how differences in marital status influenced the access to resources of black women workers. The boundaries between compound and work, domestic and public, are porous within 'domestic government'. But this role of power in terms of gender is not often discussed in the representation of 'African women' in academic and policy literature and laws.

The authority of 'African patriarchy'

> This 'lobola'[1] system is so inequitable! It takes so much money
> from a young family that it ends up starving them, while at
> the same time it makes elderly African men wealthy. Besides,
> it treats women as pure property, it's like they're trading in
> cattle! In traditional days when money wasn't involved,
> [when] it was only a ritual exchange of gifts, it was all right.
> But in modern days, the transactions are in money and I
> won't stand by it!

These heavily punctuated words were delivered by a local white farmer in Hurungwe. He was telling me about the various forms of

---

[1] 'Lobola' is the Zulu word used generically in southern Africa to denote 'bridewealth'.

credit he provides to his workers and how he drew the line at 'lobola', bridewealth. 'If any of my workers come to me asking for credit to pay lobola', he declared, 'I not only refuse them but I lecture them about the evils of that system.'

This white farmer's attitude ironically resonates with that of many traditional feminist approaches to bridewealth marriages. Both emphasize how 'lobola' strengthens patriarchal African control over women by limiting women's freedom of choice, by treating them as male property. For instance, Nancy Folbre (1988) in describing Zimbabwean bridewealth as the linchpin of the Shona and Ndebele 'patriarchal mode of production' equates lobola with medieval England's feudal extraction of surplus labour. Elder males among the pre-colonial Shona and Ndebele, 'controlled the means of reproduction: marriage rules and traditional law gave them considerable control over women and their reproductive capacities' (Folbre 1988:63). Like the white farm operator, she sees this pre-colonial tradition as a handicap for a modernizing Zimbabwe, although her idea is non-patriarchal socialism, not 'free enterprise' as it is with the farm operator. Any possible transition to socialism in Zimbabwe, Folbre argues, must take into account the 'male peasants' reluctance to relinquish their own patriarchal privileges' (Folbre 1988:74).

The similarity between this type of feminist scholarship and the attitude of the white farmer quoted above (an attitude held by a number of white farmers), is not so surprising since both share the assumption, as do conventional academic approaches, of the non-modernity of Africans. Their emphasis rests on the definition of subjects in terms of their 'traditions' of 'African patriarchy' and their biology: African men versus African women (perhaps with the assistance of European men and women), and a (putative) underlying social structure. It dispenses with the historical and current dynamics of power which are tied to the intermeshing of international relations, state and localized practices, and forms of knowledge such as social science.

The invention of 'customary law' and the all-powerful state

Many scholars have pointed out how colonial officials (and anthropologists) allied with African male elders to produce legislation and judicial opinions which discriminated against African women (e.g. Chanock 1982, May 1987, Schmidt 1991, 1992, Armstrong et al 1993, Jeater 1993). Elizabeth Schmidt has been the most erudite commentator on the subject for colonial Zimbabwe.

Her thesis is that in the early decades of the twentieth century, colonial laws combined the fears of African men about losing control over their daughters and wives with the concerns of state officials that African women were undermining the migrant labour system which was built upon male Africans leaving the reserves to work for Europeans. On the one hand, African men were reticent about migrating while their wives remained behind (the colonial authorities prohibited workers from bringing their spouses with them). Men feared that their women would run away from their families to live with foreign African workers on farms and mines, or move to towns and missions to work on their own, as some women were doing. As a result, many African men and chiefs petitioned the colonial authorities to help control 'their women'. On the other hand, this African male anxiety posed a threat to colonial officials. They wanted to ensure that life functioned smoothly in the reserves to maintain the interests of European capitalism through subsidizing the reproduction of labour – a system of indirect rule which rested on those very African authorities who were complaining. 'With its own authority at stake, the colonial state sought to mollify male discontent by helping African men regain control. For unless patriarchal authority was, in some measure, restored, the growing disenchantment of older men and their female charges could throw into jeopardy the whole colonial enterprise' (Schmidt 1991:756).

However, Schmidt's thesis allows that this 'creation of customary law' was not always against African women and that 'there were some instances in which women gained from state intervention in the legal sphere' (1992:110). Her comment refers to the official attempt to ensure that African women consented to marriage. Although colonial laws treated African women as minors requiring their guardians' approval of their marriages in the 'interests of maintaining law and order' (ibid.), it was also a legal requirement that all marriages be registered. This requirement aimed at ensuring that women (or girls) gave their consent to the union; it formed part of the colonial prohibition against child-pledging and forced marriages. This provided new 'avenues of opportunity for African women' (Schmidt 1992:111). She argues that the colonial practice of treating African women as individuals whose consent to marriage was legally and administratively promoted, while punishing them for extra-marital affairs, was an example of 'legal contradictions' (ibid.). However, if one does not take 'the state' as a homogenous unit serving pre-determined interests of race, class, and gender, another explanation for these various laws can be found in Schmidt's own arguments.

Colonial officials placed great emphasis on the role of 'the family' in maintaining the bonds of 'African society' within the colonial system. As Schmidt argues, 'The viability of the migratory labor system was predicated upon family stability' (1992:98; see also Mittlebeeler 1976, Jeater 1993, and Chapter Two). This treatment of the 'nuclear family' as the glue of the social fabric emerged in nineteenth-century Europe. By then, it had become a way for governments and, increasingly, professional 'experts' to define the capacities and conduct of individuals to maintain, regulate, to 'govern', in the Foucauldian sense, the health, morality, and reproduction of 'society' (Rose 1987). In Southern Rhodesia, however, there was an ambivalent discourse over which notion of 'family' to maintain: the European or the indigenous.

When it came to choosing a partner, the colonial officials deemed that forcing anyone into the intimate bond of marriage was immoral, 'repugnant to natural justice or morality' since it violated their idea of individual rights (Mittlebeeler 1976:58ff., Jeater 1993). However, when it came to bridewealth, polygyny and adultery, 'custom' was reinforced, though as Schmidt herself shows, not without a struggle amongst colonial officials and other European settlers and interests (e.g. Schmidt 1992:113-115). In either case, colonial officials assumed that they were bolstering the bonds of the 'institution of marriage'. In other words, legal definitions of marriage were driven by discursive and institutional requirements other than a need to 'control African women'.[2] Such actions also helped to extend the growth of the administrative state over Africans (Jeater 1993).

Schmidt has made valuable insights into the interaction of law and society in colonial Zimbabwe. Yet she reduces these disparate actions to a single explanation and criterion of evaluation. In terms of positing an underlying, homogenous cause of action, Schmidt's investigations of the 'inventions' of customary law, like others (cf. Ranger 1993b), have not differed greatly from the more straightforward modes of production argument. An essentialist reading of pre-colonial and colonial social structures is now combined with an essentialist reading of the state: the gamut of diverse laws and policies serve the predetermined interests of capital,

---

[2] For instance, colonial law defined the marriageable age for girls by chronology as opposed to biological development to ensure precision (Mittlebeeler 1976:75). Others have shown how the colonial rule that made the eldest son the sole heir to his father's estate in an intestate succession was driven partly by legislative requirements of having a sole heir to immovable property outside the reserves (Armstrong et al 1993:18).

147

Europeans, and men. Although Schmidt, Folbre and others have provided worthy scholarship on the interaction of 'the state' and its subjects, it has been at the expense of providing an understanding of the differentiated discourses, laws, and regulatory mechanisms at different periods of time. I would rather see these laws interpreted as the result of a series of discourses and arguments amongst colonizers and colonized, chief among them being the concern of 'maintaining the family'; a 'family', which by the 1950s, was becoming more defined as the 'nuclear family' serving the needs of 'development'.[3]

Such a discourse was not only promoted by the colonial state, but increasingly by civil society organizations that took responsibility for the 'welfare' of Africans in general and African women in particular. Groups like the Federation of African Women's Clubs (Ranchod-Nilsson 1992), finishing schools (Kirkwood 1984a), churches and municipal welfare organizations (Holleman 1958), emphasized the important 'domestic' role for African women in (Southern) Rhodesia.

This promotion of the 'modern' nuclear family is still apparent in the 1990s. For example, newspaper articles dealing with issues of marriage and family tend to stress the importance of these institutions to Zimbabwean society.[4] Women (generally not men) who transgress the proper marriage arrangements become, from the perspective of such a discourse, the antithesis to this imagined social community for both whites and blacks, namely prostitutes (McClintock 1992).[5]

---

[3] Diana Jeater (1993) shows how the colonial promotion of 'proper' domestic arrangements for Africans in the early 1900s tended to serve the upholding of traditional 'African culture', a means to ensure the stability of African society within the Reserves, not as a way to 'develop' Africans as in post-World War Two official discourses. I think, however, Jeater overemphasizes the notion that by the 1930s colonialism had disassociated African assumptions and identities of gender and sexuality from broader lineage identities and replaced them with notions of individual morality (e.g. 1993:266). She not only leaves the impression that patrilineal obligations became moribund after World War Two – quite a contestable claim – but she also neglects that even for the colonizing Europeans, the morality of 'individuals' was closely bound with notions of the proper morality of 'the family' (see, e.g., Stoler 1997).

[4] For example, a woman representing an organization devoted to helping women subject to domestic violence took a very 'pro-marriage' stance towards pre-marriage cohabitation by women: 'If a woman cohabits, she is taken as loose and if the relationship does not lead to a marriage she is in trouble because she is left to stand on her own and look for someone to cohabitate with again' (*Sunday Mail Magazine* 12 July 1992).

[5] As a long-serving colonial official told Emmet Mittlebeeler, if a woman kept persisting in having affairs, 'the commissioners exhorted the wronged husband to consider the wife only a prostitute' (Mittlebeeler 1976:134).

Since Independence, the Zimbabwean police have, on several occasions, rounded up all women in particular public places in the major cities, especially if they were not 'with' a man, on the pretext that they were 'prostitutes', although there was no direct evidence that they were publicly soliciting sex. Their main 'crime', it seems, was being unaccompanied in sites associated with men, or being economically independent of men (see *Sunday Mail*, April 12, 1992). By their presence in these locations and their ability to live without (immediate) ties to men, they transgressed the spatial inscriptions of gender, marriage and respectability. By being labelled 'prostitutes', they were placed outside the proper social boundaries (see Seidman 1984:435, McClintock 1992:84-85, Gaidzanwa 1993).

However, such state actions have come under critical attack from a number of Zimbabwean organizations, a government ministry, various newspapers[6] and many national and international scholars. Their criticisms derive from a perspective that assumes women should have the same rights, obligations, and opportunities as men (e.g. Muchena 1980, Seidman 1984, Kazembe 1986, May 1987). This is a position that I support politically, not ontologically. When 'gender' is employed as a social science category reflecting the essential (ahistorical and prediscursive) attributes of 'women', it neglects the many sets of power relations that produce different gendered meanings, including those concerning its own normative practices. In other words, it is important to question an essential 'gender identity' that serves to found these discourses within, at least, academic and policy circles. As Judith Butler has argued concerning this 'foundationalist frame' of identity politics in feminism, '[t]he internal paradox of this foundationalism is that it presumes, fixes, and constrains the very 'subjects' [i.e. 'women', B.R.] that it hopes to represent and liberate' (Butler 1990:148; see also Sylvester 1995b, 2000).

For instance, there has been a lot of interesting work undertaken since the late 1970s on African women as workers in Zimbabwe and elsewhere on the continent (e.g. Muchena 1980, Cheater 1981, Bozzoli 1983, Vaughan and Chipande 1986, Adams 1991a, 1991b). Many of these studies have indicated the differences within the category of 'African women', particularly in terms of class, region, kinship and

6   The private newspapers (e.g. *Zimbabwe Independent, Financial Gazette, Zimbabwe Mirror*) and magazines (e.g. *Parade, Horizon, Social Change & Development, Speak Out*) have carried articles periodically with a recognizable western feminist perspective.

marital status, while at the same time showing that African women are often treated homogeneously by discriminatory practices in terms of employment and the division of labour. Nevertheless, these studies tend to rest on an essentialist view of 'women' that undermines this close attention to various forms of differences within that category. For instance, Jennifer Adams (1991a) states that many rural women in Zimbabwe are wage-earners and have different social and health conditions from those who are *de facto* owners of farms in the Communal Lands, whose husbands work year-round in town. She concludes by calling for development policies that aid both types of women. Class distinctions between women are swept away under the assumption that 'our' (an equally unanalysed subject position) 'help' will benefit all African women.

This scholarship has focused on the different forms of entitlements given to women who are married, as opposed to those who are divorced, widowed, or are single mothers. Pointing out that, as a group, women are the most discriminated against, it argues that married women tend to have greater access to land and other resources than women who are not attached to men as wives, daughters, or mothers. But such a nuance is easily lost, as these authors retain as their jural subject, 'women', an ontological identity with essential (ahistorical and prediscursive) interests. I am more interested in problematizing such jural subjects, looking at the modes of power that sustain 'women' as a category, including varieties of marriage, practices that inform administration and policies of 'the state' and, equally importantly, those categories and epistemologies that underwrite the social scientists' own research. Although I agree with the liberal sentiments of this type of feminist scholarship on the equality of women with men, I – along with many other feminists (e.g. Mohanty 1983, Butler 1990, Manicom 1992, Sylvester 1995b) – do not agree with its ontological representation of women (or men) sharing essentially the same interests.

'Men do not think': 'single' women as workers

'What are you going to do with my story?' asked Mai Godi, a woman in her late thirties, as we were standing in the middle of the coffee fields on a cool day in July 1992. She had just finished providing me with a brief snapshot of aspects of her life, which I could gloss as her 'life story' – where she was born, her marriage history, how long she had been working on Chidhadhadha, work experience on other farms, her access to a *musha*, and so forth. I had spoken with her several times. Mai Godi had been talked into answering our questions by her friend, the gregarious Mai Prudence. Mai Prudi was twenty years old and just starting to work on the farm after coming from Dzivarasekwa, one of Harare's high-density suburbs.

In some ways, Mai Godi and Mai Prudence had similar stories. Both were originally from Kazangarare, had children, were separated from the fathers of their children, and had families which could not or would not support them economically. Mai Godi had been with the same man for almost twenty years but, for undisclosed reasons, separated from him in 1990. He took the eldest five children while she and their new-born child went to live at her father's *musha* in the next 'kraal' (i.e. under a different sabhuku) within Kazangarare. Her father gave her an acre of land. In the last coffee-picking season she came to Chidhadhadha to stay with her *vakomana*, ('brothers', sons of her father's brother), who worked on the farm. She picked coffee for $1.50 per tin, averaging three or four tins during a nine-hour day, and earning about $30 for a six-day week. She used the money to buy food, clothing, and soap for herself and her daughter.

She had hoped that during the 1991-92 growing season she and her aunt would sell enough maize to allow her to stay at the *musha*, but drought wiped out their crops. That year she left her daughter at the *musha* and returned to live with one of her vakomana, although by September, near the end of coffee-picking season, she was living with Mai Prudence and another woman in the dorms. She was earning less since the farm was then giving only $1 for every ten-litre tin of coffee beans picked and graded. John, the coffee foreman, said the operators often calculated the rate to average out at the minimum daily wage. But this year since there were so many workers, the farmers decided to lower the piece-rate for coffee.

Mai Prudence was, in her own words, 'fooling around' with a boy in Dzivarasekwa and became pregnant. He was not willing to pay damages and her father forbade her to live with him without receiving any money. Nor would he give any money to look after her daughter Prudence. Since she had no one to look after her child in Dzivarasekwa if she was to look for work there, and as there was no money to be found at her father's *musha* in Kazangarare, she went to work at Chidhadhadha. Here, she explained, 'I am able to earn some money to buy clothes and soap and, at the same time, look after my daughter'.

These two women arrived at the farm for similar reasons as numerous other women I came to know or casually met in the coffee fields. Mai Coni came to Chidhadhadha after a nearby farm stopped giving work to single women. Mai Coni was eighteen, her child not yet a year old. The baby's father had agreed to pay Mai Coni's family, but his own mother did not approve of the marriage and threw Mai Coni and her new baby out. Mai Chengetai was a divorced mother who left her three children at the *musha* while she worked to pay their school fees. Another three women lived together in a dorm room by the beerhall. One was in her late forties whose husband of nineteen years had left her. She had been living with her daughter in Kazangarare but was having 'problems' and had decided to return to her natal *musha* in Hwedza where her paternal cousins still live. But she needed money for the bus fare, so she came to the farm. The other two were sisters. One had left her husband and six of her seven children at a nearby resettlement farm, because he had been mistreating her for years. Her sister had divorced in 1985 and had been living at their parents' *musha* near Chinhoyi, scraping a living panning for gold. She came to Chidhadhadha because her sister had told her that 'work never ends' there.

Many of the women who picked coffee were single mothers who were looking for money to provide food, clothing, soap and school fees for themselves and their children. Some were regular 'casuals', coming each cold season after the harvest in the *musha*. Others, whose husbands were either too old or too irresponsible to try and get money for their family, came because of the drought. 'Men do not think!' exclaimed one old woman who was working with her teenage daughter. 'When kids are hungry,' she continued, 'they come to their mother, not their father.' Many workers said that the number of single women workers increased after 1980 when many 'foreign' farm workers were able to get land in the Communal areas and no longer worked full-time on the farms. The lack of regular income from farming in the Communal Lands, however, often meant that these households needed other ways to earn money to buy food, soap, clothes, and even maize seeds and fertilizer. Given that the wives tended to be considerably younger than the husbands of these farm workers turned peasants, it was often the wives who came to the farms as 'single' women to earn money for this purpose.

Other single women came to Chidhadhadha, like many of the women described above, because circumstances in their life changed. This usually meant that they were separated from their male partner, their fathers refused to support them, or they had a child, or children, to look after without any other financial support. In other words, they lost access to resources gained through their husbands, fathers, brothers, or some other patrilineal or affinal relative. If they had been living at their husband's *musha* and doing most of the agricultural work there, they would inevitably have to leave after being separated, because land rights are generally vested in men. Even if they had access to land at a paternal relative's *musha*, it was usually small in size and they would probably have little capital to invest in it. Moreover, as one woman put it, money from farming only comes once a year, but she needed money year-round for school fees, clothes, soap, and to buy inputs for next year's crops. These women formed the majority of 'casual' workers on Chidhadhadha. Most of them lived in the dorms beyond the compound or in the two dorms by the beerhall.

Coffee-picking was the largest employer of these casual workers during the dry season. Coffee pickers were predominantly women. There were also some teenage boys and men employed in the coffee fields, and their numbers had also increased significantly with the drought. While they were picking, the women talked or sang. Their children played in the nearby water channels, where pesticide residues collected. Coffee-picking often involved more people working than were actually receiving payment from the farm.

The main skill in picking coffee involves selecting the ripe beans as quickly as possible without breaking the branches of the tree. In 1992, the schedule of work was as follows. In the morning, John, the foreman, would assign each worker to one side of a row of trees and would tell them to pick all the ripe beans from that row. After picking one or two buckets of beans, the workers went to the tarpaulin, found an empty space, dumped the beans out and began to sort through them, taking out any green ones. After grading, they would replace the beans in the tins and take them to Ringson, the twenty-year-old cousin of Bornwell, who was the coffee clerk. For each tin, he made a tick next to the picker's number.

The tarpaulin was called the 'scales' since the coffee was 'weighed' by Ringson who marked down how many '13kgs' – the weight of a full tin – were submitted. Ringson was supposed to make sure that none of the pickers picked too many green beans, or mixed them with the ripe beans in their tins. He also occasionally told them to hurry up and get back to picking coffee. When pickers finished weighing the tins, they returned to continue picking anew until all the ripe beans were picked from their row.

The picked coffee beans were taken by trailer each day to the 'pulpery' by the compound. This was a water-driven machine that de-skinned the coffee beans and sorted them by size. Workers then laid out the graded beans on mesh tables for drying in the sun. When they were dried, other women contract workers did a final grading, earning 75c a kilogram. On average they earned $33 to $42 a week, more than the average coffee picker who picked two to four tins a day for $12 to $24 weekly earnings. Women who became coffee graders were selected by the male clerk in charge of the pulpery.

When I first arrived on the farm in May 1992, there were 130 coffee pickers. They started arriving in April when the coffee was ready to be picked. Several weeks later the farmers felt that there were not enough pickers for the anticipated crop and arranged with neighbouring farmers to pick up any available and interested workers – i.e. 'women workers' – in their compounds to come and pick coffee. By early July, there were 230 pickers, including about forty from neighbouring farms. In August, there were over 300 workers, as many school-aged children came to earn money in their holidays. Throughout the season, some women (and men) had their children help them pick coffee, though a few children picked under their own number and earned their own money. By September, the number of pickers had fallen to around 150, and a month later there were less than fifty people working in the coffee fields.

This rise and fall of workers' numbers followed the rhythm of the agricultural cycle in the Communal Lands as well as of the coffee picking. By September, those women who had access to land or who helped out on a relative's *musha* left the farm to start preparing their fields for planting. By this time, too, most of the coffee beans had already ripened and been picked. But there were other factors that shaped this seasonal rhythm.

Negotiating the margins of the margins

For a period in July, 1992, the coffee pulpery was inoperative. When it broke down, the farmers shifted the graders to the 'scales' to do the initial grading for the coffee pickers. The numbers of coffee pickers increased because their work was made easier as others were grading their picked coffee. A few women even picked up to 17 tins a day during that period, albeit with help from a number of their children.

At another time, however, a number of women refused to accept the increased work-load. Near the end of picking season, they were asked to strip the beans off all the coffee bushes in certain sections, since the operators wanted to cut them down. Removing all the beans was a relatively quick procedure, although the pickers' arms got rather scratched from the branches, but then they had to single out all the green beans from the ripe ones, which was an arduous task. Many women remained in the dorms during this period, waiting until they no longer had to strip the bushes.

'I'm not working these days,' declared Mai Prudence with a grin as she and Mai Godi walked along the bank of the workers' fishing dam. 'Like you, Mr Blair, we can go where we want, to do what we want. And with the hard work in the coffee for little money, we aren't going to the fields.' She and Mai Godi laughed and slapped each other's hands to signal delight over their decision not to work, as well as over her comparison with me.

They continued walking along the bank, while I sat with Sekuru Kamutengo who was fishing with a home-made pole and line. The old man shook his head. 'Those girls are so disrespectful of everything,' he said. He observed that the large stone Mai Prudence was carrying would be used to kill fish. 'Ya, they wait by the bank until they see fish feeding in the shallow area and then, splash! they stun the fish with the stone and grab it.'

Sure enough, half an hour and several splashes later, the women returned with two small fish in their hands. They chided the old man for not catching any fish, saying that at least *they* would eat tonight. I watched with amusement while he became slightly upset at their mocking of him.

Single women were known on the farm for what may be called 'back-talk' (Tsing 1993). Many of them were not afraid of telling off African men at work and some even challenged the foremen themselves. 'That old widow, she is a crazy person. When Mr John, the foreman, said he would dock her a day's pay for not finishing her *mugwazo* [task], she threatened to fight him. When John and the other foreman, whom she also cursed, threatened to bring in the *murungu*, she said "tell him to line up behind you two because I'll fight him too!"' This story was told with great mirth by Felistus and her husband Takunda in their roof-less kitchen. 'She never did fight them. But John was impressed by her strength and said he wouldn't dock her pay,' Takunda said. 'Ehee', repeated Felistus, 'some women, especially those without husbands, are strong!'

Rinse and I each experienced this back-talk, in different ways. Many women teased Rinse about being in his early twenties and still without a wife. Some single women went further and offered themselves as potential partners. He bantered with them, asking, 'Why should I go out with you, someone without any nice clothes?' And a woman would respond, 'You, you should talk! Someone who does not work in the fields, surely cannot be strong enough to attract women! But I pity you. You should come to my hut tonight...' Sometimes he was embarrassed, if the women got the better of him.

I faced the back-talk when it came to carrying out my research. Single women were the ones who most obviously resisted my inquiries. Tembai was an eighteen-year-old woman who lived in the dorms by the bar. We had mutual friends. Although Tembai joked coyly with me and Rinse about her background in Kazangarare and chatted about being a casual worker on Chidhadhadha, whenever I became serious about asking her questions, doing serious research, she kept her mouth closed. Literally. She would not say anything until I relented and began talking about a 'non-research' topic, such as Mai Bhibho's relation with Jasoni, or witchcraft in Kazangarare.

Many single women workers, including Mai Chido, resisted my pointed questions and search for hard 'facts' about the lives of single women workers. Their position on the margins of the margins, on the edges of the domestic government that marginalizes (male) commercial farm workers from dominant government programmes, allowed some women to be more cavalier about the power stakes from which they were so distanced. For example, in response to the boycott which many of the single women workers launched against the increased workload in the coffee fields at the end of the season, the farmers increased the price they paid to $1.30 a tin. John told me that two years earlier Mr Schmidt was only paying 85c a tin until one day most of the workers decided to remain in the dorms. Schmidt sent John to negotiate with the women because there were not enough casual workers in the compound to replace them if they were fired. The price went up to $1.35 a tin.

Women workers do negotiate within the limits imposed by the power relations of domestic government. As will be argued in the next section, the one advantage enjoyed by unmarried 'casual workers' was that the management had less leverage over them than over married women. The farmers and the foremen could not pressure their husbands to make them work, as they could in the case of women married to permanent workers. Single women were aware of this power, and would point it out to foremen and other men.

Nevertheless, single women workers could not as 'single' women improve their housing or receive credit as married women could, through their husbands; aside from wages, the only other 'resource' these contract workers received was subsidized maize meal on credit. Even this was restricted when I was on the farm, as a way to ensure that single women truly 'worked' for it.

In June 1992, the farmers decided that each coffee picker would have to pick thirty tins of beans in order to get a thirteen kilogram tin of subsidized maize meal (ground at the farm). They told me that this was necessary to maintain sufficient stock of maize to sell at a subsidized rate to their permanent workers. Many coffee pickers were outraged at the new rule; it meant working for about a week and a half before they got their entitlement. They could still buy maize meal at the farm store, but it was significantly more expensive. They were particularly angry because many of them had come to the farm that year for the cheap food as much as for money, the drought having eliminated their usual sources of food. 'How can I feed my children on this?' cried one woman as she waited in line to buy five kilograms of non-subsidized packaged maize meal on credit. 'Are the *varungu* that cruel to us black people that they don't want us to eat?' she continued. But no one took up her question in the line and she became silent.

In many ways, these single women workers were marginalized from most of the resources usually available to farm workers. They did not have time, nor were they permitted, to build and maintain a garden on the farm. Instead, they either had to buy their vegetables or to gather them wild in the fields. Their housing was of poor quality, overcrowded, and full of bed-bugs. And although some women, such as Mai Godi and Mai Prudence, became friends from working together, most women appeared not to make friends unless they had known each other before coming to Chidhadhadha.

In fact, the goal of many of these single women, as I discuss in the next chapter, was to find a man and get married, thereby opening up opportunities and access to resources, including the greater possibility of getting work the whole year around. As the situation of Mai Chido has shown, single women could work virtually the entire year, for several years, without a 'husband'. But most of those who received the steady jobs and access to other resources, were married to permanent workers on the farm.

'I want your women to help me': married women as workers

Official conventions of women farm workers in Zimbabwe made them into spouses or daughters of male farm workers. In an editorial, the state-controlled national daily newspaper, *The Herald*, praised 'the women from Hippo Valley' for 'helping their husbands in planting a new crop of sugar-cane' (4 May 1993). According to an accompanying article, the women had donated their labour for this task as a sign of their appreciation of the Anglo-American-owned company, Hippo Valley Estates, for providing benefits to the workers through the drought, which had almost completely wiped out the sugar-cane industry in south-eastern Zimbabwe. Aside from the editorial's one-sided view of the history of this provision of benefits,[7] it portrayed the women as heroines, sacrificing themselves for the greater good of the company and their husbands: with more sugar-cane planted, 'the action by the women could result in more work, and possibly increased incomes in the form of overtime for their husbands, which in turn would mean an improvement in their general conditions of living.' For the editorial writer, such action was not only a positive sign of management and workers working together, it was also yet another sign of the importance of 'women': 'Many negative things have been said about women. Isn't it nice for once to remind the nation how women are underrated?'

Whereas *The Herald* editorial characterized women farm workers as sacrificing wives of their husbands and multinational employers who should be, 'for once', praised by 'the nation',[8] other official commentators simply depicted them as 'wives'. From the GAPWUZ development projects (such as soap-making) for women farm workers aimed at 'income generating' to supplement their own and their husbands' standard of living, to what I have described in earlier chapters as the farmers' practice of hiring only men as permanent

---

[7] Firstly, the editorial ignored that the 'benefits' that the company offered came as a result of negotiations with GAPWUZ. Secondly, it ignored that an article in the same paper just ten months previously called Hippo Valley Estates a 'battle ground' when a number of farm workers who were members of GAPWUZ went on strike to protest against the company's reversal of a previously negotiated deal on benefits (*Herald*, June 24, 1992) and to protest the introduction of a company union by Anglo-American (see *Horizon* March 1993).

[8] Such a claim is quite ironic given that Jennifer Adams' (1991a) research on a neighbouring Lowveld sugar estate found that the majority of women in her survey were not 'wives'.

farm workers and using their wives and children as casual workers, the women who work on commercial farms have been distinguished more by their conjugal status than, say, their class position within the discourses of domestic government.

My research indicated that married women workers had a better chance of working year-round if they felt like it and were generally considered by management as 'good workers'. Whereas 'casual workers' picked coffee during the cold season, these women tended to work in the grading shed, or tying dhukes. They would then do the planting, weeding, and topping of tobacco until the next grading season began. This is not to say that only the wives of permanent workers got these jobs; but women who were married to permanent workers were more likely to get them, for a variety of reasons: operators wanting to 'help out their chaps' by employing family members for casual jobs; foremen picking the women they knew the best from living with them in the compound. Another reason, one that neither foremen nor farmers told me, but women and men farm workers did, was that married women were more amenable than single women to the discipline sustaining the *mitemo yepurazi*, the rules of the farm. In most oral histories I gathered, it was generally the married women, not the single ones, who were called upon to work on farms in the colonial period.

A Malawian man who started working on Hurungwe commercial farms in the early 1970s remarked that when he arrived he saw many women working. When I asked whether these women were married to men of the compound or came to the farm on their own as unmarried women, he replied, 'That time there were no women who used to come from the reserves who came to work here. These women were ours, they belonged to us, the men who worked here. Every person who had a wife, it was said to him [by the farmer] that the woman must work.'[9] Another old male farm worker explained these lines of communication, 'The *murungu* was talking with their husbands saying "I want your women so that they help me with this work." If you, the husbands, agree with the *murungu*, then they [the wives] would go to work.'[10] Before examining these 'lines of

[9] Taped interview with man farm worker. Karoi North farm. January 10, 1993. This was the common response I received in my oral histories. Taped interviews with retired man farm worker. Karoi North commercial farm. May 25, 1992; taped interview with retired woman farm worker. Karoi North farm. April 22, 1993; taped interview with retired foreman from Karoi North farm. Mukwichi Communal Land. July 9, 1992.
[10] Taped interview with man farm worker (2). Karoi North farm. April 25, 1993.

communication' a bit more critically, I will note some characteristics of the 'work' these women performed before Independence.

Women and children received lower wages than men. As one woman recalled, 'Men received eight dollars. Women received seven dollars and, like me, a girl, I received three dollars per month.' There were also occasions when women (and children) worked for no pay at all. The women would help out their husbands, fathers, and male friends when the latter were given *mugwazo* (task-work). One retired foreman explained:

> They were not paid because if they were wives, they used to help their husbands and if they were children, they used to help their parents so that they may finish their mugwazo quickly. So the mugwazo was for one person [i.e. man] only and the murungu used to give money to that one person only, these others were helpers. The man was the one, then, who used to pay his wife and children.[11]

This practice, as noted earlier with reference to coffee picking, still occurs on farms today. Occasionally the white farmers did more than just ask their (male) workers to bring their wives and children to work.

> If you were unfortunate and your wife went one week without working you were denied maize meal because they [management] said 'we are not giving any to you because your wife is not working'. So the man used to tell his wife, 'my wife if you stop from going to work we die from hunger'.[12]

An older woman observed that,

> Back then women used to go to work on their own. When women who go to work were few, the murungu used to send the foreman into the compound saying that, 'please, it has been said by the murungu that every woman must come to work. A woman who does not come to work, her husband will be fired from work'. So on certain times, women were forced to work in order to safeguard the jobs of their husbands.[13]

---

[11] Taped interview with retired foreman from Karoi North farm. Mukwichi Communal Land. July 9, 1992.

[12] Taped interview with man farm worker. Karoi North farm. January 10, 1993.

[13] Taped interview with woman farm worker. Karoi North farm. April 22, 1993.

In short, women workers in the colonial period were viewed mainly as a supplement to men's labour, even though some worked the whole year round. They were paid lower wages than men and, on occasions, they were forced to work, for free or for payment, when the farmers required more workers. They were forced through the pressure put on their husbands.

Although most of the farm workers were men from one of the northern colonies, many took wives locally. 'Some *matandizi* [recruited workers] were coming to work here as young men without women, so they then grew up in here. These men could not return to their *musha* when they wanted to marry so they were supposed to marry in here.'[14]

All of the workers with whom I talked emphasized how few were the single women who came to work on the farms from the reserves in the colonial period. This was partly because there was no accommodation for them, if they did not have a relative there, and partly because there were family sanctions against such actions. When I asked an older woman farm worker whether the women coming from Kazangarare were married or single, she answered:

> *Teenage girls who were not married were the ones who used to come to work here from the reserves, but they were few. Young married women were not coming to work [on their own] because they feared that their husbands would come to take them back to the* musha. *The parents prohibited teenage girls who were not married from working on the farms, saying that when they would go to work on the farms they would do some mischief. That was why they were few... They did so because they knew that if their daughters became accustomed to life on the farms, they were not going to have good marriages. So there were very few girls, not even more than five who were working here then. Now these days the compound has filled up with women without men.*[15]

Accordingly, most of the women who worked on the farms were wives or daughters of farm workers. 'Foreign' men commonly married local women, who they often met at beer-drinks in the reserve. There was another way that 'foreign' men met local women, as will be discussed in the next chapter. But the convention was

---

[14] Taped interview with man farm worker (2). Karoi North farm. April 25, 1993.
[15] Taped interview with woman farm worker. Karoi North farm. April 22, 1993.

that local (which was equated with 'Korekore') parents prohibited their daughters and wives, more so than their sons, from coming to work on the farms in case they got into 'mischief' with the largely foreign-born farm workers. For, as will be discussed in the next chapters, despite the propensity of 'foreigners' to marry 'local' women, it was not something actively encouraged by Korekore parents. The politics of marriage have also included calculations of ethnicity and citizenship.

The story presented to me by workers about the background of the women who worked on farms in the past was similar to that portrayed in official discourses. For instance, in a glowing depiction of where white farmers usually got their extra seasonal work force, a colonial official wrote: 'In many instances no increased accommodation is required, since… it merely requires the wife and her capable daughters to go out to daily work on or near the farm where they normally live. Or, as is also often the case, a relative or two arrive from the tribal home to stay for a seasonal working holiday' (Du Toit 1977:2).

Three years after this report was written, there was, from what I learned, a substantial change in who was taking these 'seasonal working holidays' on Chidhadhadha.

In the early 1980s, Mr Schmidt began to grow coffee, and this marked the beginning of the increase in single women on the farm. If they did not have relatives to stay with, they lived on their own in the dorms. But there was another factor which, a few women pointed out, encouraged more single women to come to the farms after 1980: the equalization of pay between men and women after Independence. As one woman worker observed,

> *These unmarried women became to be many in 1980 when the country was taken by blacks. After 1981, it was said that the money which men receive has become the same with the money women should receive. This was when unmarried women became many. Again, divorce started to be too much as women were saying 'even if you divorce me, I will work for myself because the money which you are receiving and which I am receiving is just the same'.*[16]

---

[16] *Ibid.*

Some men farm workers complained to me that women received the same pay as they did – 'they do less work than I! Why should they get the same daily rate!' But many others were happy, especially if their wives worked. Due to the intersection of government policies, farmers' rules of residence and employment, and local regulation over the movement of wives and daughters, women have worked on farms largely through their dependent position within the 'conjugal unit'. Their housing and access to credit on farms improved dramatically if 'married', as did their chance of getting land in Communal Lands (since it was difficult for a single woman to get more than a small piece land from her father).

Although many of the single women who came to work on Chidhadhadha arrived to make money for themselves, their children, and perhaps their family (including husbands) back in the Communal Lands, many also became, intentionally or not, targets for marriage or sex. One older woman coffee picker was telling me and her teenage daughter about the increasing 'looseness' of young girls today compared to 'long back'. As she was talking, a few young men walked by and Rinse asked if they were picking coffee. 'No,' one of them said with a smile, 'we are looking for our *roora*, our future brides.'

Mai Prudence told me how she was under constant harassment by men farm workers who wanted to sleep with her. They even promised to look after her daughter Prudence, she explained. By the fact of living in the dorms, she was thought of as a person who wanted to be 'married'. But no, she continued, she wanted to marry someone who lived in town and has a *musha* in the reserves, so that she could spend time in both places. 'I don't want to marry one of these farm workers!'

Her bias against farm workers was similar to that of local Korekore parents, expressed in the quotation above, but not shared by other single women. As one coffee picker told me, problems do not end for a divorcee. More and more single women came to live in the dorms because the farm wanted more casual workers. She disliked the fact that the dorms were overcrowded, that they were filled with strangers, and that she could not have any relatives come to visit her as there was no room for them to sleep. She would like her own house. But only by getting married in some manner could she have a place of her own. She then extended the implications of this logic by explaining that she had to work hard to get enough money to buy nice smelling soap so that men would come and ask her to marry. 'The worst part of being a single woman,' she concluded sadly, 'was that if you are sick there is no one to look after you. Not only are you by yourself but you lose your day's wages. If you are married, your husband would not only look after you but he would also be earning wages.'

Although this was not the desire of all single women, the high value placed on the domestic family within the power relations on the commercial farms and beyond made marriage in its different manifestations a crucial arena where conflicts over resources took place on Chidhadhadha.

Conclusion

Like other scholars who have discussed African women workers, I too have indicated both the differences among, and the similar treatment of, women farm workers. Whether married or single, women farm workers were marginalized on commercial farms in Hurungwe. They were generally prohibited from getting permanent jobs. As contract or seasonal workers, their status on the farm was more vulnerable than that of the permanent male workers. They were even excluded from representation by the workers' committee. Luke, the chairman, informed me that women were outside his purview and most female workers knew that they had no representation to management other than themselves. Based on my discussion with its officials, it seems that GAPWUZ also shared a tendency to neglect women farm workers, seeing them more as temporary workers, who assist their husbands, rather than as workers in their own right.

And yet there was no unambiguous 'feminist identity' held by any of the women farm workers I knew – if there exists any such thing anywhere (e.g. Butler 1990). I have discussed forms of power on the farms, particularly the forms of differentiation along the basis of 'family' within and beyond the farm's domestic government. Access by women workers to resources available to farm workers rested predominantly along the axis of marriage to a permanent worker. Although single women like Mai Chido might virtually be permanent workers and be able, like the coffee pickers who refused to work for a reduced piece-wage, to occasionally exert some pressure on their level of remuneration, they were generally more marginalized in terms of access to better housing, gardens and credit, and were more vulnerable than married women to male harassment and attacks. However, despite acquiring access to resources through their spouses, married women farm workers were also more attached to the power relations of domestic government, and subject to pressures and obligations basically unknown to single women workers.

The number of single women – divorcees, widows, unmarried mothers, and wives without husbands – working on farms seemed to have increased after 1980, a fact which some people attributed to the rise in the number of divorces in Zimbabwe. I found no evidence to support that claim as an 'empirical fact', although many are observing that more and more single women are working in the fast-growing horticultural sub-sector. Moreover, the frequency with which I heard the claim indicates that many people on commercial farms (men and women, operators and workers) were concerned about women transgressing conventional regulations of space by gender, perhaps because women were able to get the same wages as men after 1980.

As I have argued in this chapter, factors of marriage, gender, and sexuality have been crucial influences on the politics of space and entitlement on Zimbabwean commercial farms. This is especially so concerning power relations found on the site of 'the compound'. Understanding the constraints and tactics of women farm workers requires an investigation of the debates, dialogues, and forms of control that have comprised the different types of marriage. In discussing the spatial politics of the compound, the next chapter examines, amongst other things, the situation and presence of 'prostitutes' and the question of 'marriage' itself, for, as James Ferguson has argued in relation to the Copperbelt during the days of Northern Rhodesia, 'in a social world characterized by fluid and transitory relations between the sexes, boundaries between prostitutes and girlfriends, and between girlfriends and wives, were often blurred' (1990b:407).

Mai Godi, the woman who asked me my purpose in writing down her 'life', was still working in Chidhadhadha in April 1993, just before I left. At that point, she was sweeping up the curing barns loading and unloading. Before then, I had given her a transcript of her 'life history' from my notes. She was surprised to get it from me and said, with little inflection, that she would get her eldest daughter who was attending secondary school to read it to her. I interpreted her lack of enthusiasm more as a function of her scepticism of my project than, say, as a sign of embarrassment at her illiteracy. I, too, felt unenthusiastic, looking at the two single-spaced pages that represented to me her 'life' as a contract worker. The conventions of social science once again seemed so starkly irrelevant to the forms of power that marked the life of farm workers.

But perhaps I am being disingenuous here, focussing more on my subject construction as a social scientist and deflecting attention away from what some may attribute to my identity as a 'white heterosexual male'. Perhaps my calling attention to the historical contingency of identities formed within power relations is suspect since it inhibits an examination of power based essentially and unequivocally on entailments of gender and race.

I like to think that is not the case, that my attention to the dynamics of 'knowledge and power', which infuse claims to represent the unambiguous interests of a particular group, assists in the critical production of new ways of understanding the political terrain that mediates resource-access of commercial farm workers. I suggest that this approach assists in anticipating what Donald Moore has called 'affinities of difference' which minimally 'entails recognizing radically different positions in a global political economy, in circuits of cultural capital, and in relation to histories of travel, mobility, and colonization' (1994:127). However, I cannot answer this definitively; I invoke it to show the importance of critically exploring particularities, unsettling overlapping domains of identities, in order to try to reshape power relations – a task that perhaps is as utopian as Nancy Folbre's call for non-patriarchal socialism. Yet rather than relying on pre-scripted agendas rooted in essentialist notions of sociological categories, I try to follow the weave of (inter)national political and economic relations within the social fabric of 'the local' in which I participated, the lives of commercial farm workers in Hurungwe. I look for the loose threads within the power relations of domestic government and, with announced intentions and explicit recognition of the constructed fictions, pull on them.

Chapter 6

The farm compound: work's domestic space

The case of the foreman at the beerhall

The compound beerhall was the main area used for socializing by men farm workers. Although they occasionally congregated at Chidhadhadha's beerhall after work during a week-day, men more often went there on Saturday after work and on Sunday, their regular day off. There they would sit down with their friends and pass between them a bucket of *chibhuku*, the commercialized sorghum/maize beer. There were often a few women present, mainly unmarried older women, drinking with men or dancing. But the beerhall was mainly a men's place. A woman entering the place was treated very differently from a man. Women present during the selling and drinking of beer were commonly regarded by other women and men as *mahure*, 'whores', regardless of their actual activities.

After pay-day, many men would congregate at the beerhall to drink, dance, talk and play *juga*, a card game on which they would gamble with some of the money they received. The odd Saturday night, Bornwell, the second senior foreman, used to set up his 'disco', a stereo-system with a record player and a cassette deck, and throw a dance party, charging everyone $1 as an entrance fee. This event would draw more women than the usual beer-drinks.

'But people aren't buying beer as much as they used to,' bemoaned Sekuru Kamutengo and his wife, the two retired workers whom the operators put in charge of the beerhall. Usually they only opened up the beerhall after pay-day, when people had some spare cash; they did not give credit to anyone at the beerhall. 'Before the new owners came,' they reminisced, 'Mr Schmidt gave so much credit to everyone that workers were able to drink throughout the month, not just the weekend after they received their paycheck.' During my research, the beerhall was quiet by the second weekend after pay-day, with only a few men having a beer, while others either waited outside looking for a friend who had money to buy them a beer – a role I occasionally played – or, more likely, spent their time gathering firewood, repairing the grass roofs of their huts, visiting relatives elsewhere, working on their Chidhadhadha garden or at their *musha* in Kazangarare.

Even during those periods when workers had enough money to drink, the foremen rarely joined them. 'It's not good to drink here,' the coffee foreman John informed me. 'Problems at work may resurface under the influence of beer,' he explained. 'Workers will also demand that you, *Mista Foromani*, should buy them a litre or two of *chibhuku*, since you make that much more than they do.' Instead, foremen went to the business centre of Mwami to drink bottled beer at the bottle stores or headed over to another farm to drink there, away from the workers of Chidhadhadha. In turn, foremen from other farms would often be found at Chidhadhadha's beerhall.

In addition to the informal gatherings of men drinking beer, the beerhall also served as a public *dare*, a meeting place or court. Yet the gendered and class associations of the beerhall still resonated during these public *matare* (plural of *dare*). I witnessed one such *dare* at which the foremen were represented in a different way from the time they were explaining the farm's policy; on this occasion, 'they' were on trial and were not administering policy.

Akimu was a junior foreman who was a cousin of George, the senior foreman. He had a reputation for fooling around with women, even though he was married and had five children with his wife. Before I had arrived to do fieldwork, he had been publicly confronted on a few occasions for having sex with other men's wives, but nothing came of it.

Usually, cases (*mhosva*) concerning adultery in the compound were handled at a private *dare* involving the accused and their families and presided over by the village chairman, Ezia, at his hut in the compound. But in 1992, there were a number of adultery cases that led to severe beatings or 'hut-burnings', including, on two occasions, the dorms beyond the compound, and the police were called to the farm. There were two targets for popular discontent in adultery cases. One was single women, who were accused *en masse* by married women of stealing their husbands.

The other were foremen, tractor drivers, and other senior men workers, who were accused by other men of stealing their wives. A more public *dare* for Akimu was meant to try to settle some of these problems, Ezia told me, though, as he and everyone else soon found out, Akimu had a different idea of how that should be done.

The beerhall was packed with people inside and outside. Only a few were buying beer during the *dare*, but the breath of many of the men, young and old, suggested that many more had been drinking before the court began.

Ezia stepped into the cleared space inside the beerhall and called the *dare* to a start with three *Pamberi neZANU* ('Forward with ZANU') and a *Pasi neruvengo* ('Down with hatred'). Akimu then stood up and took Ezia's place. In his well-ironed slacks and colourful long-sleeve shirt, he stood out from the rest of the crowd who were still in work clothes. With a slightly angry tone, Akimu declared that there were rumours that he had been fooling around with a married woman and they had to be put to the test tonight. He sat down next to the cleared space. Ezia then called Tambu, the married woman who was accused of sleeping with Akimu, into the cleared space.

After giving a few salutes, Tambu sat with her legs beneath her on the floor and quickly recounted, over a period of fifteen minutes, the various rumours she had heard about different women fooling around and how she was told by a few friends that there was a story about her having sex with Akimu. She finished by declaring that she would want to hear someone say that they actually saw her and Akimu having sex.

One of the women who was said to have spread the story was called into the space. While kneeling on the floor, she said she heard the rumour from another woman. Several other women were asked to confirm the story. A few, including the wife of another foreman, declined to speak. Only two others went into the space to declare that they had only heard rumours, and actually had not seen anything. Ezia finally called the three women who said they had passed the rumours, all of whom were married to permanent workers, to enter the floor together.

By this time, young men along the edges began to heckle the women, calling them 'whores' and 'liars'. A few men, notably the former village chairman, Karata, took the floor to berate the women for spreading rumours. These three women occasionally stood up and accused each other of being a 'whore' with other men, an action that usually enraged the accused woman's husband. During the next hour, these accusations against the loyalty of wives continued. There also was explicit tension between Akimu and Ezia – Akimu declared that if Ezia dared to find him guilty without any evidence, he would have the farmers take the position of village chairman away from him. Ezia responded to the last accusation with anger, saying that he would resign rather than accept this intimidation from a foreman.

Although Ezia did not resign, it was Akimu who eventually closed the *dare* about two hours after it started by declaring that he would either go to the magistrate's court in Karoi or to the 'barns' with these women and their *vanababa*, 'parents' – meaning their husbands – to settle things. By this time the space between the women sitting on the floor and the audience had narrowed considerably and passions were running high.

Workers took different messages away from that *dare*. A few, like Ringson the coffee clerk, thought Ezia mishandled it by not directing questions to the witnesses, which permitted the audience, who had less interest in the guilt or innocence of Akimu than in venting their anger, to heckle and berate the women. Ringson admitted, however, that it would be difficult to punish Akimu since he was a foreman with a known temper who could take revenge on you in the fields.

This very point was made by Ezia and Luke, the workers' committee chairman. Both felt that Akimu was guilty but that the women were scared to reveal what they knew because their husbands were in the work force. If the women testified against Akimu, he and the other foremen – for 'they all stick together' (*vanobatana*) – would make their husbands work extremely hard. That was why the wife of the one foreman refused to say anything, they surmised. Her husband probably threatened her to keep quiet or he would divorce or beat her. 'The foremen have too much power on this farm,' concluded Luke. That, they both agreed, is the problem of holding a public *dare* on Chidhadhadha, for the 'public' is saturated by the hierarchies of domestic government.

The power of the foremen was such that it transcended the class inscriptions of the beerhall as a place of general workers in Akimu's *dare*. Yet part of the power of the foremen in this case was based on forging an alliance between male workers and male foremen against married women; an alliance that resonated with the gendered inscription of the site of the *dare*.

None of the men I talked to questioned the power of the label 'whore' and how it was used as a way of dismissing the women's stories both by men in the audience and by the women themselves. This sentiment was reinforced by the 'public' *dare* being held in a site inscribed through gendered notions of sexuality and marriage. The only women found in the beerhall on a regular basis were considered to be 'whores', women who actually made a living by selling sex or who were assumed, especially by men in the beerhall, to be available for sex. They were not 'married'.

'Marriage' was a crucial way to define access to resources for women. It also was implicated in various forms of authority on the farm, acting as a means for management to exert leverage over workers and as a source of contention between husbands and wives, wives and single women – forms of authority which have been (re)produced by the associations generated by spatial distinctions.

The compound was a space where decisions and struggles took place over access to resources such as housing, wages, credit, and labour. Although some of these struggles were shaped by 'indigenous' assumptions and expectations, they always involved the presence of the farm. The 'domestic' debates were thus firmly embedded in the concerns of the 'government' of the farm operators and, by extension, of the policies of the wider government.

As a number of scholars have argued, domesticity refers to the particular arrangements and assumptions about 'home life' that have emerged as a crucial component of the discourses concerning 'modernity' among the bourgeoisie, governments and administrations within the north and within their colonizing efforts in the south (e.g. Hansen 1992, Comaroff and Comaroff 1992). The importance placed on the privately-owned home as the domain of the nurturing wife, of a husband pursuing public affairs, that is, on bourgeois 'domesticity', underpinned a series of edifying attempts by missionaries, government officials, and, increasingly throughout the twentieth century, 'experts' with social science credentials to reshape the architecture and practices of targeted populations, such as the 'poor' in the north and the 'natives' in the south, as part of their civilizing and modernizing endeavours (Rose 1987, Comaroff and Comaroff 1992).[1]

On the white farms in Southern Rhodesia, however, I have argued that there was a slightly different process at work, in which the farmers assumed, with state support, the discursive role of 'edifiers' and tried to prevent any outside authority from exerting influence over 'their' Africans. Although farmers have heavily influenced the lives of their farm workers through the form of 'government' in place and by enforcing a work schedule, I came across few examples of attempts by farmers to try to directly change the 'domestic' practices of their workers, in contrast to the efforts by missionaries, government welfare officers, and organizations such as the Federation of African Women's Clubs in the native reserves (e.g. Ranchod-Nilsson 1992, Worby 1998).

Nevertheless, even without direct attempts by farmers to mould their workers into such domestic arrangements, discourses of modern (bourgeois) 'domesticity' still influenced the various identities and contestations over resources within the farm compound. These practices were informed by both the workers' understanding of the *murungu's* life and their own involvement in extra-farm circuits, such as school, organized religion, government bodies involved in promoting 'modern' ways, and the media. Domesticity shaped the distribution of resources, the limits of law, the differences amongst workers, and specific aspirations. It helped to suggest that the compound was a separate space from the work sites while, simultaneously, it reinforced the notion that the entire commercial farm was under the *mitemo yemurungu*, 'rules of the white person.'

In this chapter, I examine two important practices which are part of the compound but are also integrally part of the workplace, falling within the intersection of domestic government and state rules. The first concerns marriage and non-marriage, with their various entailments, and the forms of jurisdiction over these choices on the farm. The second is the role of credit and consumption in sustaining differences within the compound.

---

[1]   'Most [nineteenth century] missionaries understood that the construction of the 'private' domain was fundamental to the anatomy of their social world.... [I]n its routines and conventions were vested the signs and practices on which was based the social order *tour court*. At the dawn of modernity in Europe, moreover, the nuclear family was becoming the point of articulation between civil society and the (ostensibly) free individual, the ideological atom upon which bourgeois economy and society depended' (Comaroff and Comaroff 1992:67-68).

Marriage and *Mahures*: dorms, domestic labour, and violence

Marriage politics

As indicated in the previous chapter, some feminist scholars have focused on bridewealth as the main source of inequity in African social relations. I disagree with that argument as an essential explanation, a 'master narrative', of rural Zimbabwe, but it is still important to investigate how it contributes to shaping the power relations on farms.

One of the most explicit form of politics involved with marriage was its use in becoming related to the 'big workers'. Those who were 'big workers' (*vanhu vakuru*) were often linked through marriage and kinship ties. When they changed jobs, they tended to move within this category. A gardener might become a lorry driver, a lorry driver a senior foreman, a foreman's son a clerk, a foreman's brother a tractor driver, and so on.

The key managerial position, in the sense of both being the top 'worker' and being the broker of dynastic access and careers, was the senior foreman. One retired senior foreman told me how, after arriving on a Hurungwe farm from Zambia in the late 1950s, he started dating the young daughter of the farm's senior foreman. 'A few months later I was then promoted at work. When I was promoted I saw that the father of my wife [then girlfriend, B.R.] was the one who had allowed me to get promoted. This was when I saw that it was better that I could marry his daughter so that I could be his real child.'[2]

Although the advantages accruing to a man who marries into a powerful family are rather obvious, though not guaranteed, the unequal balance between the wife-giving and wife-receiving families also offered the already 'big worker' family an advantage. The wife-giving family tends to have more respect than the wife-receiving family, as reflected by the series of obligations of the latter, the greatest being the paying of bridewealth itself (Bourdillon 1987). The actual amount of this is rarely set out in precise terms, an ambiguity which enables the *tezvara*, or receiver (the wife's father or brothers), to periodically call up favours or funds from the *mukuwasha*, the son-in-law. A senior foreman with a son-in-law as junior foreman could expect to appeal beyond the work hierarchy to ensure that his authority is obeyed.

---

[2] Taped interview with retired foreman of a Karoi North farm. Mukwichi Communal Land. April 12, 1993.

173

On Chidhadhadha, George and Bornwell were the senior foremen. In the 1970s, George had been a mechanic and a farm militia leader (guarding the farm against guerrillas and spying on the workers looking for informants) on another Mashonaland West farm. His father had been born in Malawi, but he himself was born in Southern Rhodesia. In the early 1980s he was looking for a new job as his boss was giving up farming. As George and other workers put it, Mr Schmidt learned about George's characteristics of toughness, loyalty, and skill in driving. Mr Schmidt was looking for a possible replacement for Maoko by this time, and he hired George in early 1984 as a lorry driver. Shortly afterwards, Maoko was fired and George was made the senior foreman.

George has only daughters from his wives, and his parents had no other sons. However, he has been able to get jobs on Chidhadhadha for his 'brothers' (*vakoma/vanin'ina*, his father's brothers' sons). One started as a security guard and was then promoted to a foreman. Another came as a general worker, and although he remained in that position when I was there, he was given a brick house in the compound ahead of other workers (he was made a foreman in the mid-1990s). Another worked as a mechanic on Chidhadhadha and then was selected by Mr. Schmidt's son to be the manager on his new farm near Harare.

Bornwell's history was more connected to the life of Chidhadhadha than George's. His father, Sekuru Kamutengo, began working for Mr. Schmidt's father in 1941 on a farm north of Salisbury. Sekuru Kamutengo accompanied his father's younger brother from a chiChewa-speaking area of Tete Province in Mozambique to Mr Schmidt's father's farm in Mazowe, where his own father was working. In the early 1950s, when Mr Schmidt started on his own farming career in Urungwe, he took Sekuru Kamutengo with him along with three other workers. One of these four workers was already a foreman. Another was Sekuru's relative, his mother's brother's son, Maoko, who became the 'garden-boy' while Sekuru worked in the fields. Maoko was soon promoted to 'house-boy' and then, in 1960, to senior foreman, becoming the fourth 'boss-boy' of Chidhadhadha. Sekuru became a crop-guard and then a mechanic. He was not promoted to foreman since, other workers claimed, he was not fearsome enough to become a manager of workers. This opinion was reinforced by Sekuru himself, who said that he did not 'want problems with people', and by his wife who said he refused to become a supervisor for fear of witchcraft from those under his control.

Bornwell was born on Chidhadhadha in 1962, the eldest son of the family. After finishing his Grade Seven education, he started working on the farm, and in 1981 became the first clerk of Chidhadhadha. According to workers, Maoko had chosen Bornwell to be 'his' clerk since he was not only literate but was also a relative and had shown 'foreman tendencies' in the compound by beating up his peers. However, when George arrived in 1984, Bornwell worked with him to oust his *sekuru* Maoko. As clerk and senior foreman respectively, Bornwell and George worked closely together for a number of years. In the late 1980s Dan, who was now the senior manager on the farm, discovered that Bornwell and George were defrauding the loan account. They were lending out more money to workers than they marked down in the books and had workers repay the excess amount to themselves. Each accused the other of perpetrating the fraud, and Dan removed Bornwell as clerk and made him second senior foreman.

Bornwell's family was well secured in the management structure when I arrived on the farm (see Figure 1). His younger brother, Clever, was a junior foreman; his father looked after the beerhall, which involved opening the building when the beer delivery truck arrived, and passing the money to the operators and the cheques from the operators to the delivery drivers; his mother was the cashier at the beerhall; and until mid-1992, his brother-in-law was the workers' committee chairman. Sekuru Kamutengo's younger brother was a senior tractor driver until the mid-1980s when he returned to Mozambique to fight with Renamo. When he left, Bornwell was sent to retrieve his cousin, Fred, the senior tractor driver's son, from another farm to come back to Chidhadhadha to train as a tractor driver. When I arrived, Fred was the tractor driver in charge of the seed-beds. Bornwell's father's sister's son worked as a general labourer in the 'spans'; his son, Ringson, was a junior clerk. They were known as the 'big family' on the farm, a fact which occasioned a lot of antagonism from other workers and from George. Bornwell's departure, as discussed below, had major repercussions for his relatives.

Marriage practices commonly enabled senior men to benefit from both bridewealth payments, and the labour of the daughter-in-law. Although some women, particularly senior women, also benefited from these practices, it was less typical.[3] The usual ramifications of

---

[3] For instance, one older single woman who lived with her twenty year old son who worked on Chidhadhadha adopted her young niece, the second child of her unmarried younger sister. The niece carried out household chores for her. The woman also hoped to collect bridewealth payments if the girl married, since she looked after her 'like a father'.

marriage practices for women workers came to the fore during disputes between married women and their husbands' lovers, most of whom were single women.

Jasoni was a permanent worker in his late twenties. His wife of two years was twenty years old and was pregnant with their first child when I arrived on Chidhadhadha in May 1992. After the birth of a son five months later, she was known as Mai Bhibho. She was a muzukuru, a 'sister's child', to Rinse since his older sister had married her 'brother' (her mother's step-brother). To signal the relative importance Rinse had as part of the wife-giving family, he was called a *sekuru*, grandfather or maternal uncle, and Mai Bhibho and Jasoni were his *vazukuru*, sister's children. As I got to know them better, I learned of a growing dispute in their relationship: Jasoni wanted a second wife.

Although I did not find polygyny to be widespread in Hurungwe, it was not uncommon among members of certain independent churches, often called *vaPostori*, Apostolics.[4] These African-originated Christian churches are theologically known for emphasizing the work of the Holy Spirit and sociologically known for being centred around prophets, for having schismatic tendencies, and for being shaped by the experience of labour migration (Daneel 1987, Werbner 1989:299ff.). Jasoni and Mai Bhibho belonged to a small independent church. As they were its only members on the farm they tended to go to other *vaPostori* services held in the compound. Jasoni had a vision of eventually becoming a prophet himself with his own following. Part of that vision included having numerous wives who not only would form the core of his church but also who would work the lands in his Communal Land *musha* and look after his domestic needs at his work-place. The only difficulty with his vision was that Mai Bhibho did not agree to being a senior wife.

In January 1993, there was a bad fight between Jasoni and Mai Bhibho in the compound. Jasoni did not come home during the night and Mai Bhibho had good information that he had spent it sleeping with a single woman in the dorms. Their yelling attracted the attention of their neighbours who managed to calm them down that day. But they did not dampen Jasoni's enthusiasm for another

---

4   Although *vaPostori* has a specific connotation of members of the Apostle Church of Johane Maranke (Daneel 1987:39), during my research it was a general term to describe a member of any of the Independent Churches.

wife or overcome Mai Bhibho's resistance to the idea. Over the next month, they fought with each other on other occasions. Mai Bhibho even went to the dorms beyond the compound and fought with the woman who was Jasoni's lover. The tension was only relieved when Mai Bhibho relented to Jasoni's pressure to go to his parents' *musha* in Hurungwe Communal Land, sixty kilometers to the south, to look after his mother.

Although my sympathies were extended more to Mai Bhibho than to Jasoni, I recognized that becoming a second wife to a permanent worker was considered to be an 'improvement' by many single women workers. Another woman worker I knew, Mai Magi, had lived in the dorms with her one-year-old daughter and her mother's widowed sister (*amai*). Mai Magi's older son lived with her mother in Kazangarare where he went to primary school. Both she and her *amai* picked coffee during the dry season. By September I had not seen her for some time in the coffee fields. I presumed that she returned to her *musha* to prepare for planting. I was surprised when I bumped into her at a water tap in the compound during a work-day. She explained that she stopped working once she began living with a permanent worker in the compound. This man now provided money and food for her and her daughter, while she helped out by maintaining his huts. She 'helped out', as opposed to being in charge of it all, because he already had a wife of more than ten years who also lived with him (and who was angry about his new living and sexual arrangements).

The arrangement between Mai Magi and the man she lived with was not considered to be a marriage but a union called *mapoto*, or pots, 'suggesting simply a convenient sharing of cooking arrangements' (Bourdillon 1987:319). The Zimbabwean anthropologist Bourdillon notes how *mapoto* unions emerged mainly in the urban areas due to changes in domestic relations induced by migrant labour. It was, he explains, a less formal structure which permitted men to have somewhat stable cooking and sexual relations without the concerns of the formalized bridewealth transactions and which allowed women who would have difficulty getting married (because they were divorcees or already had children) to have the security of a home and maintenance (see also Jeater 1993, Scarnecchia 1994). Bourdillon notes that 'many Shona think that *mapoto* unions are similar to prostitution' (1987:321). Although he argues that the two are sociologically distinct, he downplays what I found to be reasons why many farm workers I knew, both men and women, also associated *mapoto* unions with prostitution: both transgressed notions of respectable marriages and proper gender relations.

The transgressions of *mahure* and *mapoto*

'On the farm compounds long ago,' according to Sekuru Kamutengo, 'there were hardly any registered marriages (*muchato*). Even bridewealth marriages were rare. Instead men and women *vakachaya mapoto*, they lived together [literally, 'they beat the pots']. They had a cooking arrangement. The reason this was popular,' he claimed, 'was that the parents of the women were hesitant to attempt to get bridewealth from their sons-in-law if they felt their daughters were *mahure*, whores.' It would be difficult, he implied, for parents to get even 'damage money' (compensation paid by a wrongdoer for harm or wrong done) for a daughter who slept around (*meso-meso*). As many foreign farm workers came to Southern Rhodesia in the 1940s, 1950s, and 1960s without wives – they were 'masoja' (soldiers), single men[5] – they would pay money for sex to women from the 'reserves' who would come to beer-parties in the compound or in Kazangarare. Eventually they might live with these women in a *mapoto* arrangement, a temporary union which enables the man, as Sekuru Kamutengo put it, to easily throw out the woman if she returned to prostitution.

Many older men and women, both 'foreign farm workers' and local Korekore farmers in Kazangarare, confirmed that many Korekore women, both unmarried or divorced, came to farms to earn money through prostitution. But it was initially unclear if *mapoto* arrangements were that distinct from prostitution. One old Malawian farm worker noted that foreign workers eventually entered real bridewealth marriages, *kuroora*, to stop spending their money on prostitutes: 'Marrying reduced prostitution [*uhure*]. People from afar [foreign workers] were giving a lot of their money to prostitutes. That was why they were marrying. When you wanted a prostitute, you were supposed to give her some money.'[6]

As another Malawian worker related, *mapoto* could also cost money and, from his perspective, this was a strategy of accumulation for local Korekore women:

---

[5] The label 'soldiers' to describe 'single men' probably comes from the World Wars when soldiers, black and white, stationed in Africa were known to be sexually promiscuous (e.g. White 1990).
[6] Taped interview with man farm worker (1). Karoi North farm. April 25, 1993.

> *You are seeing all the cattle in the reserves [pointing in the*
> *direction of Kazangarare]? They are ours, the Blantyres*
> *[Malawians], which we used to buy. The women were*
> *knowing that if I beat the pots [enter into a mapoto*
> *arrangement] for two or three days, she could say 'I will be*
> *able to buy a cow.'*[7]

The above farm worker also talked of how local women pretended
to engage in other activities to disguise the fact that they were *mahure*;
though as the following shows, his definition of prostitution blended
into notions about marriage:

> *Some used to carry things for selling, but in their minds they*
> *were really wanting to become more visible to the men of the*
> *farms. When they were moving around without things people*
> *would then know that she is a prostitute. 'It was better that I*
> *carry a thing for selling when I will be moving around.' So*
> *when they will be moving around now, you, the man, having*
> *seen them would then say 'mother who has the groundnuts,*
> *these groundnuts you are carrying come from where?' 'I come*
> *with them from such and such.' At that point, the 'marriage'*
> *would have started. She, the woman, will have gone to her*
> *musha and say to her mother, 'Mother, I have seen a man*
> *who stays on the farm which is called so and so. He said he*
> *will come here such and such a day.' You, the man, now will*
> *no longer be having good sleep because you will be saying, 'I*
> *am going to Kazangarare. If only Saturday will arrive, I am*
> *going to sleep in Kazangarare.'*[8]

Here, the farm worker raises the likelihood that women who
were 'prostitutes' one day would become 'wives' the next. The other
relevant feature of the above quotations is that women were
commonly seen as potential sexual partners, particularly when they
were walking around on their own, without a husband or a male
relative. As noted in the previous chapter, simply by the fact that
single women workers were 'single,' most other workers, men and
women, assumed that they were prostitutes. By being in particular
places, in what could be glossed as 'public spaces' in general and
men's places specifically, women could easily be classified as *mahure*.
For instance, when I asked an older woman farm worker whether

---

[7] Taped interview with man farm worker. Karoi North farm. January 10, 1993.
[8] *Ibid.*

there are more 'prostitutes' now compared to the colonial period, she answered by noting the increasing number of single women: 'Now prostitution is too much because there are too many divorces. So women with no men now have become many.' I asked her to explain why there are more prostitutes, suggesting that perhaps lack of money was a key factor. Instead, she discussed the transgressions of spatial boundaries:

> *I can just say that 'pleasures' [kunakwirwa] now have become too many. The records [music], drinking beer.... Back then, a girl was not allowed to drink beer. But as it is now, a girl who has not yet been married, you see her drinking beer and getting drunk. This was the beginning of prostitution now and the dancing to the records in the public. Back then, girls were not allowed to come to the beerhall where parents would be drinking beer.*[9]

I had already encountered this notion that women were not supposed to be in particular public places on certain occasions. While drinking *chibhuku* in Chidhadhadha's beerhall, younger male friends told me that they would not permit their wives to enter the establishment as others would call them prostitutes. Women and girls who attended the Night School, the adult literacy centre Rinse and I helped set up (see Rutherford and Nyamuda, 2000), or to evening *vaPostori* services were often considered to be prostitutes. Whereas all the women who lived in the dorms were considered to be *mahure*.

Women and men informed me how these single women would gladly enter into a *mapoto* arrangement with men who were permanent workers in exchange for the men looking after them and, especially, their children. The situation of Mai Magi is a case in point. Another, was a cousin of Mai Bhibho, Mai Coni, an eighteen-year-old woman with a ten-month-old baby, who initially lived with Jasoni and Mai Bhibho when she arrived at the farm in July, 1992. Eventually, Mai Bhibho asked her to move to the dorms by the bars because she kept bringing men to her hut (she slept in the small kitchen hut) and Mai Bhibho feared that Jasoni would start assuming that she too was sleeping with these men. By November that year, Mai Coni found a young man with whom to live *mapoto*. The next month, she and her 'husband' started to work and live on a neighbouring commercial farm.

---

[9] Taped interview with retired woman farm worker. Karoi North commercial farm. April 22, 1993.

Kuchaya mapoto is distinguished by this emphasis on a cooking arrangement, the creation of domestic ties, whereby the woman does the household chores for the man. Prostitution, *uhure*, was defined as men paying women money or food for sex. *Kuchaya mapoto* blended into prostitution because a man occasionally paid a woman in a *mapoto* arrangement. This, combined with the fact that bridewealth had yet to be paid, made most married men and women view *kuchaya mapoto* as a disrespectful marriage, a 'marriage of prostitutes.' At the same time, however, *mapoto* was a form of marriage. Such arrangements, workers observed, could occasionally lead to a 'respectable' marriage whereby bridewealth was paid, and could be the only chance former prostitutes, single mothers, or older, unmarried women to become married. In other words, *mapoto* arrangements contained both the scars of condemnation and the seeds of respectability for the women involved, but not for the men. African women were the bearers of 'domestic' respectability and unrespectability to the point where the living space of single women became marked as the place of 'whores'.

When Mr Schmidt, the original owner of Chidhadhadha, began producing coffee he required more casual workers than before to work as pickers. As noted above, this led him to gather some 'Ndaus' from eastern Zimbabwe, where coffee has traditionally been grown, and to encourage more single women, who were more eager to work on a seasonal basis than men, from neighbouring farms and Kazangarare to live on the farm during coffee picking season. To this end, he had a dorm constructed in the middle of the compound in 1985. A few years later it was burnt down following a conflict between single women and married women over the latter's husbands. It was rebuilt and a wire fence put around it to keep men from visiting the single women at night. The domestic arrangements of single women were thus physically circumscribed, because of their putative sexual promiscuity, and segregated from the rest of the compound as a means of keeping the peace in the compound, to maintain 'stability' with the emphasis on proper domestic arrangements of man and wife within the domestic government. Although by the time I arrived the fence had fallen down, the separateness of the dorms, the sense of illicitness and marginalization, continued to mark the site.

Thus the marginalization of single women from resources such as steady employment and wages, reasonable accommodation, and

181

credit was shaped by notions of proper behaviour for women and by farm operators' assumptions about proper African families. It also was reinforced to an extent by some of the forms of enforcement of proper marital relations on the farm.

Enforcement of proper marriages

When I talked to farm workers about how their marital disputes were resolved during the colonial period, I received different answers. Some said that family problems, like all other non-criminal problems within the compound, were initially judged by the boss-boy. Others said that issues of adultery and marriage payments were handled 'traditionally' (*pachivanhu*), initially by the father and any family 'elders' who were in the compound. Then, if they could not resolve it, or if there were no elders nearby, the case would go to a *sabhuku* or a chief. If the workers were local, they went to the nearby chief under whom they lived (the chief ruling where their or their father's *musha* was, or to whom their government registration card assigned them). If they were workers from afar, they went to the closest chief of the nearest reserve.

There seemed to be a hierarchy of cases in the colonial period. The boss-boy or foreman tried to resolve marriage problems if they were causing disruption in the compound. If he could not resolve them, or if a party wanted a fine paid, they went to a chief since he was able to levy fines. At the same time, if a worker was seen to be the cause of disruption in the work force, the farmer might fire that person.

A similar hierarchy was instituted after Independence, though this time the chiefs were, theoretically at least, excluded from judicial powers. ZANU(PF) instituted a new court system that removed formal judicial powers from the chiefs (and the former District Commissioners). A two-tiered system was established consisting of Primary Courts to hear civil cases in customary law matters: village courts presided over by a judicial officer selected by the population in the Communal Lands, and community courts in towns presided over by a trained judicial officer selected by the government (Ladley 1982, Cutshall 1991). However, in practice, the chiefs still held courts to handle matters of customary law. Moreover, there was a system of extra-legal courts within the Party itself. ZANU(PF) party cells could bring individuals who went against 'the people' to the attention of higher party structures where there would be some sort of hearing and punishment.

The village committees on commercial farms were initially Party structures. Although everyone, including Ezia, claimed that ZANU(PF)'s ties to these committees had weakened considerably since the mid-1980s, the village committees were still the conduits for some government initiatives (the national census, for instance). On Chidhadhadha at least, the village chairman held a *dare* to settle family problems. Ezia informed me that if he could not solve a problem, he would take the case to George, the senior foreman, then to the *murungu*; if the case remained unresolved, he would send it to the Community Court in Karoi with a letter to the presiding judge. Until 1991, he would also send cases to the Village Court in Kazangarare or to Chief Kazangarare himself, if the disputants so wished, but lately people on the farm had preferred going to Karoi only.

Not everyone submitted to his authority. Those who were VaPostori did so, because Ezia also was a prophet of the Zion Church, as did those who were considered to be VaNdau. Others were ambivalent, criticizing him as a 'weak' chairman compared to the earlier one, or one who favoured his friends. The most critical were those who identified themselves as Malawians or Mozambicans from Tete District (as Chewa, Yao, Sena, Chikunda, etc.), the 'traditional' labour-sending areas, from where the former chairman also came.

It was partially due to questions about reconciliation of marriage difficulties that what can be called 'ethnicity' (*rudzi*, 'type,' 'sort') would play a factor. Some workers put a high premium in marrying their 'own type' as they knew what to expect in terms of marriage payments, negotiations, and conflict resolution. Amongst the farm workers I knew, marriage payments were more or less similar, despite differences from what were viewed by elders as their 'home' communities in Malawi, Mozambique, and so forth (where, for instance, for some communities bride-service was the common form of payment between the families). Yet, for some male farm workers, particularly those descended from outside of Zimbabwe, there was a sense that it was important to marry someone from their own 'community', which typically meant someone descended from the same area in, say, Mozambique. The main benefit of such marriages derived from the assumption that the parties would know how to handle marital conflict, since it was assumed that they shared the same background. It was particularly in the domain of marriage and conflict that I heard discussions of ethnicity, although not all workers agreed with the practice of endogamy and only a few subscribed to it.

Ezia mainly heard cases concerning petty theft within the compound and marital disputes between husband and wife. Adultery was included within the latter, but only if the woman involved was already married to someone or, if single, had a father present who insisted on getting damages or making her marry to the man involved.[10] For other single women involved in a consensual sexual relationships with married men and whose fathers were not present or not interested in making claims for damages, there were no grounds for any form of court case. These women were considered to be prostitutes and men, married or not, were free to have sex with them since they could potentially become future wives of these men.

Single women were thus placed 'outside' of these forms of dispute resolution. They were marginalized because they were 'unattached', so to speak, to the forms of authority of domestic government. Unlike with married women, farmers and foremen could not put pressure on single women through their husbands. Moreover, a man having sex with a single woman was not, by definition, committing 'adultery'. This helps to explain why, for instance, Mai Bhibho fought the woman from the dorms who was sleeping with her husband, Jasoni. It also helps to explain why during my year on the farm, there were five instances of hut-burnings on Chidhadhadha. All involved married woman setting alight the grass roofs of huts occupied by single women whom they had accused of sleeping with their husbands.

Although the accused married women did not admit that they were guilty, everyone knew that they were. In discussing why she fought the 'woman from the dorms', Mai Bhibho put forward what was widely perceived as a predicament faced by married women: 'My husband is screwing around (*kupinda-pinda*), but I cannot

---

[10] Since the passing of the Legal Age of Majority Act in 1982 (and the Supreme Court ruling in *Katekwe* v. *Muchabaiwa* in 1984), women over the age of eighteen years have majority status and had no 'guardians' who could claim damages for 'seduction' cases. The customary law delict of seduction only applies to daughters under the age of eighteen (Ncube 1989:33). Yet, the strength of this act over judicially recognized customary law has been questioned by recent rulings of the Supreme Court, including *Magaya* v. *Magaya* in 1999 when the court unanimously judged that '[u]nder customary law, women did not have the right to heirship and majority status would not give them that additional right' (see 'Zimbabwean women continue to protest the Supreme Court's decision that men cannot be treated as adults according to African customary law', AFP, June 10, 1999; 'Zim Women Take to Streets Over Loss of Rights', *Mail & Guardian*, May 21, 1999).

divorce him. My family is poor [and cannot afford to pay back the bridewealth, B.R.]. I don't want this whore to push me aside or to divert his low wages to her.'

In turn, as mentioned above, many single women saw sleeping with permanent workers, especially senior workers, as a way to improve their access to resources. As one told me while we sat in the dorms, 'If he buys me soap, perhaps contributes to the school fees for my children, or even if he provides a real house to host relatives who come to visit, rather than this room I share with strangers, it is worth having a boyfriend.' But these women were not only vulnerable to attacks by wives. They were also vulnerable to sexual assaults by men. Being marginalized from the domestic government gave them a bit more room than married women in using extra-farm authorities for redress as the following two examples show, but it did not improve their safety.

Rudo was a single woman worker in her late twenties with two young children (who were living at the *musha* of her ex-husband's parents). She began working on Chidhadhadha in July 1992. In November, she was applying suckercide on tobacco plants when she was hit by George, the senior foreman. According to George, Rudo was not opening the tobacco leaves for the woman behind her to apply the suckercide properly. She reputedly ignored warnings from George to improve her work. He then crept up behind her and slapped her hard to 'teach her a lesson'. This occurred at around eight o'clock in the morning. She continued to work through the morning. However, after lunch, she did not return to the fields. The next day, police officers came to the farm and told Dan that George had to appear at the Magistrate's Court the next day. Furious that the police came so promptly for what he saw as a minor case,[11] Dan told them that he would pay George's fine and instructed them to leave the farm. There was no further interest by the police, or the courts, in the case.

Other workers who were present confirmed that Rudo was tired and not doing a good job, but they did not see George warn her and were quite surprised that he had hit her so hard. They had other explanations for the incident and for Rudo resorting to the police. Tendai, a junior foreman, was having an affair with Rudo and he

---

[11] The Karoi branch of the Zimbabwe Republic Police had few motor vehicles and were notorious among the white farmers for taking their time in coming to attend to problems on the farms when farmers contacted them.

and George were not getting along. Tendai and others claimed that Rudo turned down George's amorous proposal and, thus spurned, George got mad and hit her. After the incident, George found three people, who happened to be relatives or friends, who claimed to have seen Tendai pressure Rudo to go to the police during the lunch break. Both Tendai and Rudo denied the charge. Rudo said she initially went to the workers' committee who had told her that this was how George behaved and they would do nothing for her. She claimed that since George had caused her great pain, she went to the police.

This example indicates how the authority of the foremen allowed them to hit someone with the backing of the farmer, and how a single woman might go to the police to try and solve her problems rather than trying to deal with them within the domestic government of the farms. As a single woman, she was not only marginalized by the dominant identities within domestic government, but she was also marginal to the main means of dispute resolution. This incident also indicates how tension amongst foremen could affect relations and understandings on the farm.

The particular tension between George and Tendai derived partly from a case during the cold season in 1992 when Tendai was accused of raping a young woman from the dorms. Again, there was a delay (of four days) between the incident and the time when the woman went to the police. The woman claimed that she did not know that Tendai worked on the farm and only went to the police when she saw him at the morning assembly four days later. Tendai claimed that George persuaded the woman to make up the story about him. Although he denied any involvement with her, everyone else on the farm, including the farmers, assumed that he had some form of sexual relation with her since Tendai had a reputation of being a womanizer.

The courts threw out the case for lack of evidence. Tendai was not punished on the farm for this alleged action, nor for any of his other actions against women. The woman was soon fired from work on what all saw as a trumped-up complaint.

During my year on the farm, the police came to Chidhadhadha several times. Aside from cases of theft of farm property, most involved some form of assault against a single woman. Although the frequency of police involvement points to the vulnerability of single women within the power relations on the farm, it also shows, I contend, that these women were more likely than married ones to go beyond the domestic government on the farm and involve the police.

Both men and women recognized that women workers did not receive a 'fair hearing' from the foremen and that they received better treatment from the police. It was easier for single women to go to the police than married women, unless the latter wanted to sever their ties with their husbands. Like the women involved in the *dare* for Akimu in the beerhall, married women were subject to the control of the farm through their husbands. Although in the above cases the single women did not gain from going to the police and were perhaps persuaded to do so by conspiracies of intrigue amongst senior workers, by going to Karoi they showed that the farm was under higher forms of authority, a fact that bothered farm management, especially when women were lodging complaints against a foreman.

It was perhaps because of the frustration of men whose wives who took exception to their sexual arrangements with single women, that there was such anger unleashed against married women at Akimu's *dare*. The men were trying to equate married women with single women under the category of 'whores'. The label 'whore' made women into marginal and transgressive figures. As 'whores', women were not 'respectable' and were thus open to attack and scorn mainly from men, but also from other women. As 'whores', women transgressed proper domestic relations and the proper forms of authority which those entailed within the domestic government. At Akimu's *dare* men were lumping all women into that category. But in practice it was usually only single women who were treated and seen as 'whores'.

By being unattached to the domestic government, single women were inherently transgressive of the 'laws of the farm'. When they explicitly violated the sanctity of the rules, or rather showed that the 'laws of the farm' were under higher forms of authority, the one recourse farmers had was to fire them, to remove them from the domestic space itself. Farmers became involved in situations which disturbed the functioning of, and the stability envisioned by, domestic government. Until that point, they left it up to their senior workers and village chairmen to deal with the problem. The transgressive threat that single women posed to the domestic government and the spatialized domesticity was such that many farm operators refused to hire them.

Re-creating domesticity: the importance of 'respectable homes'

> *When I get to the farm of Mr Schmidt's son, Ed, I am going to*
> *buy myself a T.V. Chengetai, my wife will work every week*
> *and with her wages and mine, we can not only improve our*
> *living on the farm but also can save up to start planting burley*
> *tobacco in a few years at our new musha in Gokwe!*

These were the excited thoughts of Fred, one of the more senior tractor drivers on Chidhadhadha. He was telling me these plans during his last day working on the farm in early April 1993. He had given in his notice and was arranging to sell some of his household items and move the rest to the farm of Ed Schmidt, the son of the original owner of Chidhadhadha, on the other side of Harare, almost three hundred kilometres away. Fred was the last of Bornwell's relatives who had moved out to Schmidt's new farm during my stay on Chidhadhadha. When Bornwell himself left the November before to become assistant manager at Ed's small tobacco farm, all his relatives who had senior positions eventually gave notice and followed him there (save for his younger brother, Clever, a junior foreman who did not get along with Ed Schmidt). They perceived greater opportunities at Schmidt's farm once Bornwell went over there. Other unrelated senior workers who remained behind saw such movement as a dynasty broken. Helping to link these two understandings – opportunities and broken dynasty – was 'domesticity'.

Ensuring proper domestic relations was not only a strong form of regulation on the farm; 'domesticity' was also a strong marker of identity for some workers, particularly those who were closer to the farmers within the hierarchy of domestic government. I am going to sketch out how this marker of domesticity was an integral part of particular practices of consumption, accumulation, and various power relations on Chidhadhadha. Bornwell's departure is a good place to start such an examination.

During an early morning at the start of November 1992 I bumped into Bornwell entering the compound. He was dressed in 'nice' clothes, not work clothes. He told me that he was leaving Chidhadhadha that day and invited me to his place to talk.

He was living in the biggest house in the compound. The long brick-walled and metal-roofed building had seven rooms, electricity, and indoor plumbing. When we sat down on his concrete steps, he stopped speaking chiShona and started to explain in English why he was leaving Chidhadhadha after spending his life, thirty years, on the farm.

He gave two reasons. The first concerned accumulation. He complained that his wages were quite low compared to those of other foremen in the area. The new owners actually cut his (and everyone else's) pay when they arrived from $350 a month to $315. Although he did not have any formal training, he had fifteen years of experience working with tobacco. Furthermore, despite receiving handsome bonuses at Christmas time, he was dismayed that there were no criteria concerning how much he would get other than the discretion of the bosses.

'Worst of all,' he declared, 'was that Dan and Geoff limited my opportunities for making money in the compound.' They told him to limit the number of times he set up his 'disco' in the beerhall where he charged a nominal entrance fee, since he was diverting too much of the workers' money away from the farm store and butcher. Nor had they been too forthcoming, he felt, in providing transport for him to take the 'disco' to neighbouring farm compounds for dances. They also prevented him from selling kapenta in the compound.[12] He explained that he had been sending his sister to buy kapenta wholesale at Kariba (about 130 kilometres away) and he had been selling it in the compound for less than it was sold at the farm's store. Although the new owners said they did not want this competition and told him to stop, he observed that a number of other workers had since pursued the same strategy without the farmers trying to stop them.

The second reason was his conflict with George. To him, George made fifteen dollars a month more than him only because he had a driver's licence for the lorry.[13] The bosses told him that they were equal in power, yet George saw himself as the main manager of the farm. 'George would approach the bosses on his own,' Bornwell complained, 'and spread false rumours about my ability to manage his workers.'

All of this would end, Bornwell declared, on Ed Schmidt's farm. He and Ed not only agreed on a salary level substantially higher

---

[12] A tiny fish, *Lymnothrissa myodo*, from Lake Kariba, sold salted and sun-dried in packages of various sizes which many farm workers, among others, frequently use as a relish with sadza.

[13] Others claimed that George received $125.00 more than Bornwell.

than he was receiving from Chidhadhadha ($500 a month) and a bonus tied to the farm's performance, but he had also arranged with a neighbouring farmer to set up his disco at his bottlestore. What seemed to really impress him about his new job was the ability to improve his own and his family's lifestyle. Ed promised him that he would pay the fees for his eldest child, a twelve-year-old boy, to board at a nationally recognized government school. He also promised Bornwell a motorcycle and possibly a car so that he could drive from the farm to his own *musha* in Kazangarare. Moreover, he was 'going to get a real *mushe* [good] house, better than mine at Chidhadhadha, with electricity and water which,' he emphatically added, 'would really please my wife.'

Bornwell placed a lot of emphasis on the spatial arrangement of his 'domesticity'. Unlike my visits with general workers which often took place outside their huts, when I visited Bornwell we usually went inside his house to talk in his living room with its antimacassar-covered furniture, curtains over the windows and, as the centre of attention, a television and a stereo system. The style of this room conveyed modern respectability as did the refreshments served to favoured guests (which I often was) – tea with sugar and milk, a plate of bread and jam, or bottled beer from a nearby bottle store (not containers of *chibhuku* bought by workers at the farm's beerhall).

Not only the decor and culinary practices but also the household division of labour displayed domestic respectability. Bornwell told me with pride that his wife did not work on the farm or at his own *musha*, his land in Kazangarare. Instead she was a proper 'housewife' who did not 'work' (aside, I noted, from the considerable labour she carried out in maintaining the proper 'domestic' character of the house). I never got her opinion on her life and her family's lifestyle since whenever I visited and Bornwell was there, she either remained quietly seated on the floor or excused herself to work in the kitchen. If I came by and Bornwell was not home, she was not very amenable to conversation. In this way, she differed from most wives of general farm workers who contributed equally with their husbands to the conversation while also carrying out domestic chores. But she was similar to most wives of the 'big workers' who also emphasized respectable 'domesticity'.

George lived behind the farm store in a place with electricity and running water. Like Bornwell, he did not want his wife to work outside the house and he placed a lot of importance on the education of his children (his eldest daughter was doing her 'O' Levels in Karoi). The senior cook also had a house with electricity and running water, though in his case his wife did work on the farm and at the *musha*, while the senior mechanic occupied the other house with electricity. The only other place with electricity in the compound at that time was the beerhall.

Indoor plumbing was a real privilege given the few 'Blair toilets'[14] and water-taps in the compound then. There were only sixteen of these outhouses and four water-points (connected to a borehole) for most of the workers and their families to use (though by the late 1990s almost all permanent workers were living in brick houses). The twenty-seven families of senior workers living in the fifteen brick houses on the north side of the compound had seven Blair toilets and nine water-points for their own more or less exclusive use. After work, there were often long lines at the communal water-points. When I was there, the farm employed a retired man to clean the toilets. However, due to disagreements concerning his wages and what materials the farm would provide him and the fact that he fell sick for a number of months, the outhouses were often unclean. There were no water-points or toilets near the dorm beyond the compound. A number of the people in the compound proper and almost all who lived in the far dorm used the bush as a toilet, most probably contributing to the common problem of diarrhoea affecting farm workers and their families.

Aside from the houses with electricity and a row of brick houses built in the late 1980s, there were twelve other brick houses with metal or asbestos roofs. These were given to junior foremen, the senior clerk, gardeners, domestic servants, security guards, tractor drivers, lorry drivers, and checkers and shooters (senior tobacco graders). During the cold season of 1992, the farm built six brick houses and began constructing Blair toilets next to them. Apart from those who lived in dorms, the remaining male workers lived in mud and pole huts in various states of disrepair. In short, these *vanhu vakuru*, 'big people', with access to nice housing, electricity, and running water were quite privileged compared to their fellow workers.

---

[14] These refer to the style of outhouses designed by the Ministry of Health's Blair Laboratories in Harare which minimizes the number of flies and increases the longevity of the toilet's use. A number of development initiatives in rural areas promote them. Whenever I introduced myself to Zimbabweans, there often was great mirth over my name given its wide association with toilets.

191

More important than these household facilities, however, was the sense of difference based on their lifestyle. Most of the *vanhu vakuru* did not socialize with other workers, other than relatives or for business dealings. They kept within their homes, or left the farm for the local town or other farms for social gatherings. To me, they often badmouthed 'African' habits and beliefs, wondering why 'they', other Africans, did not improve themselves and stop practices such as bridewealth and belief in spirit possession. If I went to their place while they were eating, and they were eating sadza with their hands, they tended to be embarrassed and apologized about not eating the 'proper' way with cutlery or not having *chikafu cheWestern*, western food. Although I would protest that nothing was wrong, they insisted these ways were not 'good'. They did so because they assumed that I, a *murungu*, would think this way since that is how their bosses think and, moreover, because this way of distinguishing themselves from other workers was crucial to their daily life. They subscribed to what Eric Worby (1998:576) has called an 'aesthetics of modernity', a colonial and post-colonial national project in rural Zimbabwe that not only aims to transform productive practices but also promotes 'emblems of modernized status – practices that include monogamy and fidelity in marriage, the careful husbandry of scarce resources, and the display of bourgeois domestic assets (such as cups and saucers) as well as items of consumption (such as tea and sugar, bread and butter or jam).'

In other words, these *vanhu vakuru* were deploying in their lives crucial dichotomies such as 'modern/ traditional', 'work/non-work', 'husband/wife'. 'respectable/non-respectable'. Such dichotomies fuelled and generated the division between 'big workers' and general workers. 'He is acting like a *murungu*,' took on the power of scorn when said by a general worker with reference to a foreman or the senior clerk.

This was not to say that many general workers did not aspire to such 'modernist' consumption strategies and identity formation. Aside from the fact that only the *vanhu vakuru* received the housing, the cost of achieving and maintaining the declared 'modern' lifestyle was beyond their reach. They needed both (or more) partners in a conjugal household working on the farm and at the *musha* (if they had one) – they could not afford to have a 'non-working housewife'. Neither could they afford to buy much furniture or electronic equipment. This difference in the ability of general workers and *vanhu vakuru* to enjoy modern domesticity was also integrally connected to the forms of authority of 'domestic government'.

Patronage, accumulation, and conflict

Farmers helped to maintain the senior workers' consumption of goods and their image as conspicuous consumers, as being 'modern'.[15] They would sell them their second-hand household items, such as televisions or stereos, at low prices. They also supported their production activities outside of their duties on the farm. For instance, the senior cook used to have land set aside on the farm to grow burley tobacco, with the farm covering some expenses. The new owners stopped that practice but still provided him with loans to grow burley at his *musha* in Kazangarare.

These *vanhu vakuru* were key personnel in the operators' management of the farm and their own households. As Karen, Geoff's wife, put it, her gardener and cook were her 'crutches'. They really supported her and her family in meeting their daily needs. These 'domestics', like the foremen and clerks, helped to maintain proper 'order' at work, in the compound, and in the homes, for the farmers. Most farmers I knew thought these workers required special treatment and assistance to improve their lives. However, the farmers did not want senior workers to think that they were equals, people whom one could treat as possible friends. For instance, one farmer told me how after he left his town job to start working on a farm as a manager, he had invited the senior foremen to the first party he held. 'Boy, did the old man [the owner] chew me out,' he told me. The message was plain: don't bring foremen (or, he also noted, black managers) to white farmer social gatherings. On farms, he noted, the difference between owner and worker, white and black, was paramount.

The farmers also expected loyalty from these workers. The cook of one of Chidhadhadha's farmers left employment abruptly. Although the farmer and his wife were actually contemplating letting him go since he was continually sick, they were upset that he took the initiative and left them in the lurch. They were also mad at the nearby farmer who gave him a job. Another example was a lorry driver I knew who found a better-paying job on the other side of

---

[15] Farmers were not the only ones promoting such 'aesthetics of modernity'. Many of the churches promoted such practices and attitudes as did advertising and various forms of government propaganda, institutions, and events (see, e.g., Burke 1996, Alexander and Ranger 1998, Worby 1998).

Karoi. When his new employer phoned his long-time boss and found out that the latter still wanted to keep the driver, the new job opportunity was revoked and the lorry driver had to remain in his old job.

Because of this sense of expected loyalty, of bonding to the farmer, Bornwell switched to English when talking to me. He did not want any nearby women outside his compound home, none of whom knew much English, to hear that he had found a job at Ed Schmidt's farm, lest they spread the news and the Chidhadhadha farmers discovered his disloyalty to them. Bornwell told Dan and Geoff that he was leaving Chidhadhadha in order to work on his *musha* full-time. He also had arranged with Ed Schmidt to get paid for two months while staying in Kazangarare. Bornwell did not want to upset Dan and Geoff too soon by the fact that he was switching farms.

In exchange, these senior workers expected to be treated better than other workers. When it did not happen, they, and even other workers, would get upset. For instance, the child of the gardener for one of the Chidhadhadha's farmers died in Karoi. To transport the dead body back by bus would have required getting special permission and a certificate or two from the Police, so the gardener approached his immediate boss to drive his dead son back to the farm so he could bury him. The farmer refused, according to the rumours in the compound, because he was afraid that the dead boy was diseased which could then harm him and his family. So the gardener had to approach the other farmer, whose yard he did not maintain, to drive the body of his child back to the farm. Farm workers I knew were outraged at the first farmer. 'How could he not assist his own gardener in this time of grief?' they demanded of me. 'If that boss cannot help his own domestics, how can we expect him to help us?' This was the same farmer who was instrumental in cutting back the credit which, as noted in Chapter Four, led to workers becoming less enthusiastic about working on Chidhadhadha. And it was this apparent transgression of their duty to help their 'crutches', their 'big workers', that was a key cause of Bornwell's departure.

Part of this 'duty' of farmers, according to Bornwell, was to assist him in pursuing extra-employment sources of accumulation. Bornwell compared the new owners with Schmidt. Under Schmidt's ownership, he had been able to pursue various ways of making money outside of being a foreman, and this was a long-standing perk for senior workers. A position of boss-boy, mechanic, or cook

– key roles in farmers' domestic governance – brought higher pay, better housing, and closer ties to the *murungu* than that of a general worker. These resources could be used by senior workers in the colonial period to invest in other ways to make money.

The following is a quotation from a retired foreman from a Karoi farm who in the early 1990s was one of the most successful small-scale tobacco farmers in Zimbabwe. Although he emphasized the work ethic of his family as the reason for his success (he was a strong Protestant), his description of his sources of accumulation shows that he held a senior position in the work force:

> *I used to farm with my wife [on a plot given by his employer on the commercial farm] when I came from work. We used to have gardens [to grow vegetables for sale] and many other different things to help us. With the money earned, we bought a motor-bike and a car. When I was given the $18.00 as my bonus [in the 1970s], I used to give this money to my wife so that she could buy beer and a cow. Back then, cows were very cheap. We used to make a 'concert' and people gave us money by drinking beer, buying meat and dancing to the music. We were growing in money and [were able] to send our children to school.[16]*

Only those male workers at the apex of power like the foreman or the cook could acquire sufficient money in the form of bonuses to invest and receive permission from the *murungu* and his boss-boy to hold parties in the compound. He also probably got a good deal from the farmer, or one of his neighbours, on the motor-cycle and car. Although he showed initiative in these investments, he started from a privileged position within the domestic government of the farm.

I heard similar stories about Maoko and his ways of making money outside of being boss-boy for Mr Schmidt. And I noted Bornwell's strategies of holding a 'disco' and selling kapenta. Whereas senior workers have always had schemes in the compound to make money from the workers (ranging from trading to forms of extortion), since Independence senior workers have also pursued more accumulation strategies outside the farm. This was now easier given that black Zimbabweans could legally enter all contractual

---

16 Taped interview with retired foreman of a Karoi farm. Mukwichi Communal Land. 12 April 1993.

arrangements and because foreign-born or patrilineally descended long-term residents, who still account for many permanent farm workers today, could more easily get land rights in the Communal Lands. Strategies have included buying and letting houses in towns, growing cash crops like tobacco on their *musha*, and potentially, though rarely, buying a commercial farm themselves. Furthermore, since the government has increased infrastructure support in the Communal Lands, having a *musha* can be lucrative. As others have noted, such support has spurred on class differentiation based on increased crop production for the market as well as on mercantile activities such as retail trade and transportation (Moyo 1995, Nyambara 1999). Those few who have been able to take advantage of these increased opportunities tend to have connections to such other jobs as teachers, store-owners or civil servants (e.g. Worby 1992).

By cultivating their ties to their farmers, senior farm workers were amongst the few who have been able to exploit these opportunities. George had a couple of houses in Chikangwe, the high density suburb in Karoi; Bornwell and the senior cook had each a profitable *musha* in Kazangarare.

During my research, a new type of 'big worker' emerged on Chidhadhadha. The farm began to employ a senior foreman, Trust, on a short-term contract. Trust was trained at a tobacco institute in Harare and had been working for several years at another Hurungwe commercial farm. Given his training, he earned almost double the salaries of George and Bornwell. He also had innumerable plans to make money. Although he had a *musha* in Kazangarare for which he got assistance from Dan and Geoff (for example, they gave him 150 gum poles to make air-curing barns for burley tobacco), Trust had bigger schemes in mind. He was talking to a neighbouring farmer about buying his farm store and beerhall. He was investigating the possibility of buying either a commercial farm in Mozambique or a small-scale commercial farm in Vhuti. Trust approached me to ask what I knew about getting loans from the African Development Bank and constantly asked if I could sell him my car and any other 'expensive good' I had at a cheap price.

Trust arrived a month before Bornwell departed. Although he was not hired to replace Bornwell, in the latter's absence he became the other section head on the farm, bringing about a shift in the allocation of preferred jobs in his section. For instance, Ringson, Bornwell's cousin who was the coffee clerk during the dry season, began to work in the gang during tobacco planting and harvesting. After Bornwell's departure, Trust's brother became the clerk. In January, Ringson left Chidhadhadha, the place where he was born, and went to Ed Schmidt's farm where he was training to become a mechanic. Fred, Bornwell's cousin who was a tractor driver, had been expecting to become the next foreman given his long service and his connection to Bornwell. When Bornwell left, so did Fred's opportunity to improve his situation on Chidhadhadha. Shortly after Bornwell left, Fred said that George and his allies had won the battle and that he too had better leave for Schmidt's farm. He left, as noted above, in April 1993.

I have touched upon the animosity between Bornwell and George before. I have also noted the conflict between Tendai and George and discussed the rivalry between the new foremen and Maoko which led to the latter's firing. Conflict, alliances, and rumours were crucial to the jockeying for power amongst senior workers. Key to these strategies was access to the *murungu*. Whoever could claim to be the closest to the farmer(s) could demonstrate his authority over others. The best way to demonstrate this confidence was to get resources from the farmer and get one's allies placed into higher positions at work. This authority often led these workers to be seen as the 'owners' of the farm, a position other intermediary workers such as junior foremen often resented and which often led to the use of preternatural forces both by and against senior workers (disputes amongst *vanhu vakuru* often are waged through witchcraft; see Rutherford 1996:451ff, Rutherford 1999). Being one of the *vanhu vakuru* often meant being both an instigator and a target of compound politics.

Conclusion

The compound was more than the place of sleep, recreation, and other domestic matters for farm workers. It was a place where the skein of power relations, the concatenation of discursive practices which comprised the 'domestic government' on the farm, contributed to the everyday struggles, interactions, and noticeable events that differentiated farm workers in at least three specific ways.

First, women farm workers were largely defined through their connection, or lack thereof, to a male farm worker. From access to resources such as housing and credit to the access to and reach of dispute-resolution procedures, women workers were defined by how they fitted in the 'proper' modern domestic household. Single women transgressed this domestic government. Though they worked on the farms, they were denied many of the resources given to permanent workers and their wives. Yet their transgressions also marked them as possible sexual partners for men, symbolized most openly by the barbed wire fence that once surrounded the dorms for single women. The order of domesticity defined the transgressiveness of single women, but many of the latter could become respectable wives, or almost respectable *mapoto* wives.

Secondly, senior foremen, cooks, and other *vanhu vakuru* held esteemed and privileged positions on commercial farms because they helped to maintain the order of the farm and the households, the domestic spaces, under the direction and control of the farmers and their families. They also sought to achieve the lifestyle and domestic arrangements that constitute modern domesticity itself through various forms of accumulation on and off the farm that fed into particular consumption habits (see Burke 1996 for a detailed examination of consumption in Zimbabwe) and forms of accumulation which often were intimately supported by the farmers themselves. But such efforts had to operate within subservient behaviour towards white operators who tended to see black workers 'acting' like a white person as 'uppity' and potentially subversive.

Such strategies were not impossible for other workers to pursue. As I discuss in the next chapter, getting a *musha* has been a way many farm workers have followed to try and improve their situation. However, they did not have the seniority in the farm's hierarchy to be able to acquire access to greater resources through the farmer. Bornwell felt that the possibility for greater accumulation and meeting the ideal domestic arrangements at the other farm meant that he had to cut his life-long ties to Chidhadhadha. He was lucky as he already had a close tie with Ed Schmidt with whom he had grown up. Without it he would have had difficulty finding a higher-paying job since he lacked formal training in tobacco. Unlike Trust, Bornwell and George depended on the goodwill of their *murungu*, on their valued position within the domestic government of the farm, to maintain their own power and domestic comforts in the compound. Others, like Fred, depended in turn on their ties to these senior workers.

Thirdly, the compound itself was under the authority of the farmer. This authority reinforced the importance of proper domestic arrangements through the criteria governing access to housing and credit, and through the senior workers backing the farmer up in times of conflict. Dan and Geoff paid George's fine for hitting Rudo, maintained Tendai and fired the woman who accused him of rape, while Akimu was brash in his 'trial' because he knew the bosses would support him over, say, Ezia the village chairman. They wanted to maintain order in the compound to ensure the smooth running of production (and accumulation), but they also were concerned about the proper 'modern' arrangements of family and lifestyle that were being learned by their 'traditional' workers on their farm. However, there was another source of power and opportunity for farm workers outside the farm: the Communal Lands.

Chapter 7

Becoming a 'peasant'

'Getting a stand': farm workers becoming peasants

> 'Ah, I missed out this time! A few days only. If I had heard about the musha last week, I could have got it. The owner (muridzi) was selling it for $100 and only asking for $50 down. I could have got that musha in Dunga for that price. I'll keep looking though....'.

The words of Tobia trailed off as he looked glumly around the farm compound. Originally from Mozambique, Tobia was now an old widower living with his divorced daughter and her two children in two run-down pole and mud huts on Chidhadhadha. He was finding work on the farm too difficult these days for his nearly seventy-year-old body and was wanting to retire to 'the reserve'. Tobia did not have any Korekore relatives or close friends who could recommend him to a land-giving authority in the 'reserve', and anyway, he noted, it seemed that the authorities were no longer giving any land in Kazangarare. Buying from someone who was leaving his *musha* seemed to be his best option at the moment. And he just missed a good deal at $100.

The buying of a *musha*, which is not officially allowed, is rarely discussed in the literature on land rights in Zimbabwe. Nor was it ever broached by any government officials on their own initiative when telling me about the 'overcrowding' problems in Hurungwe's Communal Lands. Yet, Africans have paid money to get a *musha* in Zimbabwe's 'reserves' since at least the 1940s (Holleman 1968:334). In Mukwichi Communal Land, the practice did not seem to have such a long history. Most people said that the selling and buying of *misha* (plural of *musha*) started after Independence when the demand for land increased.

Farm workers, particularly those of 'foreign' birth or descent, have been important in helping to create this demand. This included not only older workers like Tobia who were looking for a place to retire, but also younger ones like Fred the tractor driver and his cousin Bornwell who saw a *musha* as a place of investment, as a way to supplement their farm income, or even as a place which would eventually replace their need to work on a farm.

I heard much talk amongst these men about 'getting a stand', acquiring a *musha* in the Communal Lands. Mukwichi had been a good place for such an acquisition; before Independence, not many people lived there and the land was relatively fertile.

Many women farm workers spoke of the *musha* as another place of work. Some saw the *musha* as a better place than the *purazi*, commercial farm, given that they, not a *bhasi*, control the work schedule. Others claimed that in the 'reserves' they miss having water taps and the ability to earn money on their own from the farms. But aside from a few entrepreneurial women like Mai Chido who got a *musha* in her eldest son's name, most women saw access to a *musha* as being dependent on their husband or father.

But farm workers were not the only ones to increase the demand for *misha* in Mukwichi. There were also those who had come from the Masvingo area in south-central Zimbabwe, who were locally called 'MaVhitori'[1] but more widely known as 'Karanga'. As well, there were salaried teachers and other civil servants, the 'rural salariat' (Leys 1986), who had come to the relatively unpopulated and fertile lands of Hurungwe after Independence. In terms of 'supply', various interests – the chiefs, the local ZANU(PF) hierarchy, local Village Development Committees (VIDCOs), the councillors, the *masabhuku* (kraal-heads), the *marenda* (land spirits), the District Administrator, and individual land-holders – competed with each other to be the ultimate authority in controlling legal and practical rights to land, rights which also enable the selling of land.

These dynamics which have contributed to the gradual emergence of the buying and selling of *misha* have also influenced other practices concerning access to and use of land in the Kazangarare area of Mukwichi. The post-Independence establishment of Dunga itself, and its neighbour to the west, Chipatapata, in what is still legally 'State Land', rather than 'Communal Land', is a good indication of the changing features of Kazangarare and the 'government' of land in Zimbabwe, as are the various ties, and cross-ties, the lines of patronage

---

[1]   This term is derived from Ft. Victoria, the colonial name for the city of Masvingo.

and dependence, coercion and resistance, between neighbouring commercial farmers and peasant farmers. Yet these are still foreign to much official commentary on rural Zimbabwe today.

Instead, development discourses have sutured discussions of current and historical practices in rural Zimbabwe to the outlines of dual economy narratives, stitching the boundary between commercial farms and Communal Lands to a division between white capitalist production and black peasant/subsistence production (see Nyambara 1999 for a similar critique), leaving only a scar as evidence of the 'wound' inflicted upon one side by the other. The attribution of culpability in causing such a wound depends on whose side the commentator takes. I will not take 'sides' – either by promoting the necessity of allowing the 'market' to fully operate in the Communal Lands in order to prevent environmentally-destructive subsistence practices from destroying more of Zimbabwe's land-base, or by advocating the importance of increasing support to peasant households to enable them to farm without the need for members migrating for jobs in the exploitive 'capitalist sector'; or by praising white farmers for giving peasants jobs or calling for farm workers to become full-time peasants. Rather, to try to unstitch, or at least to fray, the sutures binding commercial farms and Communal Lands to a dual economy division in official discourses – the discursive triad of white farmer, African peasant and farm worker – I begin by examining the official picture of the land distribution system in Kazangarare. This entails discussing various attributes of local government and, especially, development in Mukwichi and how this produces an official identity of 'peasants'. I then investigate how these official discourses have helped to structure the local relations governing land access in Kazangarare. A brief sketch of the post-Independence settlement of Dunga helps to situate my argument. Next, I turn to some of the relationships between commercial farms and Kazangarare. I conclude by looking at how these relationships challenge the assumptions of dual economy narratives that comprise official development discourse and how farm workers became vilified because of their provocative act of becoming peasants.

Land and 'development' in Mukwichi

The 'order' of land acquisition and its 'violators'

The question of land is a touchy one, I was told by almost every government official in Hurungwe District. It was 'touchy' because there was a great separation between the order of land distribution and acquisition envisioned by official plans and what happened in the district's Communal Lands themselves. According to one senior official of the Hurungwe District Council, acquiring land in the Communal Lands was officially a three-step process. First, a prospective settler would approach the local VIDCO for the area where he (officially, married men typically acquire *musha* rights) wanted to live. The six VIDCO leaders, who are (notionally) elected every two years by the (supposed) thousand villagers in their constituency, would show the settler different pieces of land where he and his family could settle. After land was selected, the VIDCO leaders would call a meeting of everyone living in their area. If the thousand people approved of the prospective settler, then the VIDCO would take him to the WADCO (Ward Development Committee), comprised of the six VIDCO leaders in an area and headed by an elected councillor. If the WADCO approved, they would take the person to the District Council, the third and final step, for approval and registration. If the settler was from, or registered in, another district he was to get a letter of transfer from the District Administrator of his old district and give it to the District Administrator in Hurungwe. Such a system, the official expounded, not only better controlled the number of people settling than the old way of using chiefs, headmen and kraal-heads, but it was also more 'democratic' since it gave 'the people' a direct say in who would be their neighbours.

These two themes, 'control' and 'democracy', kept reappearing in most official discussions concerning land usage and development. As the official continued, they were currently subverted in Hurungwe, especially in Mukwichi, in two ways. First, an individual VIDCO leader could grant land without notifying any other land authority. Secondly, a 'traditional leader' – the chief or kraal-head (*sabhuku*, owner of the books) – could give land to people, an illegal action by an unelected authority. As a result of these violations, the official story went, the population had been significantly increasing in Hurungwe and Mukwichi Communal Lands, denuding it of soils, trees and other natural resources. According to this characterization, overcrowding was resulting either from corruption or from the illegal land allocation activities of traditional authorities.[2]

---

[2]   There has been a shift in official thinking about the role of traditional leaders in local government and land distribution. In 1998, the Traditional Leaders Bill was tabled before Parliament; among other things, it designates village heads as those who allocate land in Communal Lands and extends the authority of traditional leaders into resettlement areas.

The District Council had put a moratorium on new settlers coming into the Communal Lands by the mid-1980s. In 1987 they passed a by-law that allowed any unregistered person (i.e. one who was illegally settled) to register. Whoever did not do so would be evicted after a period of grace. Within one month, 34,000 people registered. Although they had not evicted people who could not demonstrate that they were properly registered, officials threatened to do so. This threat usually occurred when they discussed development plans.

The 'planning of development' versus 'the living of the people'

> *You have spoken very well, only there is one thing which confuses us about the effects of the plan, which was made at the planning level, on the living of the people. There is only one lingering sickness [denda]... The bad thing here is that [for example] this Mr M. is the one who lives on the road, that is where his field is, and I live behind Mr M. with three others. So, say the land where we three live is suitable to keep wild animals since there are good pastures there. Now when we have been removed from there, Mr M. then fails to understand that we should have some of his land. Rather, he says that my land can never be divided for other people. So what will the people do when they have been removed from the area in which they used to live [to make room for wildlife areas]?[3]*

This was a question from an audience member at a workshop organized by the District Council in the township of Kazangarare in July 1992 on setting up a local committee of Campfire (the Communal Areas Management Programme for Indigenous Resources). He directed the question towards an Agritex (the government's agricultural extension department) officer who had just finished a talk on the importance of 'land use planning'.

The official had discussed how such planning would lead to conservation and would permit Agritex to assist farmers in dividing their land into distinct, fenced-off areas for farming, residence, grazing, gardens, and wildlife. Such order would not only ensure the conservation of resources but also, he contended, facilitate attempts by local people to get money from government and donors.

---

[3]   Taped Campfire meeting, Kazangarare Township, July 14, 1992. All following references come from this meeting.

He had just concluded by talking about how some people's land may be reduced in order to make room for people moved off land set aside for wildlife, when the above question was asked. In reply, the official underscored the fact that 'planning' is done by Agritex with 'the people', so that when the plan is written up all people decide together as to who would live where and who would give up what land. He reiterated that the plan may initially come from 'the books', but it needs to work with what people know about their local resources: 'Let us take things and put them into our hands so that we be the *managers* of our wealth. There is no one who will come to *manage* you.' [Emphasis signifies the use of English words in the originally chiShona utterances.] Control was to be democratic.

He talked about wildlife because the Campfire programme in Mukwichi and elsewhere at that time was mainly about building protective areas to sustain the wild animal population to attract foreign hunters and tourists whose trophy or safari fees would be returned to, or shared with, the wards where the animals were located. The idea behind Campfire was to combine the conservation of animals with the potential to earn foreign exchange from the lucrative international wildlife industry. Like most Zimbabwean development programmes, Campfire is centred around 'land-use planning'.

As the above quotations from the Agritex officer demonstrate, officials involved in rural development programmes in Zimbabwe tend to be sensitive about the charge of 'top-down' planning. This sensitivity, as senior district Agritex officers informed me, comes from the fact that much of the development thinking in Zimbabwe today, particularly the emphasis on 'land use planning', is identical to the Native Land Husbandry Act of the 1950s which was a source of African nationalist discontent (e.g. Drinkwater 1991). The tension between these plans and their rhetoric of local control has been the subject of a number of studies (e.g. Worby 1992, Alexander 1993, Moore 1998), particularly on the Campfire programme itself (e.g. Murombedzi 1992a, 1992b, Farquharson 1993, Derman 1995, Hill 1996). Following these studies, I now sketch the power relations that come with development programmes in Kazangarare, stressing more the forms of authority they envision rather than giving concrete examples of their application.

Agritex's land use plans and (not) 'villagization'

There were a few Agritex demonstrators within Mukwichi, officials whose job was to ensure that people farmed 'properly'; they assisted and instructed people in constructing contour ridges and, especially, in planting more cash crops such as soya beans, sunflowers, cotton, and tobacco. The local Agritex officer informed me that they were especially promoting Virginia tobacco because it was the most profitable cash crop suitable for the soils of Mukwichi. Although inputs were costly, the government's Agricultural Finance Corporation (AFC) would provide loans; indeed, he claimed that tobacco was one of the few crops for which it still provided loans to peasant farmers. By promoting Virginia tobacco, he expected Mukwichi farmers to 'diversify their crops and move from a subsistence to a cash economy'.

This transition from subsistence-to-cash, as discussed before, has been the common metaphor used to describe the Communal Lands (and colonial Tribal Trust Lands/reserves) within Zimbabwe's development discourse. Such a discourse produces the notion that 'peasants' have not taken advantage of the fruits of the market place and that only through proper tutelage and planning would they 'develop' and become modern, cash-oriented farmers, thereby limiting their current soil-depleting practices and reducing overcrowding. Such a discourse has helped certain farmers. Most told me that the Agritex officers would only assist those farmers growing tobacco and cotton. Moreover, these farmers had access to significantly more credit from the AFC than other farmers. This credit, if farming went well, allowed them to increase their monetary wealth.

One Kazangarare farmer I came to know was a very successful Virginia tobacco grower. He combined loans from the AFC with family labour and farming skill to make, for a Mukwichi farmer, significant amounts of money. When he left his position as a senior worker on a Karoi commercial farm in 1988, he received a loan of $8,500 which he used to start growing Virginia tobacco. Through hard work by him and his family, investing a portion of the loan in barns and the remainder into expanding production to two hectares, he made $57,000 in profits in 1990-91 and $35,000 in profits the following year, the year of the drought, in which most of his neighbours lost their entire maize, groundnut, and sunflower crops. He was a development success story. His recent farming life matched the narrative of progress charted out in development discourse while taking advantage of the select opportunities legitimated by the charting itself. And the chart of development planning in Zimbabwean state practices tends to have land-use planning as its lodestar.

'"Villagization" is not the word I would use', a senior official of the Ministry of Local Government, Rural and Urban Development in Hurungwe District explained to me. 'Land reorganization' was the official choice of words. Land reorganization aimed to allocate people and things according to what planners and officials deemed to be their most ecological and, more importantly, most economic potential. Although land reorganization is a national plan of development for Zimbabwe, its local implementation requires the consent of the 'villagers' themselves. The 'village' meant a VIDCO, the postcolonial entity putatively containing a thousand adults. Once given approval by the VIDCO, an Agritex officer goes to an area and maps out the key variables – the human and domestic animal population, the economic and social infrastructure present and needed, the ecological topography, current land-use and capability. Next, the officer outlines the resource requirements of the area according to Ministry standards for proper land use for gardens, wood-lots, cropping, pasture, and residential space. This proposal then awaits funding from different government Ministries and, if the funding and political will materialize, the 'plan' will be implemented.

By early 1993, only two 'Planned Village Settlement Reports' had been prepared for the Kazangarare area of Mukwichi. The reports were frank about the political risks of implementation; they not only implied upsetting people's current settlement patterns and redistributing land and other resources (according to the optimal figures of economic land/person/livestock ratios for different soil types), they also proposed to relocate a significant number of the people currently farming that area. As one report for a Kazangarare VIDCO pointed out, 74 per cent of the current population, or two hundred families, would have to be moved. The report acknowledges 'constraints' to implementing this plan, including:

* Unwillingness of families to move away from developed traditional family homes.

* Unwillingness to live in consolidated villages removed from their cropping lands.

* Fear of land distribution and of being displaced.[4]

---

[4] Department of Agricultural Technical and Extension Services, Mashonaland West Province, January 1992. *Planned Village Settlement Report for Hurungwe District, Mukwichi Communal Land, Ward No. 4, Village No. 19 – Dzokamushure*. Harare: Ministry of Lands, Agriculture and Rural Resettlement. p.11.

Although the listing of these constraints could indicate the position of this official and Agritex in inter-ministerial debates about the advisability of land-use planing (of which Agritex officials have often been critical; see Alexander 1993), textually this passage was immediately countered with a standard development formula:

> *Increased yields will result from better land use and increased areas allotted to families will increase family cash income. Draught power will be adequate for all families. The greatest advantage however will be less pressure on the land resulting in the halting of erosion and the securing of the soil resource for posterity. Increased farming income may motivate farmers to*
>
> 1. *return to giving farming operations top priority rather than mining [for gems]*
> 2. *formulate by-laws to control siltation resulting from poor mining practices.*

In addition to these declared advantages having nothing to do with the identified 'constraints', the report echoes colonial-era plans of creating a full-time yeoman peasantry. The government agency assumed that providing the proper resources and optimally balancing the ratios between people, land, and livestock would allow the self-interest of the peasantry to develop; would encourage the moral imperative to 'increase family cash income'; and, consequently, would lead to their own, and Zimbabwe's, development. It was a framework that emphasized planning, with power relations of 'enframing' development (T. Mitchell 1988, 1991). To understand how people were getting land rights in Kazangarare, how they were violating the order of official policies and how the latter were affecting access to resources – in other words, how various forms of control were enabling and prohibiting different people from getting land – I now provide a sketch of the local authorities who have had a say in allocating land in Kazangarare, particularly in Dunga, and how they have related to the official plans.

The contested nature of land distribution

'Farming for business' in Kazangarare

From oral histories, I learned that in the first half of this century Kazangarare farmers practised what has been called 'shifting cultivation' (called *mutemwa*, 'slashed down', by some farmers) to farm, in order of importance, sorghum (*mapfunde*), pearl millet (*mhunga*), maize (*chibage*), nuts and beans. The first two crops were made into a stiff porridge, the staple *sadza*, while maize, which is the dominant grain for *sadza* today, was mainly eaten green (*chinyoro, chinyoko*).

Married men who were already part of the Kazangarare community were able to get land within the *nyika*, the land area, more or less on their own (*madiro*). Not even the *sabhuku*, according to a few elderly *masabhuku* with whom I talked, told people where to live. As there was generally more land than people, these *masabhuku* said, when it came to access to land, no one 'explicitly' ruled (*kutonga*) over other members of Kazangarare:

> *A person could just say, when he would have seen that the land where he is has become unsuitable, he could by himself, out of his own wishes, go to an area where he would like to live. No one rules over him. No one questions him.... About land there was no problems.*[5]

I said 'explicitly' ruled, since there were various forms of power over people, particularly along the lines of marriage, gender and strangers (e.g. Jeater 1993). I was often told that unmarried men and women could not get a *musha* on their own; they could get fields only from their guardians. Married women could not get land on their own either, although they had a series of 'secondary rights' to land through marriage and often were the people who did most of the work on all lands (e.g. Moore 1993). In general, any stranger could get land if first the *sabhuku*, and then the chief, approved of him and his family. 'Foreigners', those men who came from outside the country, however, had more difficulty getting land given colonial policies discriminating against them and local fears about them stealing local women (see Rutherford 1996:490ff).

As in many discourses about modernity, narratives about change in local farming practices provide a sharp distinction between the times before and after money was used for various exchanges (e.g. Bloch and Parry 1989). I do not have a precise sense of when money initially became used for various practices, nor is the transition as complete as some have made it out to be. Most older people I talked with in Kazangarare associated this growing importance of 'money', the 'farming for business' through selling to the Grain Marketing Board (GMB) and to other marketing boards, with Independence.

---

[5]   Taped interview with elderly *sabhuku*, Mukwichi Communal Land. January 14, 1993.

After 1980, the turmoil of the war ended and the new government began to promote the growing of cash crops. There were now agricultural demonstrators in Kazangarare and, on occasion, free fertilizer and hybrid maize seeds were distributed in the area. More people began to seek land in Mukwichi. Farming became profitable for some:

> There are now people who are doing money with the GMB over three thousand, five, six, seven, nine arriving to ten thousand dollars. Each and everyone is saying 'going to work is to waste time when farming gives so much money. Farming is right'. So land is becoming trouble now. Every person is now wanting bigger land. Long back, we were not wanting big fields. We were wanting small fields for farming our food only, for eating. This big-ness of fields came with the GMB. The young generation [vana vadiki-diki] are no longer wanting to work when they have good land. They are becoming 'master farmers' on their own. When they harvested, sent their crops to the GMB, and received their cheques [from the GMB], they become happy.[6]

'Farming for business' has not meant everyone in Kazangarare becoming monetarily 'rich' from farming. Some farmers would have preferred to work in towns because their farm land is unproductive, but they could not find jobs and so tried to make ends meet through farming. Others stay in Kazangarare in order to seek their fortune through 'stones', searching for gems (which they sell to local buyers, notably a nearby white farmer). Many families maintain a *musha* and have people working on the commercial farms. But 'farming for business' has meant changes in Kazangarare.

Elders associated this 'farming for business' with changes in technology, labour forms, and family forms. Rather than using the ashes of burnt trees for fertilizer and needing to shift fields after a number of years, the use of livestock manure and, then, chemical fertilizer and ploughs, contributed to a propensity to farm longer in one place. Labour forms changed from a range of reciprocal work arrangements to the use of money and money-substitutes as payment in exchange for labour (see Worby 1995). The ability to make money from farming (and mining) has also meant that more young men have decided to stay in Kazangarare rather than migrate elsewhere

---

6   *Ibid.*

for employment. All this has led to the increasing demands for, and conflicts over, land.

These demands have helped to fuel the sale of *misha* in Kazangarare, which itself had become a local sign of the growing importance of 'farming for business'. However, most people did not view the purchase of land as a pure market transaction. Buying a *musha* did not entail purchasing the land *per se*, but compensating for the labour the previous owner put into it. As a *sabhuku* put it, 'We do not sell fields. I the *sabhuku* am the one who prohibits the selling of land. When you came here you did not buy it, so leave it like that. Sell your strength [*simba*] which you used when moulding bricks and building your house.'[7] As Kazangarare residents informed me, if one leaves a *musha* without a brick house but with ploughed fields, one could still sell it since one has put work into the *musha*. But if one tried to sell a *musha* with unploughed fields and no brick house, that would be disallowed as no work was put into the land. 'Labour' here, it should be noted, hid a hierarchy of proprietorship within it since the head of the *musha* who received the money from the sale relied on family labour, the work of his wife (or wives) and children, and possibly hired labour.

It was this sense of labour, the implied sense of organizing people to work on the houses and land, that local leaders felt should be compensated, and not the proprietorship over things, the transfer of one's rights to the land and houses themselves. In one way they were reasserting the inalienability of land – land is owned by the land spirits called *marenda*[8] – while assuming, in an altered way, Western property rights.

Such land sales needed the approval of local authorities, some of whom also seemed to be financially compensated for sales. *Misha* sales and the increasing demand for land are indelibly connected to questions of, and conflicts over, leadership and land-distributing powers.

---

[7] *Ibid.*

[8] As others have examined in great detail (e.g. Garbett 1966b, Lan 1985), Korekore polities place a significant emphasis on the *mhondoro*, spiritual ancestors of ruling and conquered lineages, for rain-bringing rituals and chiefly succession battles, among other things. The *mhondoro* are the 'owners of the land'. Kazangarare is a Korekore polity and, consequently, has a number of *mhondoro* who historically have played important roles in rituals for rain, land ownership, and in chiefly politics. However, their power, at least in the early 1990s, was modified by the *marenda*, the 'great spirits of the earth' (*midzimu yepasi mikuru-kuru*), who were the past owners of the land, the autochthons. According to leaders of Kazangarare and one claimant to the position of spirit medium of the senior *mhondoro* of Kazangarare, it was the *marenda* and not the *mhondoro* who cause the rain to come (see Rutherford 1996:489ff.).

'Ruling' and land

The two main sources of legitimation for leaders in Kazangarare since Independence have been traditional authority linked to the royal lineage or to the *marenda*, and government authority of District Council, VIDCOs, and ZANU(PF), though the two sources were not completely separated. The chief, selected according to 'custom' (as politically defined at the time), appointed headmen and kraal-heads, usually from the ruling clan. To be official, these appointments needed approval from the District Administrator. All traditional leaders spoke of their responsibilities towards the *marenda*. In terms of government authority, the legitimacy of VIDCOs and councillors was based partly on their being elected by the people they represented and partly on their strong connections to ZANU(PF). On Hurungwe District Council, all councillors were from the ruling party. The few VIDCO leaders I knew in Mukwichi were also connected to the Party hierarchy and they often identified VIDCOs as vehicles of ZANU(PF).

Each source of authority, however, was used by leaders from the 'other side' for legitimacy. Councillors talked about the importance of the *marenda* and *sabhuku*, while the chief told their people about their need to 'develop' and the importance of villagization. The invocation of the particular rhetoric of authority depended on the discursive context and the strategies used by the parties involved. Yet the ability to negotiate one's responsibility to 'government' and 'development' was a greater asset for local leaders in most situations I came across, than the connections to the royal lineage or *marenda*.

It was around the distribution of land that the distinction between traditional and government sources of authority was predominantly made. Although chiefs and the *masabhuku* continued to distribute land after 1980, they resented what they saw as the removal of their 'customary' powers and characterized the drought as a sign of the unhappiness of the *marenda* over this action. Despite the fact that chiefs were not supposed to 'traditionally' give land, some people got land directly from them, which was criticized by VIDCO leaders and councillors. In short, an important way to demonstrate leadership was to give land (see Kopytoff 1987).

This power was also lucrative. Some used their authority to acquire money from people looking for or getting a *musha*. Many people talked about paying a small 'gift' to a VIDCO chair, a *sabhuku*, councillor, or giving a traditional gift of thanks (*badza*, hoe) to the

213

chief, to ensure that they were placed either on the waiting list for land or on the official register as someone who had paid taxes for the last few years (which would make it appear one had been in Kazangarare before the official freeze on new land distribution).

Both groups of authorities claimed to represent the people of Kazangarare who, for the most part, were defined as anyone living there. Part of the legitimacy of local leaders lay in giving land to people who became dependent on them for any land problems. This strategy, coupled with competing forms of leadership, permitted many people, including many 'foreigners', to get land in Kazangarare. The tension between the two sources of legitimacy, as well as the conflicts between both of these sources and official development plans are exemplified in the history of Dunga.

Dunga: the 'place of Malawians'

The histories of Dunga and Chipatapata indicate the intersecting relations of power within the Communal Lands and how some foreign farm workers have taken advantage of this intersection, though not without risk. By discussing the history of Dunga – the eastern part of what is still officially State Land separating the middle part of Mukwichi Communal Lands and commercial farms – I investigate how different leaders and the settlement itself were legitimated through the competing relations of authority.

The claim to be the original settler was a major source of legitimacy for local leaders in Dunga. This is not surprising given the importance placed on 'founding' status in local Korekore political discourses (Lancaster 1974, 1987, Lan 1985) and the fact that this land was basically uninhabited in the 1970s, aside from the occasional mica miners, guerrillas and soldiers.

After Independence, people slowly began to settle in Dunga. The man who was VIDCO Chair when I arrived, Mr. Moyo, claimed that he was the first settler. He had been a foreman on an adjacent farm; though originally from the Masvingo area, Mr. Moyo had received a *musha* in Kazangarare in the late 1970s. In 1980, he said, the acting Chief Kazangarare instructed him to settle in Dunga and act as a *sabhuku*.

Although there were others who tried to be the land-giving authority in Dunga and who had more substantiated claims of being the original settler, Mr. Moyo had the advantages of having been foreman of a nearby farm and, especially, of holding senior positions in local ZANU(PF) branches.

The Party's support was critical for the legitimacy of the post-Independence settlers in Dunga, especially when the District Administrator tried to remove people from this area of State Land. The District Administrator and other district officials based their decision to evict on their land-use surveys which showed that the only 'economic use' of this land would have to be built around wildlife. Their concerns were joined by local white farmers who demanded the removal of the 'squatters' near their properties.[9] In early 1984, the District Administrator informed those living in Dunga that they would be removed. Local Party leaders resisted this notice of removal and, with the support of the acting Chief Kazangarare and the local councillor, they went through the ZANU(PF) hierarchy right up to '88' (Manica Road, Harare), the then national headquarters of ZANU(PF). Senior Party officials instructed the District Administrator to reverse his decision, and he reluctantly complied.

When the District Administrator finally approved the Dunga settlement, the uncertainty over the legality of the area was (apparently) raised and more people, especially from the farms, began to move there. By this time, most were getting their land through Mr Moyo.

Although Dunga (and Chipatapata to its west) was legally still State Land in 1993, all officials admitted that these areas are administered as part of Mukwichi. However, most officials in Hurungwe with whom I talked were not happy about these settlements, for two reasons. The first was the 'impermissibility' of settlement in such hilly country according to the land-use plans. The second concern was that they saw the existing settlement pattern as too chaotic, too much like a 'reserve', and thus counter to the then policy of not extending 'communal land'. When the government redistributes land from commercial farmers to settlers, they try to ensure that orderly, well-planned settlement and land-use occur; not, these officials emphasized, like the settlement of Dunga.

Yet officials still hoped that they could plan Dunga. Agritex has prepared a 'Planned Village Settlement Report' for Chipatapata that envisions the removal of 71 of the existing 97 households based on calculations which 'show' that there is sufficient arable land for only

---

9   Karoi North ICA minutes, March 17, May 9, July 21, October 26, 1983; January 19, March 15, 1984; Hurungwe Conservation Committee minutes, May 1984.

21 households.[10] The plan also targets more than half of Chipatapata (621 of its 1,154 hectares) for a fenced-off wildlife area. Although no official plan had been drawn up by March 1993 for Dunga, Agritex officials told me that they had similar plans for that area since its soils and topography are 'most suitable' for wildlife in terms of conservation and generating profits for farmers. By that time, officials had started to collect data on the lands and peoples to map out the land-use capabilities of the area. The people most threatened by such an action are those who settled through unofficial channels, like many 'foreign' farm workers.

Commercial Farms and Kazangarare

Farm workers becoming peasants

Rinse and Blair (R/B):

How did you get a *musha* [in Dunga] last year [1992]?

Farm worker (Fw):

Last year I got the *musha* from asking my friend 'please divide your other field for me'. He said 'alright, come and I give you a *musha*'.

R/B: This year, who will go and farm in the *musha* – yourself, your wife, your children?

Fw: My wife is and I too will be helping. When I finish work on Saturday I can go to the *musha* to help... When I see that things are a bother [there] I am able to look for another person to help me. I will be giving him $30 per month. If I am unable [to find such a person], I will look for people who want to work for *piece-work*. [Emphasis signifies the use of English words.] But my wife would be staying there at the *musha*.

R/B: The person to whom you will be giving $30 per month, will he be staying at your *musha*?

Fw: No, because there are so many people at their own *musha* who are wanting to work without wanting to work for the *varungu* [white people]. They will be saying 'we please want a contract [*kondirakiti*]'. To these people, I will be saying, 'you come and do a contract here. You can be paid either by ticket

---

[10] Ministry of Lands, Agriculture and Rural Resettlement. *Planned Village Settlement Report for the District of Hurungwe, Mukwichi Communal Land, Ward No.2, Village No.10 – Chipatapata.* January 1992. Harare: Government of Zimbabwe.

for monthly payments or by piece work so that when you finished the work I give you so much money.' All these things happen in the reserves.

R/B: What crops will you plant this year?

Fw: First, I want maize and sunflowers. If I get a lot I shall sell. If they are not that many, I will just eat them. But I know the sunflowers are for selling.

R/B: To get a *musha* in Dunga, what other people did you see? Or did you just talk to your friend?

Fw: That *sabhuku* I saw him. I registered and he took the number of my *chitupa* [national registration card] and I then 'entered' into Dunga. If you want a *musha* you give $10 [to him] saying that you enter where? In the book... I paid $10 to the *sabhuku* there. The *sabhuku*, his name I have forgotten. I paid $10 because per year people pay $5 for tax. Now [I did this] myself because the people in Dunga have done what? [They say there] are enough. So I paid $10 to be as if I have had two years with a *musha*... Now that *sabhuku* told me that if you want a *musha* you must pay money for two years because if you pay money for one year only, other people will then ask 'that *musha* you were given, when were you given it since the land here was full already?' ... So when I entered last year I did as if I entered in 1991. This I did so that I do not what? To suffer a lot. Because if you want to ask for a reserve these days, they tell you that people have done what? Are enough. If you have your relative [in Dunga] talk with him so that he does what for you? He cuts for you his field [*munda*]. When he has cut it for you, you then register now so that your relative will not have the power to say that 'here it is all mine'. He will not have a way of doing this now because you have registered in the book, so that the *sabhuku* will be able to protect you when your friend wants to remove you from the place he had given you.

In this interview with a farm worker originally from Malawi carried out in 1993 (and conducted in chiChewa and chiShona, the former which Rinse also understood but not myself), many aspects of the relationship between farm workers and Dunga are apparent: a relationship which challenges many of the assumptions stitching together official discourses of development and government of the

Communal Lands. He acquired a piece of land in Dunga in 1992, five years after the District Council's moratorium on the distribution of land. He received it through a friend (to whom he was paying gifts of salt and maize-meal from the farm store), not through 'traditional' or government channels. Afraid that his title was not 'secure' enough, he registered it with a '*sabhuku*' – probably Mr Moyo, perhaps another leader. But to do so, he had to pay the *sabhuku* money to show that he had been paying taxes for at least two years. Although he imagined that his wife would do most of the work at the *musha* and was planning to grow maize, the principal food crop, any notions of 'traditional' farming practices collapse when he talks about hiring 'contract' workers and selling his crops if they are plentiful. The most salient seam-splitting attribute of the above quotation is that it is a farm worker, and a 'foreign' one to boot, who is getting land in Dunga – a common practice among the farm workers I knew, but one that has been unseen and, moreover, defined as transgressive by the official concatenation of power and knowledge.

To give an indication of how common it is for farm workers to obtain access to land in the Communal Lands in Hurungwe, I now turn to the results of my survey of Karoi North farm workers and of farmers in Dunga.[11] 354 out of 790 farm workers (45 per cent) on 15 commercial farms in Karoi North had access to a *musha*. The actual 'ownership' of the *misha* was diverse. Although only about one third of them were the principal 'owners' of the *musha*, most of these workers contributed to the farm production, and probably benefited from its output. Nearly 70 per cent of the workers with a *musha* had it in Mukwichi Communal Land: 160 in Kazangarare, 62 in Dunga/Chipatapata, and 21 in Chundu (a chiefly area to the north-west of Kazangarare).[12]

Of the 354 workers with a *musha*, 61 were born outside Zimbabwe. However, only 14 of them had their *musha* outside the country. The majority (41, or 67 per cent) had a *musha* in Mukwichi, including 19 in Dunga and Chipatapata. Moreover, the fathers of 118 other workers born within the country were born outside it. Given the emphasis on patrilineal ties in gaining access to land,

---

[11] This survey was conducted in Dunga in early 1993. The same people who assisted me in conducting the survey on commercial farms helped in carrying out this survey as well.

[12] In terms of the others: 44 had a *musha* in Hurungwe Communal Land, fourteen on a Hurungwe resettlement scheme, two in Vhuti small-scale commercial farming area. Of those with a *musha* outside of Hurungwe, 49 had one in another Communal Land, two in another resettlement area, and sixteen had one outside of Zimbabwe itself.

these workers would have legally been prevented from getting a *musha* in the colonial period. In other words, at least 179 of the 354 workers with a *musha* would have been prevented from getting one before 1980. I write 'at least' because I did not ask the respondents where their paternal grandfathers or great-grandfathers were born. I suspect that a number of other workers have patrilineal descendants from outside Zimbabwe if one goes back several generations and thus would also have been legally prohibited from getting land.

When I asked who gave the land to the owner of their *musha*, I noticed that some workers would occasionally mix up the titles, for instance calling Mr Moyo a *sabhuku* or even *mambo* (chief), when technically he was the VIDCO leader (granted that Mr Moyo also called himself a *sabhuku* at times). Nevertheless, with those qualifications in mind, it is apparent that there were a number of land-distributing authorities: a *sabhuku* gave 168 of them and a chief gave 24; a VIDCO gave 54 and a father, or another paternal relative, gave a further 54; nine were given by friends, two were purchased, and three were opened up by the person himself (*madiro*). Similar attributes were found in the survey of Dunga farmers, though the percentage of 'foreign' farmers and workers was higher. Of the 151 (out of more than a thousand) household heads surveyed in Dunga, 117 had previously worked on a farm. Seventy-seven of them were born outside Zimbabwe, as were the fathers of 94 of them. All received land in Dunga after 1980. Mr Moyo gave 66 of the *misha* (though twelve other workers referred an unnamed *sabhuku*, which could also mean Mr Moyo). Fourteen said the chief gave them their land, fifteen named another Dunga leader, and seventeen said that the neighbouring *sabhuku* in Kazangarare gave them their *musha*; five received their land from a friend and two said they bought their *musha*. However, 33 of the respondents said they paid money to get their *misha*. Twelve gave money to Mr Moyo and eleven to the chief, paying amounts ranging from fifty cents to $70. The three who paid a friend, spent money ranging from $110 to $600. The two who said they actually 'bought' the *musha*, paid $100 and $160 respectively.

In sum, this brief sketch of the results of the surveys administered to farm workers in Karoi North and to farmers in Dunga shows several important themes. The main one is that many male farm workers in this part of Hurungwe District, 'foreign' and 'indigenous' alike, are also 'peasants' in the sense that many of them have access

219

to a *musha*.[13] Moreover, many of them received land after Independence, through a variety of authorities and, occasionally, paying money to acquire it. I now turn to consider how the different forms of 'government' on commercial farms and in the Communal Lands affect farm workers who are also 'peasants'.

The *varungu* and the 'reserves'

The relations between the commercial farms and Mukwichi are multifaceted, and may be broken down into the broad categories of work, trade, assistance, and conflict.

The greatest connection between the commercial farms and Mukwichi was that many farm worker households also had access to land. Although they did not work constantly at the *musha*, their presence on commercial farms was often important to the economics of the *musha*. On the commercial farms, the workers not only received wages, but also consumer goods and food, such as soap, maize meal and salt, at a cheaper price than they were sold in shops in Mukwichi. Workers constantly sent these goods and remitted money to relatives on the *musha*. This was especially visible during my research since many in the Communal Lands were badly affected by the drought and depended heavily on those who worked on the farms and elsewhere to support them in this way.

Agricultural inputs also travelled from the *mapurazi* (commercial farms) to the *misha*. Some workers received fertilizer and hybrid seeds on credit from their farmers which they sent to their *musha*. In my survey of Karoi North farm workers, in 1991-92 most workers bought these inputs from a store and in 1992-93 received these inputs free from the government. Yet, a significant number of workers bought these items on credit from their farm operators. In 1991-92, 266 of the 370 workers with *misha* purchased seeds, 158 at a store and 80 on credit from the farm operator. That year, 245 purchased fertilizer, 103 at the store, 86 from the '*murungu*', and 38 from the AFC. In 1992-93, 269 workers used hybrid seeds, 132 of them took advantage of the free seed packets distributed by the government, 73 purchased seeds on credit from the farm operator, and 43 bought from a store. That year, 223 used fertilizer, 119 receiving some from the government, 43 from the '*murungu*', 25 from the store and

---

[13] The size of the *musha* varied from less than a hectare to over fifteen hectares. I did not delve into the quality of the land farm workers received, but others have noted how 'foreigners' to a Communal Land polity can be given poor land and be used as pawns in the political struggles of the leaders (e.g. Hughes 1998).

seventeen from the AFC. From the survey of Dunga farmers, the number of those who relied on neighbouring commercial farmers to purchase seeds and fertilizer on credit was smaller: 6 per cent of those who used hybrid seeds and 25 per cent of those who used fertilizer. Nevertheless, except in 1992-93 when the government distributed seed packs and fertilizer free, the *'varungu'* were the second most important source for these goods.

The relatively significant role played by farmers in supplying these inputs on credit to their workers for their *misha*, coupled with the fact that they typically only provided these agricultural inputs to some of their workers, underscores the importance of achieving a senior position in the workforce and of maintaining a good relationship with the farmer. If a worker wants to get these items on credit from the farmer, he needs to be recognized as worthy by the operators. By buying on credit, the worker was able to delay payment, sometimes until after harvesting, and was able to transport the goods to his *musha* more easily than if he bought them in Karoi, the usual alternative to the commercial farms. In other words, credit for agricultural inputs was a significant entailment of the post-Independence 'domestic government'.

The final attribute of 'work' between the two land categories is seasonal labour migration. There were two predominant tendencies within this migration. First, there are those workers who migrate from Mukwichi to work on the farms during the cold season (May to August), usually grading tobacco or picking coffee. As mentioned above, many of these seasonal workers tend to be women. Second, are those workers who leave the commercial farms to work at a *musha* during the growing season (typically from October to May). Again, these are often women. Their husbands or fathers remain behind to continue working on the farms, while they are sent or go on their own to the *musha* of their spouses, parents or in-laws to work in the fields. Those workers who remain on the commercial farms the entire year often assisted with the work in the *musha*. Part of their remitted money was also specifically targeted for paying labour to plough fields, weed, or even to stay at the *musha* permanently, to work 'on ticket'.

Trade was another common feature of the relationship. I knew of several farmers who bought crops from their workers who had *misha* in Mukwichi. Sometimes the worker repaid the farm credit in bags of maize, sunflowers, or groundnuts. The farm operator would use these crops for his own farm or sell them to the marketing boards himself. Such trade was illegal at the time since government marketing boards had monopoly control over external trade in Communal Lands, but it continued with minimal government intervention.

The trading relations transcended the specific ties between farmer and workers. A number of Communal Land farmers who had never worked on a commercial farm also sold crops to farm operators. A few operators who lived next to Mukwichi ran a maize grinding mill and charged significantly less than other businesses there. Mukwichi farmers also sold gemstones to a few known buyers amongst the *varungu* and some (illegally) sold firewood as well.

A different sort of 'trade', which farm operators called 'assistance', also occurred. Some operators who shared a border with Mukwichi assisted their neighbouring farmers in various ways such as providing water-carts and allowing access to their dams or rivers during the drought. The operators did this, they said, both because they were concerned about the effects of the drought and because it was strategic in terms of a 'good neighbour' policy. In return, they would ask the Mukwichi farmers to put up fire-breaks in front of their boundaries with commercial farms and to prevent annual cold season fires from spreading onto the farms. One farm operator even sent his equipment into the neighbouring area of Mukwichi to build a rain-fed dam. In exchange, the local Party leader gathered people living under him to work for free on that farm for an agreed number of hours. Indeed, it was commonly through the idiom of employment that white farm operators explained their greatest assistance and edification of peasant farmers: by giving them work, white farmers often saw themselves as not only giving Africans access to money but also modernizing them into the 'Western', or 'European', way of life, and out of the 'traditional' world that was assumed to exist in the 'reserves'. In other words, such 'assistance' involved a paternalism and a form of control, a control which was exercised when farm operators were displeased with the actions of Mukwichi farmers or their leaders. This was one side to the type of 'conflict' I heard about between Karoi North farm operators and Mukwichi farmers.

When neighbouring farm operators were upset with actions taken by peasant farmers – ranging from stock theft to fence-cutting, from illegal grazing to trespassing – they often would take actions to punish the nearby residents if they could. As one operator who lived next to Mukwichi informed me, 'it's important to have a lot of sticks to use as leverage against the reserve farmers'. Actions taken by farm operators included cutting credit, prohibiting access to water-sources, closing down the cheap grinding mill they ran, holding the mail they received for Mukwichi residents, shooting stray animals, and fining trespassers. Like the feelings of dominance assumed by farm operators towards their workers, these actions were buoyed by notions that operators were providing (modern) assistance to their neighbours. If the peasants did not want to 'play by rules' of modernization, then many operators did not feel any compunction to carry out the activities described above.

The reasons given by Mukwichi farmers for conflict with the *varungu* were in turn diverse. Some claimed that people stole fencing wire and let their cattle and goats graze on the commercial farms because of their relative poverty compared to that of farm operators. Others gave more overt political reasons for the conflict, claiming that a few neighbouring white farmers stole land from the Kazangarare area. From such a perspective, the cutting of fences and the 'trespassing' were interpreted as assertions of ownership of these areas.

But such claims were not unambiguous, nor were they made by all Kazangarare farmers and leaders to whom I spoke. Even the history of Dunga was a contested field, with different evidence and claims about when, and if, the land had ever been farmed by Kazangarare people who were then removed by colonial officials. However, more often than not, local officials and politicians told me that Dunga and Chipatapata were settled by peasants reclaiming their 'home'. Although they might not have agreed with the unplanned way such settlement had occurred, these officials supported the 'return home' taken by 'local peasants' since it fitted within the dominant narratives of 'development', of 'government', of the Communal Lands and of the identity of 'peasants' with their 'home' areas. Farm workers did not fit so neatly into these narratives.

Betwixt and between: farm workers in Mukwichi Communal Land

> *If you are living well [with your neighbours], we do not call you 'strangers' (vauyi). There is not reason to do so. We are all people [vanhu]. Tell me, we can call you 'strangers' on what grounds? That is why you hear in the reserves people saying 'why are these local [Korekore] people calling us 'strangers', 'strangers'?' However, the mistakes some of you*

> *are doing, they are the ones which are causing local people*
> *to speak like that... There are some who live by offending.*
> *Look, there are drums which live in here, belonging to the*
> *local marenda, to the local spirits (midzimu). We [citizens of*
> *in here] do not know them [the drums], but you who come in*
> *here yesterday went and unearthed them... We knew that if*
> *we ever arrived in this place [where the drums were hidden],*
> *it was sacred. [This violation of our local sacred areas] is*
> *why you hear us saying the word 'strangers'. Even though*
> *we know it upsets some, there are some of you causing us to*
> *say that. Now, we do not want the custom of calling every*
> *new person a 'stranger'. No, we do not want that.*[14]

These words were spoken by the Ward 3 councillor in Kazangarare at a February 1993 meeting in Dunga. He was addressing concerns of some Dunga residents, who were originally (or patrilineally descended) from 'afar', that 'citizens', the 'owners of the land', or Korekore people, were calling them '*vauyi*', a derogatory word for 'strangers'. Although the councillor was trying to calm tensions and point out that there were no differences between 'them' and 'us', he was also blaming 'them', the foreigners, for bringing such insults upon themselves by not living according to local rules. In addition to those who 'dug up the sacred drums of the *marenda*', he noted that some planted a type of sorghum which violated the prohibition from the *mhondoro* Chimhuka against growing the crop: 'Look, the rain has been a problem, the blame is with the people who planted sorghum. In our area, we do not want it. You hear a person say, "at our old *musha* we eat sorghum, I want to plant it". Now, is it not that we all suffered because of this case of sorghum? You see now, this is when we say "you are strangers now"'.

The councillor was warning 'foreigners' that they needed to obey the rules of Kazangarare not only in order to live well with the 'citizens' without being insulted, but also to be able to continue living there. Although he did not make such an open threat, he did digress into the above topic after discussing the importance of everyone who came from 'Zambia, Malawi, Mozambique or Botswana' bringing their citizenship cards when they registered to vote in the upcoming Rural District Council elections (held in June 1993). Moreover, he went on to warn those who settled illegally:

---

[14] Taped meeting between Councillor Chigutiro and people of Dunga, Chikoro school. February 23, 1993. All quotations come from this meeting.

Now see your badness, you who have been given land so that you could farm here then say 'friend, I found land in Kazangarare'. Then another one would come also, 'friend, I have my relative, also this one'. You see now. This would mean that all of you will be chased away because you were not given land for many of you [but only one of you].

He then let it be known that those who were giving land to friends, who had 'badness', were the 'foreigners': 'We the owners, we are failing to get land for our children.'

The councillor was aiming his veiled threat at 'farm workers', most of whom were these 'foreigners'. If they did not abide by local rules and regulations, he implied that they could be removed from Kazangarare for not being national 'citizens'. Although he specified those who were not registered properly, the tenor of his speech gave the impression that all people from afar, all *vauyi*, could be targeted for removal. Colonial legislation which had discriminated against 'foreign' Africans has continued to have salience in post-colonial Zimbabwe. Moreover, the colonial concatenation of power and knowledge regarding 'development' has also continued to marginalize farm workers on the basis of their assumed liminal morality.

When I asked 'indigenous' Africans in Kazangarare who had never worked on commercial farms before (but rather worked in towns or on mines) why others from the 'reserves' have worked on farms, they inevitably mentioned 'laziness', the person was a 'lazy person' (*nyope*). For instance, in answer to my question about whether people from Kazangarare in the past worked seasonally or year-round on *mapurazi*, an old *sabhuku* replied, 'Usually *nyope* (lazy people) were already living there, they were already 'lost ones' (*machona*) living at work [year-round]. People who were not enjoying working in the reserve were wanting to sit only on the farms, drinking beer themselves.'[15] The *sabhuku* emphasized that people would work seasonally on farms to get money to, for instance, buy clothes and pay for bridewealth. But the responsible man from Kazangarare would then be able to return to his *musha* and live, more or less, by farming. Commercial farm work should have been a temporary affair for Kazangarare farmers. Going elsewhere for work – to Salisbury or to South African mines, for instance – was a respectable endeavour for, the assumption went, one earned more and lived in places with more opportunities than found on *mapurazi*. Farm work was for *nyope*.

---

[15] Taped interview with elderly *sabhuku*. Mukwichi Communal Land. January 14, 1993.

For me, the underlying message resonated with the one that politicians and the media occasionally put forth: People who work on farms are 'lazy' because they do not work for themselves but work for a *murungu*. They work in the low-paying rural areas rather than in the (generally) higher-paying and 'modern' urban areas. They lack the self-discipline to become developed on their own, to improve the farming potential of their *musha*. Therefore, they require the supervision of a farmer to do farm work, for which they receive money to spend on frivolous things like beer. These people, in other words, lack the 'development' ethos that has been promoted since at least the 1940s by government officials, school teachers, missionaries, and national and international non-development organizations for and within the Communal Lands.

If 'indigenous' Africans who have worked on farms for long periods get typecast as those who fail as subjects of development in local discourses in Kazangarare, 'foreign' farm workers are devalued by a similar moral discounting over and above their 'foreign-ness'. 'Farm workers,' opined a senior government official in Hurungwe, 'came here to look for jobs on mines and farms. If they have lost those jobs I do not think it is proper to give them land. They are non-citizens, what other country in the world allows non-citizens to get land? Land is an economic unit. For resettlement and other development policies, the government should now consider economic potential and citizenship as the main criteria in selecting candidates.'

I queried him about the practice of giving citizenship to long-time residents after 1980. He dismissed the 'one dollar citizenships' (as discussed in Chapter Two) as having no legal weight, explaining that the granting of such citizenship was an electioneering gimmick by ZANU(PF) to ensure that farm workers vote for them. 'The difference between such citizenship status and authentic citizenship,' he pointed out, 'is evident on the metal national registration cards which everyone has. *Bona fide* citizens have cards which say 'CIT'. Cards that have 'NCR' on them are held by non-citizen residents, those who were born in another country but have lived in Zimbabwe for most of their lives. Recent immigrants to the country have cards that have 'ALIEN' imprinted on them.' He suggested that the recent government 'policy shift' concerning resettlement and development meant that those with the latter two national registration cards would be automatically disqualified from getting land. He even hinted that those 'foreigners' who had found land were the cause of the overpopulation and the disregard for land-use planning in Hurungwe and that they may be purged from resettlement schemes and from Communal Lands. 'Foreigners should only look for jobs not land,' the official stated emphatically.

In his portrayal, farm workers in general are 'foreigners', originally born outside Zimbabwe. Farm workers born in Zimbabwe but patrilineally-descended from outside are also included as 'foreigners': their national registration cards, if they have them, tend to have 'NCR', not 'CIT', inscribed on them. Falling back on the colonial assumption about rights of immigrant workers, this senior official assumed that farm workers as 'foreigners' should be in Zimbabwe to work for someone, not for themselves. He assumed that those farm workers who have found land and have dedicated themselves solely to peasant production have violated the terms of their implicit contract with the government.

This idea of 'working for someone' has also marked farm workers as morally weak candidates for 'development'. In Chapter Two, I discussed how editorials and comments by politicians since the late 1980s have portrayed farm workers as lazy and undisciplined for development projects like resettlement. I heard such a portrayal first hand from a senior district Agritex officer who shed light on what future resettlement schemes might look like in Hurungwe.

He said that since the soil in Hurungwe is generally ideal for tobacco production and this crop tends to be the highest earner of cash per unit input, Agritex had been planning future resettlement schemes in the district along the lines of the ZTA's 'small-scale producers' scheme' (see ZTA 1992:31ff.). The government would settle commercial farms that it had purchased according to a formula which permitted one person to plant ten hectares a year on a four year rotation, or forty hectares per person. Unlike previous resettlement models, which gave either an individual a permit to farm a small piece of land or a collective as a whole the rights over the farm, these settlers would be under what he called a 'resident manager' who would supervise them and be in charge of financial management for the group as a whole. He intimated that retired (white) commercial farmers might be candidates to be these resident managers, given that they have the skills in farming and experience in managing people.

Whereas commercial farm operators could potentially play a role in future resettlement projects in the District, this Agritex official informed me that farm workers would probably no longer have a presence in resettlement schemes in Hurungwe. 'The candidate should have some tobacco training at one of the teaching centres or at least a Master Farmer's certificate given out by Agritex and should be approved by his VIDCO and councillor.' When I inquired about farm workers who lack formal training but have vast experience in tobacco, he granted that such background is important. But, he added, based on previous resettlement experience, when farm workers won political sympathies for their 'squatting' rights and places on resettlement schemes, it did not work out. It had been 'proved' that without the supervision of a farmer, farm workers were not successful.

The identity of 'farm workers' in official configurations has led to the common assumption that as 'foreigners' they should be prohibited from getting land and should only work for others, and that as 'farm workers' they are too accustomed to working for others and thus lack the proper moral disposition for 'development'. They were betwixt and between the already considered agencies of modernity (commercial farmers) and the already constituted subjects of development (traditional-to-become-modern peasants). To put the predominant assumptions in official discourses succinctly, farm workers in the Communal Lands and resettlement schemes are in the wrong place. The combination of their official identity of being foreign and dependent on farmers, in conjunction with the inscription of the space of 'the reserves' and resettlement schemes as the site of modernization through planning, transgresses the historically sedimented contours of power and knowledge within the government and development of rural Zimbabwe.

Conclusion

The history of domestic government and the genealogy of development has produced an identity for farm workers that portrays them as lacking the 'development' ethos, the self-interest to be productive and to transform themselves into modern subjects. Farm workers should not have land because the responsibility for edifying them lies with farm operators, rather than with the government or themselves.

And yet, as discussed above, many farm workers in Karoi North do have access to land in Mukwichi. Farm workers have taken the initiative to obtain a *musha* as a way to supplement their income, as a place of retirement, or to help them to leave the commercial farms themselves. They have played an important part in the increased settlement of Kazangarare and in creating a demand for land that has led to both the sale of *misha* (albeit on a small scale) and the increased rivalry between competing land-delegating authorities. Utilizing patron-client ties forged within the arrangements of domestic government, farm workers have substantially added to a series of ties between commercial farms and Communal Lands, acting as a source and conduit of labour and credit, marketing and assistance. They have also contributed to the rise of 'farming for business' initiated by the growing government presence in Mukwichi after Independence.

Overall, the effects of these ties between farm workers and Mukwichi are many; the varied economic practices and motivations of farm workers who also farm cannot be narrowed down to some either/or evaluation of 'development' spin-offs and constraints. In local politics, 'foreigners' occasionally becomes a synonym for 'farm workers' in the contests over positions of authority and land distribution but, in my experience, 'farm workers' were never described as *persona non grata* by Mukwichi farmers. Although 'locals' who had chosen farm work over *musha* farming were considered to be *nyope*, lazy people, such assumptions about their work ethic tended to disappear once they and 'authentic' farm workers (*vanhu vemuserefu*, people from afar) entered into the *misha yenyika* (rural homes of the land). Although Korekore farmers stated that farm workers farming in Kazangarare periodically violated the *mitemo yenyika* (laws of the land) by ignoring various taboos imposed by the *marenda* and *mhondoro*, they never claimed, at least in responding to my questions, that 'people from afar' transgressed the 'plan of *budiriro*' (development). Government officials and statements, however, made such claims based on the 'facts' that farm workers are 'foreigners' and that they lack the ethos of development, an 'ethos' defined largely as an ability to follow the rules of planning.

Dunga epitomizes the 'place' where such conflicting portrayals of farm workers as peasants are most apparent. Farm workers provided the impetus for the settlement of Dunga. With the assistance of the Party, the District Council, and Chief Kazangarare, they legitimized their presence in the face of antagonistic government officials and white farmers. Yet, at the official level, there was great concern over the disregard for development plans in Dunga and suggestions were made to remove the 'foreigners' and implement a land-use plan to bring 'success' to the remaining farmers and to Hurungwe itself.

By examining the overlapping spheres of knowledge and power that define the 'local' and 'official' discourses of places such as Dunga where farm workers are also peasants, I have tried to explain how the modernizing assumptions of development have been challenged. Narratives on the modernization of Africans, the development of the reserve, the stabilization of workers, and the foreign-ness and dependence of farm workers made farm workers-becoming-peasants a transgressive subject in the early 1990s, a violation of the jural identitics and teleological histories inscribed in the entailments of different spaces within the genealogy of power.

It is through critically understanding this genealogy that I contrast my position with those more firmly ensconced in development practices and discourses. Such official forms of edification rely on jural identities, subjects made authoritative in bureaucratic government and/or disciplinary government, identities which underpin interventions, arrangements, and self- and other-definitions. By saying that farm workers have been marginalized from development efforts, I am not advocating the inclusion of farm workers into the development apparatus as currently constituted. Rather, I am suggesting that the experience of farm workers within these institutions of colonial and postcolonial Zimbabwe indicate the problems with much official thinking about 'development', its institutional arrangements more broadly, and the way it deals with farm workers in particular.

Chapter 8

The limits of official edification

The formal identities in official discourses about development in rural Zimbabwe have been used to empower certain forms of action and marginalize others. Bound to these identities are norms of proper conduct and subjectivities that, in return, have instilled and distilled the relations of rule in historically and spatially distinctive ways, in a particular 'spatial order of things'. I approach these by representing the heterogeneous lives of commercial farm workers who, while homogenized by the jural identity of 'farm workers', historically have fallen betwixt and between the figures of 'European farmers' and 'African peasants' in official discourses; they have been placed more or less under the personal responsibility of (white) farmers. The resulting regime of what I call domestic government has empowered certain forms of activities and strategies on commercial farms, such as patronage by farm operators and the dominance of the *mitemo yepurazi*, laws of the farm, over any existing or possible national regulations governing work and non-work activities. Domestic government has also constrained activities, such as more women gaining permanent jobs and the establishment of effective and autonomous organizations of workers.

My argument has a double thrust. The first is that domestic government is a base for a plausible explanation of the power relations informing the lives of commercial farm workers in Zimbabwe (as opposed to the more conventional dual economy arguments). Second, my ethnographic discussion of local discourses in Hurungwe District aims to amend the tradition of domesticity in modern Zimbabwean politics. In conclusion, I now bring together some of my arguments concerning the dynamic interplay between official and local discourses – an interaction of which I was, and continue to be, a part – and underline my proposed amendments to the arrangements of domestic government. I also discuss possible implications of this new-found visibility of farm workers in discussions of land distribution and rural development in the late

1990s and for those advocating on behalf of, and trying to develop, farm workers.

Domestic government and land distribution

As changes occurred within the government of Southern Rhodesia during the 1940s (see Chapter Two), colonial officials and academics began to shift their attitudes towards, and understandings of, 'natives'. A sense of a secular missionarizing towards Africans in the form of modernization, bringing 'natives' into the 'modern' world of values and practices, became widespread and legitimate in the relations of rule. This entailed both an expansion of state interventions in African lives and a consolidation of particular identities within official discourses. Both activities depended on, and reinforced, certain social territories, places which became saturated with certain identities and which justified particular actions. Thus, in the rural areas, native reserves became marked as the responsibility of government and its development programmes. Farm workers by contrast, being located on European farms where white men were able to represent themselves to a sympathetic government, became the responsibility of white farmers.

The liberation war and Independence itself in 1980 signalled certain shifts within the relations of rule. In particular, the legal status of farm workers changed from 'servants' to 'employees' and ZANU(PF) cadres and trade union officials began to be active on commercial farms. However, as the decade progressed the economic importance of commercial farms, as forcefully articulated by farmers' organizations, international agencies, and some government officials, weakened this wider support for farm workers and gave fresh strength to the domestic authority of farmers.

After 1980, the development apparatus in the newly named Communal Lands continued to target African peasants for modernization. In Chapter Seven, my account of the government of Mukwichi Communal Land investigates the practices through which farm workers, particularly those who are called 'foreign', fit themselves into localized contours of peasant areas. Here, the official depiction of farm workers helps to make visible the administrative relations in the development of 'peasants'. Those who have worked on commercial farms for most of their lives have been active participants in the rise of 'farming for business' in the Kazangarare area, given their desire to farm and their connections to credit from farmers. Yet, many officials with whom I talked, and official commentary in the media at the time, portrayed farm workers as disrupters of 'development', as a group of people more suited for working under the discipline of commercial farmers than for themselves and for the prosperity of Zimbabwe in future resettlement schemes. However, the frequent transgression of local administration by farm workers, local leaders and Communal Land farmers indicates to me that the problem lies more with the top-down thrust of local government and development planning than with a category of people like 'farm workers'.

Policy-makers typically dismissed GAPWUZ's consistent demand that the workers on farms taken over for resettlement should be offered the chance to be given land. However, the pressure on policy-makers has been increasing since the formation in 1995 of an advocacy group composed of organizations working with farm workers (the Farm Workers' Advocacy Group) and with the growing interest by donors and non-governmental organizations in farm workers. Their clear message is that policy-makers need to take farm workers into consideration in plans for land distribution.[1] This has had some positive effects on raising the visibility of farm workers in policy-making circles. For example, the Ministry of Public Service, Labour and Social Welfare carried out a survey in 1998 to look at the effects of land distribution on farm workers living on designated farms and by 1999 official land policy documents recognize farm workers as a target group for land resettlement (see Moyo, Rutherford, and Amanor-Wilks 2000 for further discussion).

But this begs the question whether those policies will ever be implemented, given the very politicized history of the land question in Zimbabwe (Rutherford and Worby 1999) and the fact that as I write in July 2000 over 1,600 white-owned commercial farms (according to the CFU) across the country have been invaded by people organized largely by the Zimbabwe National Liberation War Veterans Association in tandem with leaders of ZANU(PF) and the government. The operations of many of these farms have been disrupted, the movable property of both farmers and workers in some instances has been taken or destroyed by the invaders, farmers and workers have been threatened, physically attacked, and even killed while the police look on and President Mugabe praises the

---

[1] Personal communication with Godfrey Magaramombe, coordinator of Farm Community Trust of Zimbabwe.

'war vets' for retaking the land 'on their own' (see on-line stories from February 2000 onwards on, among other sites, *Daily News, Financial Gazette, The Herald, Weekly Mail & Guardian,* and *Zimbabwe Independent*).

The stated objectives of the invaders, according to their leaders, are to forcibly retake the land stolen by 'whites' and to punish the white farmers for their vote in the February referendum, in which a new constitution assembled by a Presidentially-appointed Constitutional Commission was rejected by over 55 per cent of those voting. Given that before the referendum the ruling party had modified the Commission's draft to enable, among other things, the government to expropriate farms without fully compensating (white) owners, the spokesmen for the land invaders said farmers mobilised farm workers to vote against the referendum. The other initial purpose was to intimidate people, particularly farm workers, into voting for ZANU(PF) in the June parliamentary elections, rather than for the opposition Movement for Democratic Change (MDC). The MDC emerged in September 1999 out of the Zimbabwe Congress of Trade Unions and other civic groups and whose popularity grew dramatically before and after the referendum as Zimbabweans reflected on their declining economy and the numerous cases of corruption.

Just as the guerrillas viewed farm workers ambiguously during the liberation war, so again they are viewed on the one hand as puppets of 'the white colonisers', as people whose interests, like those of the 'whites', are said to be against those of (indigenous) Zimbabweans, and, on the other hand, as people who are exploited by settlers and whose interests lie with Africans against whites. For instance, President Mugabe alleged at a rally that white commercial farmers influenced their workers to vote No, and so are being punished by the land occupations. As he declared, 'We will discuss with the ex-combatants to have the land they occupied demarcated. But we want the whites to learn that the land belongs to Zimbabweans' (*Herald* on-line, March 11, 2000). At a later rally on a commercial farm in Mashonaland West, another ZANU(PF) Minister, Ignatius Chombo, also notes the allegation that farm workers are 'foreigners' but gives it a different interpretation:

> 'We know that there are some people who are saying you will
> be sent back to Malawi or Mozambique,' he told supporters
> at Maplanka Farm near Mutorashanga. 'I want to assure you

*that no one will be sent back anywhere...you belong here
and you will die here in Zimbabwe,' he said, adding that
blacks were united and never knew of any boundaries
separating countries before the coming of the whites.* (Herald
on-line, April 10, 2000).

Even if sufficient stability emerges for a policy to be implemented,
I suggest that farm workers' organizations need to attend to some
historically embedded attributes of the identity of farm workers to
assist in their arguments. As the above quotation intimates, the
suitability of certain identities for policy discussions is undermined
by the assumption that farm workers (like 'whites') are 'foreigners'
who lack a right to land in Zimbabwe, and by the notion that they,
as a category, require supervision in order to be productive (see
Moyo, Rutherford, Amanor-Wilks, 2000). For example, in 1999 before
the current Party- if not state-led farm invasions occurred, district
and provincial ZANU(PF) politicians in Mashonaland East were
telling me that the mere listing of farm workers as a category to be
resettled did not mean they actually will be resettled, becuase many
senior Party and government officials and leaders still saw them as
'foreigners' who should have no rights to land in Zimbabwe. As
farm worker advocates argue, there is a need to revisit the process
of granting citizenship to those born in the country as many farm
workers do not have documentation, thus limiting their participation
in elections and the educational chances of their children (see, e.g.
GAPWUZ 1997, *Herald* on-line, May 26, 2000). But legislative and
policy changes will not automatically alter the dominant identity of
farm workers with its attendant consequences for official access to
land. My discussion of farming activities of farm workers (including
those of foreign birth and descent) outside of commercial farms,
however, challenges this dominant imagination of farm workers in
the nation of Zimbabwe.

Domestic government and rural development

In Chapter Three, I investigate the space of white farm operators,
a pervasive and singular site. 'European' is associated with the
commercial farming sector at large in Zimbabwe, an identity that
informs policy discussions, academic analyses, debates over the
land question, and the forms of authority on white-operated
commercial farms. In other words, 'race' has been a strong factor
in shaping what I have called 'domestic government' on white-
operated commercial farms, producing concrete practices and

expectations that are somewhat different on black-operated commercial farms.

Aside from my 1993 survey that included two black-owned commercial farms, and some brief discussions in 1999 with workers on such farms, my research has not addressed the situation of farm workers on the growing number of black-owned commercial farms (which perhaps comprise twenty per cent of the total). Judging from my brief experience, anecdotal evidence from farm workers, white farmers, government officials, GAPWUZ officials, and members of non-governmental organizations, it seems that a different set of idioms and social practices operates on many of these farms, tending to disadvantage farm workers in terms of living and working conditions more than those who work for white farmers: farm workers can be treated more like junior kin, similar to those working for owners of *misha* rather than as 'African workers' as on white-operated farms. This gap in my own research will, I am sure, be filled by future research. But given the history, demographics and dominant representations of agriculture – by national and international media, farmers and workers, and members and some officials of the CFU – ownership of commercial agriculture is significantly marked as 'white'; a racial identity intimately connected to notions of modernity, edification, and the sanctity of the paternalistic relationship between white farmer and black workers and its precedence over any outside forms of 'government' intervention.

It would be easy to single out this paternalism, given its prejudice that 'African farm workers' are not yet modern, as the major barrier to the creation of sustainable and autonomous workers' organizations on farms. Paternalism, marked by hierarchical, arbitrary decision-making and, in the case of some Zimbabwean commercial farms, its possible use of violence, goes against any commitment to more equitable industrial relations, where workers and their representatives have an institutionalized say in the decisions affecting their working lives.

However, many farm workers are accustomed to this domestic government. They know how to get resources from farmers, be it for their lives in the compound or at the *musha*. In Chapter Four, I examine the practices by which the arrangement of 'domestic government' is played out in 'work', a domain of activity that is officially defined, in the main, for men. After describing the different aspects of tobacco production, I discuss the 'culture of capitalism' as it is modulated by the work practices on commercial farms in Hurungwe District. My point is not that Zimbabwean commercial farms are, say, 'semi-feudal' rather than 'capitalist'. Instead, my ethnography underscores the importance of attending to particular arrangements on farms in order to understand labour relations and work conditions. It is misleading to presuppose a particular organizational form or cultural outlook because of its attributed identity (e.g. capitalist, modern, racist, sexist, etc.).

In Chapters Five and Six, I approach the gendered entailments of commercial farm work. The sites associated with women farm workers, particularly the dorms, are marked by notions of casual labour, sexuality and, especially, family arrangements (or lack of them). Puncturing the story propagated by many farmers that women only work seasonally, an arrangement which farmers claim 'suits them', does not lead, however, to the assumption that all women workers share the same identity or are discriminated against solely because of their gender. Rather, I examine how gender is refracted strongly through the lens of a patriarchal family on commercial farms, how access to resources such as good jobs for women depends on their husbands or male relatives. In turn, by being attached to the domestic government through a husband, a woman worker is more closely connected to the forms of discipline within the farm itself. Women who are not attached to permanent workers, those who are 'single', are marginalized from many of the available resources, though they tend to have recourse to judicial options outside of the domestic government. They also are marked, along with their work and living sites, as sexually promiscuous by other men and women workers and thus are vulnerable to sexual and physical attacks.

In Chapter Six, I discuss the compound as a crucial site within the arrangements of domestic government. Necessary resources for day-to-day living (e.g. water, housing, gardens) are differentially distributed according to criteria based on the intersection of gender, marital status, and type of labour contract. Access to these resources not only plays into differential power amongst workers but also into styles of consumption, particularly the style distinguished by marks of modernity, of respectable bourgeois domesticity itself. Integral to this mode of consumption and access to resources are the decisions of the farmer and his senior workers, particularly regarding credit.

One of the more innovative strategies promoted by NGOs which have recently been providing rural development projects for farm workers is the development of Farm Development Committees (FADCOs), modelled on the VIDCOs in the Communal Lands.[2] Their principal aim is to conscientize farm workers about development issues such as hygiene and health care, mobilize them to carry out related development activities (such as building latrines), and to liaise with farm owners about the needs of farm workers in the compound. These NGOs are thus building upon the sense of obligation towards their workers that many farmers have, but have not always acted upon (though, of course, in some cases the NGOs are building on long-standing efforts of farmers to improve living conditions for workers). The impact of these FADCOs is somewhat unclear, as is the use to which different farm workers and farm operators are putting the projects. Some critics argue that they are being used to harness free labour from farm workers to make improvements to the farmer's property. In a few cases of which I am aware, they are being used by management as quasi-workers' committees, as substitutes for GAPWUZ. Moreover, although efforts are being made to solicit the 'felt needs' of farm workers, establishing FADCOs through 'participatory rural appraisal', there is often an unwarranted faith in the representativeness of methods which claim to be 'participatory' (e.g. Mosse 1994, 1997). Such committees have to be interrogated constantly if the aim is actually to change the power arrangements of farm work. Of course, such radical rear-rangements are likely to meet stiff resistance from farmers (e.g. Gardner 1997). If NGOs are to forge alternatives with farm workers, they need to take into account differences amongst farm workers. To achieve such change, needless to say, requires strong and persistent struggles with and against workers, farmers, their organizations, government officials, and NGOs themselves.

Domestic government and anthropology

My suggested amendments, and my political appraisal of arrangements of power and possible changes, rest on a series of hierarchies in the intersection of official and local discourses, as

---

[2] This strategy was initially implemented in Mashonaland North Province by Save the Children Fund (UK), but is now being promoted in Mashonaland East by the Dutch non-governmental organization SNV and in other provinces by the Farm Community Trust of Zimbabwe. I thank Lynette Mudekunye, Diane Auret, Peter Struijf, Godfrey Magaramombe and Lynn Walker for discussing FADCOs with me in 1998 (see Auret, 2000). My current research is examining these and other NGO-initiated projects in more detail.

did my actual field research and as my writing of this book now does. My analysis indicates what I think are the crucial hierarchies and marginalizations which shape, on the one hand, attributions of identity within the intersection of power and knowledge concerning commercial farm workers and, on the other hand, their (differentiated) access to various resources. I have also discussed some of the deflections, the talk-back, and the creative use of these power relations by different farm workers in Hurungwe District.

I valorize 'power' as an heuristic tool to assist my critical analysis of commercial farm workers. I use it to bolster the points of view embedded in my critical ethnographic (re)presentation. At the same time, I make plain that it is a provisional point of view, which I hope others will engage with and perhaps be swayed by – it is not a metaphysical concept supported by epistemological claims. To free my argument of appeals to epistemology, I disclose the influence of the intersection of official and local discourses on my own study: I highlight the situated-ness of the 'I' carrying out the research and writing the book.

Yet in doing so, I also privileged the 'I' as the singular 'eyes' and 'ears' of most encounters that comprise 'local discourses' in this study. Such a representation glosses over some of the negotiations, conversations, and power dynamics which inform my under-standings and interpretations (see Briggs 1996 for an excellent discussion of metadiscursive authority within anthropology). Here I must raise, self-critically, the question of my representation of Rinse, who, as my assistant, interpreter in various ways, and friend, played an immense role in my research. Ironically, in a book which places great theoretical weight on 'domestic government' and which criticizes some of its attributes, I tend to downplay 'Rinse' by collapsing his actions and thoughts under an imperious 'I'. This embarrassing truth is itself a comment on the politics of doing anthropology.

As others have shown, conducting ethnographic research is not 'outside' of politics and power (e.g. Fabian 1983, Faris and Wutu 1986). Rather, the condition of anthropology itself has been predicated on global power inequalities. Even those ethnographies which seek to change the world 'for the better' do not escape this field. An example comes from the anthropologist Leigh Binford in his moving ethnography based upon the testimonials of survivors from the 1981 El Salvador massacre by the US-backed and trained

Salvadorean army. Binford (1996:196) aptly summarizes this predicament, or what he calls 'contradiction':

> *In anthropology, this contradiction – between those who are at liberty to describe the cultures of others and those others less able to contest their objectification, whose beliefs and practices are described – lies at the heart of the ethnographic enterprise; it will exist as long as some people have the desire and, more significantly, the opportunity and the power to make objects of the lives of others.*

Although I have tried to put forward my own positioning and politics, this does not give me or this book immunity from criticism. Rather than situating one's politics on what Richard Rorty has called a 'metaphysical' mode of reading – a demonstration that common sense and other 'surface phenomena' are really the effects of something deeper, a 'larger shared power–rationality, God, truth, or history, for example' (1989:91), a hidden system of meaning revealed by one's epistemology – I follow a growing concern within the current theoretical moment of postcolonialism, whereby critics are concerned about locating their critique within the nuances, arguments, and discussions already going on amongst those in the political field they endeavour to join (see Sylvester 1995a). As David Scott (1995:42) proposes, postcolonial criticism is above all strategic, an act which must,

> *self-consciously understand itself as a practice of entering a field of moral argument, of gauging that argument's tenor, of calculating stakes (what might stand or fall as the result of a particular move), of ascertaining the potential allies and possible adversaries, of determining the lines and play of forces (what might count and what might not as a possible intervention).*

While bringing attention to the way I conducted this ethnographic study, I advance suggestions about the need to amend the arrangements of 'doing anthropology'.

Working on the margins

But this book is not just about my political opinion, for politics as discourse is also about narrative, about story-telling. I thus use a narrative to end my critical ethnographic re-presentations of the social arrangements on Chidhadhadha farm in Hurungwe District. I intend this narrative ending to tell the story of the departure of my physical presence from the farm, while I underline the contested, provisional authority of this study itself.

*** *

The night before I left Chidhadhadha farm for my return to Canada in May 1993, I helped organize a party to show my appreciation to the workers. I bought beer and food. Rinse had organized the students of an adult literacy centre called the Night School (which he and I had helped to establish; see Rutherford and Nyamuda, 2000) to prepare some plays for the party. The plays were wonderful, with themes ranging from AIDS to insensitive foremen, from witchcraft to insolent school kids. Individual members of the Night School, including Mai Chido and two of her children, also sang songs, recited poetry, or performed dances. Afterwards, the Nyau dance troupe[3] performed with the tok-tok-tok of the beating drums while the crowd taunted and was taunted by them. The crowd itself was in the hundreds.

Soon after the performances ended, the free beer, bread and tea were served and the music started to blare loudly in the nearby beerhall. There was much handshaking, joking and dancing. The party continued through the night to dawn. It was a *pungwe*, a 'dusk-to-dawn gathering'.[4]

Then, with everyone bleary-eyed in the dawn light of the holiday, Ezia had a member of his Zion Church congregation collect his drum and, to the accompaniment of its beat, he began singing a song while I was saying my final farewells. Rinse and others collected hand-made tambourines and rattles and sang along. Soon, a number of people, many of them friends, were dancing and singing in a circle around the *mufundisi*, the prophet, who also was the village chairman. I was deeply touched. Not because the song was meant

---

[3] Nyau historically comes from Chewa traditions in Malawi regarding men's organizations and ceremonial rituals (e.g. Kaspin 1993). Among other things, Nyau or *zvigure* as it is commonly called in chiShona has become a form of entertainment on commercial farms (and in urban areas) in Zimbabwe.

[4] There is irony here. *Pungwe* is associated with the liberation struggle, in which guerrillas would hold rallies in villages, having people sing liberation songs and listen to speeches on liberation (see Lan 1985). This is also the form used by the Party in 2000 to 're-educate' farm workers away from MDC by making them sing and shout slogans promoting ZANU(PF) and denigrating the opposition, with beatings and other forms of violence also being used (see, e.g., 'Farm Labourers bear Brunt of Invasions', Reuters, April 22, 2000; 'Zimbabwe Farm Workers Targeted', BBC, April 24, 2000; 'Inside Zimbabwe's Terror Camps', *Independent* (UK), May 9, 2000; 'White Farmers Not Going to Vote', *Zimbabwe Independent* June 2, 2000).

solely for me, for I do not think it was. It was a song that brought many workers, not all from the Zion Church, or even Christian for that matter, together in a form of solidarity. Ephemeral as it might have been, it was an emboldening sign, at least for me.

The others present will have different memories and stories about this event and others discussed above. But this event in particular is a lasting one for me because I videotaped it, along with the performances the night before. Only in my last week on Chidhadhadha did I feel that the camera might be another medium to help give insight into the lives of commercial farm workers. With encouragement from Rinse and those workers who helped to organize the *pungwe*, I videotaped much of it. But in so doing, I remained highly conscious of my status as distant observer, physically symbolized by the two kilogram electronic lens in front of my right eye. Although I showed the tape to interested workers later that night on a television borrowed from the headmaster of a nearby school, it did not quell the sense of great inequalities between my life and theirs. The video-camera emphasized the lack of solidarity between me and the farm workers, friends and non-friends, men and women, senior and general workers.

But the lack of solidarity was not surprising given the overlap of identities which form the power relations I have discussed. Solidarity cannot be presumed in postcolonial writings. In this respect, the video camera also shows (some of) the limits of my book. I have discussed events and encounters in which I have been involved as 'local discourses'. My ethnographic discussion of these is limited in the same way as videos are limited: they miss what is happening outside the frame of reference, on the margins of representation. Some scholars have pointed out that this is the nature of representation. Many others try to claim that their representations are closer to more secured truths by appealing to the authority of a greater power (i.e. epistemology). I have instead relied on the provisional authority of a political critique.

Given my place as a 'foreign white male anthropologist', I believe that my critique should not try to be representative of a larger solidarity, for this would disguise the fact that I have not been 'united' with those I studied: neither with farm workers nor peasants, white farmers nor black government officials, men nor with women. Indeed, glimpses of other interpretations, political points of view, and subversions of my discussion may be seen on the margins of my framing of this book, in the various and varied lives of the people I studied. My critical discussion of the local practices among farm workers in Hurungwe District and their intersection with historical and current official discourses indicates that the margins coexist with the dominant identities; identities that are not in any way naturally 'unified' but are formed through the spatially significant arrangement of power relations, the differences and similarities that have informed social practices through the intertwining of localized, national, and international genealogies and through creative play in daily practices. In this book, I describe this privileging of (white) paternalism in capitalist enterprises in rural Zimbabwe, the discursive entailments and effects of the arrangement of domestic government on the lives of farm workers. I also point to some possible amendments. In so doing, I join the emerging critique of conventional ethnography, pointing to the need for an explicitly political engagement in 'the field', which entails overlapping 'heres' and 'theres' (see Gupta and Ferguson 1997). I have worked on the margins trying to understand and critique the unequal social order which keeps so many people working on the margins.

The space of commercial farms, and through that, the lives of farm workers became a national and international concern after the constitutional referendum in February 2000. This first defeat of ZANU(PF) over a national issue, the crucial role played by the National Constitutional Assembly in campaigning for the 'No' vote, and the anticipation of the June parliamentary elections, led many Zimbabweans who wanted a change in government – including a number of white farmers – to embrace the best organized opposition party. Some of these white farmers helped to establish, and often co-ordinated, MDC support units throughout the countryside to raise funds and to assist in organizing activities for the party. According to some of the farmers involved, the acceptance of MDC by many, including farm workers, was rapid and widespread. This political mobilization continued even when the first farms were invaded shortly after the referendum.

Initially the invasions were carried out in Masvingo Province by the provincial members of the Zimbabwe National Liberation War Veterans Association (ZNLWVA) to demonstrate against white farmer support for the 'No' campaign; this support was said to be motivated by antipathy towards the insertion by President Mugabe of a constitutional clause permitting the government to pay only for improvements made to expropriated land, and calling upon the United Kingdom government to pay for the land itself. The ZNLWVA soon co-ordinated invasions on a national level, with input from ZANU(PF) leaders, the Central Intelligence Organisation, and members of other branches of government. But as the MDC continued to set up structures on the commercial farms and in the Communal Lands, the demonstrations for land reform also became explicitly political, turning into an extremely blunt tool for coercing people to vote for ZANU(PF). And commercial farm workers were the biggest target of this intimidation.

Within a matter of days in late March and early April 2000, most of the countryside became prohibited areas for MDC activists, structures and campaigns. War veterans and ZANU(PF) youth groups subjected anyone involved, or suspected of involvement with the MDC, to physical beatings, torture, and even death. Their belongings could be destroyed and their relatives harassed and also beaten. White farmers generally, but especially those who were campaigning openly for MDC, were threatened, their farming operations disrupted, and a few were killed. Farm workers in many areas were forced to attend nightly political re-education *pungwes* and if they resisted, were beaten and had their property stolen or destroyed. Management workers such as foremen were especially targeted for being tools of the *murungu*. In some areas, women and girls have been raped and thousands of farm workers fled the farms for their *musha* or to towns. The rest have continued to work under threat of violence. The top officials of the Zimbabwean Republic Police have ignored High Court orders calling upon them to evict the land invaders, arguing that land occupation is a 'political' issue beyond their jurisdiction.

In the June elections ZANU(PF) won 62 and MDC 57 of the 120 contested seats (ZANU-Ndonga won the remaining one). Almost all of the seats in the three Mashonaland provinces, the sites of the worst violence, went to the ruling party. As I write in August 2000, the farm occupations have continued and in some places have become more intense, with war veterans issuing death threats to some farmers and workers and continuing their beatings. The demand to redistribute land from whites to blacks returned to prominence after the elections, and retribution against (alleged) MDC supporters continues. In early June, the government gazetted over 800 farms for compulsory acquisition and in early August a ZANU(PF) land committee announced that a further 3,000 farms will be compulsorily acquired by the state and resettled before the rains begin in November. A few of the 800 or so gazetted farms that were not contested have been settled so far. These events have created a climate of intense uncertainty and speculation for all Zimbabweans regarding the pace and process of the actual resettlement programme.

In Hurungwe, the invasions began in early March. Today, 160 or so of the 171 white-owned commercial farms (out of 190 commercial farms or so in the Karoi farming area, excluding Tengwe) and one black-owned commercial farm have been occupied, many of which are still housing camps of 'war veterans'. The district has become known to be one of the 'hot spots' in the country in terms of violence, with the town of Karoi and a number of commercial farms closing down for two days in late July in protest against the violence.

In my short visit to Chidhadhadha, which was briefly occupied but whose neighbouring farms still house permanent war vet camps, farm workers told me of their fear of talking about certain issues and of even interacting with others during their daily activities. Politics, particularly support for the MDC, became a taboo subject after the occupations began. Farm workers on many farms in the district were forced to hand over their MDC t-shirts and membership cards to war veterans on pain of being beaten up. War veterans also targeted a few white farmers, and many black managers, foremen, tractor drivers, and cooks on farms, accusing these *vashandi vakuru* (big workers) of being close to the *murungu*. If a worker were to annoy another at work or in the compound, there is a good chance that the offended party will tell the 'comrades' in a nearby camp that the person 'sold out' the comrades and the country by being an MDC supporter, exposing the reported person to the risk of instant punishment. 'It is like the [Independence] war', said one worker. 'We are scared of saying or doing anything or the comrades may inflict pain on us.' As in the war, simply working for whites is enough for one to be viewed as a 'sell-out' by the war veterans. Although workers told me that the MDC held rallies in the area after the referendum, its activities stopped with the invasions and people voted out of fear. The ruling party won the two parliamentary seats in Hurungwe during the June elections.

'Politics' is a word of fear for many farm workers in Hurungwe. Some may want '*chinja*' (change), the rallying cry for MDC, and others may want land (not – or not only – work), the slogan of ZANU(PF), but it seems that for the majority this year politics has only brought misery, fear, and uncertainty of their future. For whenever farm workers mobilised en masse for political change outside of ZANU(PF) in part through white farmers, in part through GAPWUZ, and in part through their own initiatives, war veterans and others with the backing of the state have violently suppressed that mobilisation. This fear may have helped to ameliorate some of the harsh conditions on some commercial farms, for farmers fear their own workers can tell the war vets about their 'oppression'. Yet many people are not certain of their future as farm workers given the claims that over 3,000 of the 4,500 or so commercial farms will be acquired by the government for resettlement. Given the lack of jobs and ever-rising prices, the farm workers I know in the district are anxious about their future; they do not know if they will be selected as resettlement farmers and even so, what type of support they will get from the state and where they can source the money they need for school fees, clinic fees, and daily survival.

There were two dominant narratives at play concerning farm workers and these invasions. Leaders of ZANU(PF), war veterans and the state media saw farm workers as being used by their white

247

bosses to vote for the MDC and carried out a variety of terror tactics to ensure they do not vote that way. For them, the political symbolism of white farmers openly supporting an opposition party was the return of colonial rule, the time when the *baas* coerced people for his own ends. As farm workers were the ones farmers have historically used, the power of the farmers had to be counteracted by the power of the Party. Farm workers had to be 're-educated'. On the other hand, the MDC, many NGOs, donors, the independent (read 'private') Zimbabwean press and international media saw farm workers as victims of state-mobilized thuggery, victimized for exercising their right to freedom of association. They, like white farmers, were the ahistorical liberal citizens whose human rights were being violated and national and international concern and protests had to be mobilized.

As I have talked to Zimbabweans in Harare and on commercial farms from June to early August 2000 about the events in the first half of the year, these narratives are both all-powerful and partial. They have strongly shaped the interpretations given by individuals, especially those aligned with ZANU(PF) or MDC. Yet they also downplay the complexity of power and identities for farm workers, how the hierarchies of domestic government influence their political choices and actions. Whereas the former narrative views domestic government as all-powerful and simply a tool for oppression, the latter ignores it or portrays it in a benign light, as a form of unity between white farmers and their black workers. Given the level of violence and intimidation still affecting many farm workers and thus their interactions with me, it is hard right now to provide a fuller picture of what has happened. But I can draw initial probable consequences for farm workers in the body politic of Zimbabwe, at least for the short-term.[1]

Firstly, the invasions have reinforced a fear of 'politics', of farm workers participating in a wider public that is not engineered by the ruling party. In the early 1990s, farm workers were scared to talk about politics not only because of farmers' sanctions against it, but also because Party cadres had inculcated in them the metaphor *politikisi ihondo*, politics is war, meaning that if anyone ever goes against ZANU(PF), in word or at the polling booth, the cadres will return to the bush, to restart the liberation war. By the late 1990s

---

[1] These thoughts were first presented at a workshop at Yale University in May, 2000 entitled 'Zimbabwe: The Politics of Crisis and the Crisis of Politics. A Meeting of Concerned Scholars.'

the fear of that threat was waning as more and more farm workers I talked with (and Zimbabweans more generally) were openly criticizing the Party and even President Mugabe himself, given declining living standards for the majority and notable incidents of government corruption. The invasions and their violence and 're-education camps' have been carried out in part to revitalize that fear of politics.[2] Some farm workers, of course, have enthusiastically supported the invasions and ZANU(PF), and others have supported MDC. But given the history of domestic government that proscribed participation in any extra-farm 'public', and this reinforced intimidation against participating in any public forums not sanctioned by the Party, it will be extremely difficult for most, if not all, farm workers to contribute to public debate and dialogue outside the contours defined by ZANU(PF) and, perhaps increasingly, by MDC, including on the nature of the 'public' itself.

Secondly, farm workers are once again further marginalized from being officially recognized as a group who should be resettled. The policy documents of 1998-99 on the second phase of land reform and resettlement have been discarded; it seems clear that those to be resettled will be members of the ZNLWVA, which has taken the leadership position in the land invasions, and members of ZANU(PF). There is a strong demand for land amongst farm workers – as shown by my research, by studies on 'squatters' settlements which show that former farm workers comprise the majority in many of these communities (e.g. Zishiri 1998), and by media accounts of the invasions.[3] Indeed many farm workers I have talked with have expressed genuine demand for land, agreeing, in part or wholeheartedly, with the land invasions, though often hoping to retain employment opportunities on commercial farms. Although some of

---

[2] This message has been repeated by many of the leaders of the invasions. For instance, on Trianda farm seventy kilometres north of Harare, a journalist observed the following threat being made: "If ZANU(PF) loses this election, you will not say that I did not warn you. If we lose, we will get out our guns. We cannot allow the MDC to sell our country', said a leader of the veterans, identifying himself only as 'Comrade Zimbabwe'. 'We will be at the voting stations. If ZANU(PF) loses, the way forward will be filled with war', he said in the local Shona language" ('Zimbabwe Veterans Say Poll Defeat Would Mean War,' Reuters, May 7, 2000).

[3] As a foreman in Hurungwe told a reporter, concerning farm workers' rights to land, 'We have worked here. We will die here. We deserve it first.' The reporter then contrasted that viewpoint with that of the people who currently have the power on the farm: 'But veterans' leader Gwagwa, who said he spent decades in guerrilla camps across southern Africa before returning to Zimbabwe, said his men had just as much right to the land. "I fought so that I could make my life better. Now I am back and I have nothing. These people (whites) have taken all our farms. We are only taking some land back and have not done enough yet", he added.' ('Zimbabwe Farmworkers Brace for Violent Night', Reuters, May 5, 2000).

the occupiers have promised land to farm workers, in other cases they have prohibited them from being allocated stands on occupied farms. Given the larger assumption amongst government, Party officials, and war veteran leaders that farm workers have been tools of the farmers and are 'foreigners', it is unlikely that farm workers will be officially welcomed onto whatever resettlement schemes result from the invasions.[4] More farm workers lose their jobs in the wake of redistribution, and farm production will fall as a result of disrupted activities and the resistance of banks to lend to occupied farms. When combined with their marginalization from land resettlement, it seems certain that more farm workers will be moving into the difficult existence of 'squatter' communities.

Finally, there is likely to be a growing dependence on farmers by those workers who do retain their jobs. The land invasions have exacerbated an already declining economy, resulting in growing scarcity of imports and higher prices for most consumer goods. The paternalism of domestic government has already cushioned some farm workers from this deterioration and more will be turning to its hierarchies for assistance in the short term at least; and there will probably be a concomitant reluctance by farm workers to challenge those hierarchies. For those on the margins of domestic government like single women, there will be growing desperation as the inadequacy of their wages turns them more and more towards gathering wild foods, begging, and prostitution.

Although domestic government has provided some, usually minimal, security for farm workers, its hierarchies have also been used by politicians and state-controlled media to question the citizenship and the belonging of white farmers in Zimbabwe. For example, the then Minister of Information, Posts and Telecommunications, Chen Chimutengwende explained away the presence of high numbers of farm workers at MDC rallies by arguing that:

---

[4] According to Philip Munyanyi, the secretary-general of the farm workers' trade union, GAPWUZ, as of August 2000 only 50 of more than 700 farm worker households on the redistributed farms in the fast-track resettlement program had been resettled in two districts in Mashonaland Central province. Fanuel Jongwe, 'Land reform leaves 15,000 families homeless,' *Daily News* on-line, August 28, 2000. In October, the director of an NGO working with farm workers said a total of only 318 farm workers had been resettled so far in the accelerated land resettlement scheme. 'Only 318 farm workers resettled,' *Daily News* on-line, October 6, 2000. A recent article discussed how a government-owned farm in Mashonaland West province has seen the influx of 12,000 families from former white-owned farms looking for a place to live. These former farm workers came of their own volition, were chased away by war veterans, or were dumped there by their employers. Grace Mutandwa, 'Dumped farm workers suffer double blow,' *Financial Gazette* on-line, December 7, 2000.

> *White farmers threaten their workers that they will lose their*
> *jobs if they do not attend the rallies. The truth is that these*
> *workers are ZANU(PF) members who know that their vote is*
> *secret... Commercial farmers were forgetting that some*
> *workers are well informed and know that the whites despise*
> *and treat them badly... Farm workers can never support their*
> *employers because they are ill-treated, underpaid and made*
> *to work like slaves. They know that an MDC victory, which is*
> *a white victory, will not be to their benefit... Farm workers*
> *also know that during colonialism their working conditions*
> *were much worse than they are today and have been*
> *improved through the ZANU(PF) Government* (Herald on-line
> April 4, 2000).

My discussion of domestic government in the colonial period and its altered forms in postcolonial Zimbabwe may help to explain how commercial farmers can be depicted that way, although my intention is not to question their citizenship, or their belonging to Zimbabwe. But the attitudes and practices of domestic government are pervasive, so that when white farmers do publicly promote the good deeds they do for their workers, as more and more have been doing through their involvement with NGO programmes, what they take as a sign of being a good citizen can for others be another sign of dependence of blacks on whites, a reiteration of colonial relations of rule despite the sincerity and goodwill which farmers and some of the workers involved may have. Until domestic government is radically rethought by all, given the memories of colonialism and understandings of race in Zimbabwe, such attitudes towards commercial farmers and their relations with farm workers are likely to continue.

Despite the persistence of domestic government and how it plays out in the imagination of Zimbabwe, the recent events signify a radical shift in tone and outlook for farm workers compared to the end of 1999. By then, farm workers had been thrust more into the public eye than ever before and it seemed possible that for some their situation might change. The unprecedented national wildcat strikes in September and October 1997 made everyone aware that farm workers can fight for their rights as 'workers', a category that has taken on national importance given the growing strength of the country's labour movement. Their franchise in the 1998 local government elections meant that council candidates, mainly from

251

ZANU(PF) but also including white farmers, recognized them as a political constituency with particular grievances and demands, at least during the election period. Their increasing involvement in NGO projects enabled some of them to be regarded by management as having a role to play outside the workplace. Although none of these activities have had totally unambiguous benefits and have been shaped by hierarchies within and beyond domestic government, they do show that the prognosis for farm workers is not uniformly gloomy, that possibilities can re-emerge, that those working on the margins are capable of challenging the power relations which situate them in such a precarious existence.

Adams, Jennifer. 1991a. "Female Wage Labor in Rural Zimbabwe." *World Development* 19: 163-177.

Adams, Jennifer. 1991b. "The Rural Labor Market in Zimbabwe." *Development and Change* 22:297-320.

Alexander, Jocelyn. 1991. "The Unsettled Land: The Politics of Land Distribution in Matabeleland, 1980-1990." *Journal of Southern African Studies* 17 (4):581-610.

Alexander, Jocelyn. 1993. *The State, Agrarian Policy and Rural Politics in Zimbabwe: Case Studies of Insiza and Chimanimani Districts, 1940-1990*. Ph.D. thesis. Oxford University.

Alexander, Jocelyn, and JoAnn McGregor. 1997. "Modernity and Ethnicity in a Frontier Society: Understanding Difference in Northwestern Zimbabwe." *Journal of Southern African Studies* 23(2):187-201.

Alexander, Jocelyn, and Terence Ranger. 1998. "Competition and Integration in the religious History of North-Western Zimbabwe." *Journal of Religion in Africa* 28 (1):3-31.

Alexander, Jocelyn, JoAnn McGregor, and Terence Ranger. 2000. *Violence & Memory: One Hundred Years in the 'Dark Forests' of Matabeleland*. Oxford: James Currey and Harare: Weaver Press.

Amanor-Wilks, Dede Esi. 1995. *In Search of Hope for Zimbabwe's Farm Workers*. Harare: Dateline Southern Africa and Panos Institute.

Appadurai, Arjun. 1986. "Introduction: Commodities and the Politics of Value." In A. Appadurai (ed.) *The Social Life of Things: Commodities in Cultural Perspective*. Cambridge: Cambridge University. pp. 3-63.

Appadurai Arjun. 1990. "Disjuncture and Difference in the Global Economy." *Theory, Culture and Society*. 7:295-310.

Appiah, Kwame Anthony. 1992. *In My Father's House: Africa in the Philosophy of Culture*. New York: Oxford University.

Armstrong, Alice, et al. 1993. "Uncovering Reality: Excavating Women's Rights in African Family Law." Paper prepared out of a Women and Law in Southern Africa Research Project seminar.

Arrighi, Giovanni. 1967. *The Political Economy of Rhodesia*. The Hague: Mouton.

Asad, Talal. 1986. "The Concept of Cultural Translation in British Social Anthropology." In J. Clifford and G. Marcus (eds) *Writing Culture: The Poetics and Politics of Ethnography*. Berkeley: University of California Press. pp. 141-164.

Auret, Diana. 2000. *From Bus Stop to Farm Village: The Farm Worker Programme in Zimbabwe*. Harare: Save the Children (UK).

Baker, D.G. 1979. "Time Suspended: the Quenet Report and White Racial Dominance in Rhodesia." *Zambezia* VII(ii):243-253.

Beinart, William. 1984. "Soil Erosion, Conservationism and Ideas about Development: A Southern African Exploration, 1900-1960." *Journal of Southern African Studies* 11: 52-83.

Bhabha, Homi. 1994. *The Location of Culture*. London: Routledge.

Bhebe, N., and T. Ranger (eds). 1995a. *Soldiers in Zimbabwe's Liberation War*. Volume One. Harare: University of Zimbabwe Press.

Bhebe, N., and T. Ranger (eds). 1995b. *Society in Zimbabwe's Liberation War*. Volume Two. Harare: University of Zimbabwe Press.

Binford, Leigh. 1996. *The El Mozote Massacre: Anthropology and Human Rights*. Tuscon: University of Arizona Press.

Black, Colin. 1976. *The Legend of Lomagundi*. Salisbury: Art Printopac.

Bloch, M., and J. Parry. 1989. "Introduction: Money and the Morality of Exchange." In J. Parry and M. Bloch (eds) *Money and the Morality of Exchange*. Cambridge: Cambridge University Press.

Bourdillon, M.F.C. 1987. *The Shona Peoples*. 3rd edition. Gweru: Mambo Press.

Bozzoli, Belinda. 1983. "Marxism, Feminism and South African Studies." *Journal of Southern African Studies* 9: 139-171.

Bratton, Michael. 1990 . "Ten Years After: Land Redistribution in Zimbabwe, 1980-1990." In R. Prosterman et al (eds) *Agrarian Reform and Grassroots Development: Ten Case Studies*. Boulder: Lynne Rienner.

Bratton, Michael. 1994. "Land Redistribution, 1980-1990." In M. Rukuni and C.K. Eicher (eds). *Zimbabwe's Agricultural Revolution*. Harare: University of Zimbabwe Press.

Briggs, Charles. 1996. "The Politics of Discursive Authority in Research on the Invention of Tradition." *Cultural Anthropology* 11(4):435-469.

Burke, Timothy. 1996. *Lifebuoy Men, Lux Women: Commodification, Consumption, and Cleanliness in Modern Zimbabwe*. Durham: Duke University Press.

Bush, R. and L. Cliffe. 1984. "Agrarian Policy in Migrant Labour Societies: Reform or Transformation in Zimbabwe?" *Review of African Political Economy* 29: 77-94.

Butler, Judith. 1990. *Gender Trouble: Feminism and the Subversion of Identity*. London: Routledge. Callan, Hilary. 1984. "Introduction." In H. Callan (ed.) *The Incorporated Wife*. London: Croom Helm.

Caute, David. 1983. *Under the Skin: The Death of White Rhodesia*. Harmondsworth, UK: Penguin.

CFU. 1991. *Proposals for Land Reform for Zimbabwe, 1991*. Harare: Modern Farming Publications.

Chanock, Martin. 1982. "Making Customary Law: Men, Women, and Courts in Colonial Northern Rhodesia." In M.J. Hay and M. Wright (eds) *African Women & the Law: Historical Perspectives*. Boston University. Papers on Africa, VII.

Cheater, Angela. 1981. "Women and Their Participation in Commercial Agicultural Production: The Case of Medium-Size Freehold in Zimbabwe." *Development and Change* 12: 349-377.

Cheater, Angela. 1984. *Idioms of Accumulation: Rural Development and Class Formation among Rural Freeholders in Zimbabwe*. Gweru: Mambo Press.

Cheater, Angela. 1991. "Introduction: Industrial Organization and the Law in the First Decade of Zimbabwe's Independence." *Zambezia* 18: 1-14.

Chinemana, F. and D. Sanders. 1993. "Health and Structural Adjustment in Zimbabwe." In P. Gibbon (ed.) *Social Change and Economic Reform in Africa*. Uppsala: Nordiska Afrikainstitutet.

Clarke, Duncan. 1977. *Agricultural and Plantation Workers in Rhodesia: A Report on Conditions of Labour and Subsistence*. Gwelo: Mambo Press.

Clifford, James. 1986. "On Ethnographic Allegory." In J. Clifford and G. Marcus (eds) *Writing Culture: The Poetics and Politics of Ethnography*. Berkeley: University of California Press. pp. 98-121.

Clifford, James. 1988. *The Predicament of Culture: Twentieth-Century Ethnography, Literature and Art*. Cambridge: Harvard University Press.

Cohen, David William and E.S. Atieno Odhiambo. 1989. *Siaya: The Historical Anthropology of an African Landscape*. London: James Currey, Nairobi: Heinemann Kenya, Athens, OH: Ohio University Press.

Comaroff, Jean, and John Comaroff. 1991. *Of Revelation and Revolution: Christianity, Colonialism, and Consciousness in South Africa*. Chicago: University of Chicago Press.

Comaroff, Jean, and John Comaroff. 1992a. "Home-Made Hegemony: Modernity, Domesticity, and Colonialism in South Africa." in K. Tranberg Hansen (ed.) *African Encounters with Domesticity*. New Brunswick: Rutgers University Press.

Comaroff, Jean, and John Comaroff. 1993. "Introduction." In Jean Comaroff and John Comaroff (eds) *Modernity and its Malcontents: Ritual and Power in Postcolonial Africa*. Chicago: University of Chicago Press.

Comaroff, John, and Jean Comaroff. 1997. *Of Revelation and Revolution: The Dialectics of Modernity on a South African Frontier*. Vol. 2. Chicago: University of Chicago Press.

Cooper, Frederick. 1989. "From Free Labor to Family Allowances: Labor and African Society in Colonial Discourse." *American Ethnologist* 16: 745-765.

Cooper, Frederick. 1992. "Colonizing Time: Work Rhythms and Labor Conflict in Colonial Mombasa." In N. Dirks (ed.) *Colonialism and Culture*. Ann Arbor: University of Michigan Press.

Cooper, Frederick. 1996. *Decolonization and African Society: The Labor Question in French and British Africa*. Cambridge: Cambridge University Press.

Crapanzano, Vincent. 1985. *Waiting: The Whites of South Africa*. New York: Vintage Press.

Crapanzano, Vincent. 1994. "Kevin: On the Transfer of Emotions." *American Anthropologist* 96: 866-885.

Cutshall, C.R. 1991. *Justice for the People: Community Courts and Legal Transformation in Zimbabwe*. Harare: University of Zimbabwe Publications.

Daneel, Inus. 1987. *Quest for Belonging: Introduction to a Study of African Independent Churches*. Gweru: Mambo Press.

Darby, H. C. 1932. "Pioneer Problems in Rhodesia and Nyasaland." In W.L.G. Joerg (ed.) *Pioneer Settlement*. Special Publication No. 14. New York: American Geographical Society.

Davidoff, Leonore. 1973. *The Best Circles: Society, Etiquette and the Season*. London: Croom Helm.

Davies, Dorothy. 1975. *Race Relations in Rhodesia: A Survey for 1971-73*. London: Rex Collins.

de Jong, J. 1975. *A Simplified Approach to Labour and Equipment Planning*. Conex Project Preparation Resource 19. Salisbury: Department of Conservation and Extension.

Derman, Bill. 1995. "Environmental NGOs, Dispossession, and the State: The Ideology and Praxis of African Nature and Development." *Human Ecology* 23(2):199-215.

Drinkwater, Michael. 1989. "Technical Development and Peasant Impoverishment: Land Use Policy in Zimbabwe's Midlands Province." *Journal of Southern African Studies* 15: 287-305.

Drinkwater, Michael. 1991. *The State and Agrarian Change in Zimbabwe's Communal Areas*. London: Macmillan.

Du Toit, Andries. 1993. "The Micro-Politics of Paternalism: the Discourses of Management and Resistance on South African Fruit and Wine Farms." *Journal of Southern African Studies* 19: 314-336.

Du Toit, F.P. 1977. *The Accommodation of Permanent Farm Labourers*. Technical Bulletin 17. Salisbury: Rhodesia Agricultural Journal.

Du Toit, F.P. 1978. "Alternative perceptions of Agricultural Employment in Rhodesia." *Zambezia* 6(1):75-86.

Dunlop, H. 1971. *The Development of European Agriculture in Rhodesia, 1945-1965*. Department of Economics, University of Rhodesia, Occasional Paper No. 5.

Edwards, Stephen J. 1974. *Zambezi Odyssey: A Record of Adventure on a Great River of Africa*. Cape Town: Bulpin Press.

Ennew, Judith, et al. 1977. "'Peasantry' as an Economic Category." *Journal of Peasant Studies* 4: 296-322.

Escobar, Arturo. 1988. "Power and Visibility: Development and the Invention and Management of the Third World." *Cultural Anthropology* 3: 428-443.

Escobar, Arturo. 1995. *Encountering Development: The Making and Unmaking of the Third World*. Princeton: Princeton University Press.

Fabian, Johannes. 1983. *Time and the Other: How Anthropology Makes its Object*. New York: Columbia University Press.

Fagan, Brian. 1969. "Excavations at Ingombe Ilede, 1960-2." In B. Fagan, D. Phillipson, S. Daniels. *Iron Age Cultures in Zambia*. London: Chatto & Windus.

Fanon, Frantz. 1967. *Black Skin, White Masks*. New York: Grove Press.

Faris, James. 1992. "A Political Primer on Anthropology/Photography." In E. Edwards (ed.) *Anthropology and Photography*. New Haven: Yale University Press.

Faris, James, and K. Wutu. 1986. "Beginning Anthropology." *Critique of Anthropology* 6: 5-23.

Farquharson, Laura. 1993. "Commercial Wildlife Utilisation in Zimbabwe: Are Commercial Farms the Appropriate Model for CAMPFIRE?" Unpublished Paper. Montreal: McGill University, Faculty of Law.

Ferguson, James. 1988. "Cultural Exchange: New Developments in the Anthropology of Commodities." *Cultural Anthropology* 3: 488-513.

Ferguson, James. 1990a. *The Anti-Politics Machine: Development, Depoliticization and Bureaucratic Power in Lesotho*. Cambridge: Cambridge University Press.

Ferguson, James. 1990b. "Mobile Workers, Modernist Narratives: A Critique of the Historiography of Transition on the Zambian Copperbelt." *Journal of Southern African Studies* 16: 385-412, 603-621.

Ferguson, James. 1999. *Expectations of Modernity: Myths and Meanings of Urban Life on the Zambian Copperbelt*. Berkeley: University of California Press.

Featherstone, Mike. 1990. "Global Culture: An Introduction." *Theory, Culture & Society* 7: 1-14.

Feierman, Steven. 1990, *Peasant Intellectuals: Anthropology and History in Tanzania*. Madison: University of Wisconsin Press.

Fields, Karen. 1985. *Revival and Rebellion in Colonial Central Africa*. Princeton: Princeton University Press.

Floyd, Barry. 1959. *Changing Patterns of African Land Use in Southern Rhodesia*. Lusaka: Rhodes-Livingstone Institute.

Folbre, Nancy. 1988. "Patriarchal Social Formations in Zimbabwe." In S. Stichter and J. Parpart (eds) *Patriarchy and Class: African Women in the Home and the Workforce*. Boulder: Westview Press.

Food Production Committee. 1943. "Food Production Committee." *Rhodesian Agricultural Journal*. 40: 165-177.

Foucault, Michel. 1965. *Madness and Civilization: A History of Insanity in the Age of Reason*. Tr. R. Howard. New York: Random House.

Foucault, Michel. 1972. *The Archaeology of Knowledge*. Tr. A.M. Sheridan-Smith. New York: Pantheon.

Foucault, Michel. 1983. "The Subject and Power." In H. Dreyfus and P. Rabinow (eds) *Michel Foucault*. 2nd edition. Tr. L. Sawyer. Chicago: University of Chicago Press.

Friedman, Jonathan. 1990. "Being in the World: Globalization and Localization." *Theory, Culture & Society* 7: 311-328.

Gaidzanwa, Rudo. 1993. "The Politics of the Body and the Politics of Control: An analysis of class, gender and cultural issues in student politics at the University of Zimbabwe." *Zambezia* 20:15-33.

Gapwuz. 1997. *Report on the Workshop on Living Conditions of Farm Workers in Zimbabwe*. 23-25 February, 1997. Darwendale, Zimbabwe.

Garbett, G.K. 1966a. "The Rhodesian Chief's Dilemma: Government Officer or Tribal Leader?" *Race* 8: 113-128.

Garbett, G.K. 1966b. "Religious Aspects of Political Succession Among the Valley Korekore (N. Shona)." In E. Stokes and R. Brown (eds) *The Zambezian Past*. Manchester: Manchester University Press.

Gardner, Katy. 1997. "Mixed Messages: Contested 'Development' and the 'Plantation Rehabilitation Project'." In R.D. Grillo and R.L. Stirrat (eds) *Discourses of Development: Anthropological Perspectives*. Oxford: Berg.

Gennep, Arnold L. Van. 1960 (1909). *The Rites of Passage*. London: Routledge and Kegan Paul.

Gupta, Akhil, and James Ferguson. 1992. "Beyond 'Culture': Space, Identity, and the Politics of Difference." *Cultural Anthropology* 7: 6-23.

Gupta, Akhil, and James Ferguson. 1997. "Discipline and Practice: 'The Field' as Site, Method and Location in Anthropology." In A. Gupta and J. Ferguson (eds) *Anthropological Locations*. Berkeley: University of California Press.

Handler, Richard. 1988. *Nationalism and the Politics of Culture in Quebec*. Madison: University of Wisconsin Press.

Hansen, Karen Tranberg. 1992. "Introduction: Domesticity in Africa." In K. Tranberg Hansen (ed.) *African Encounters with Domesticity*. New Brunswick: Rutgers University Press. pp. 1-33.

Hardin, G. 1968. "The Tragedy of the Commons." *Science* 162: 1243-1248.

Hecht, David, and Maliqalim Simone. 1994. *Invisible Governance: The Art of African Micropolitics*. Brooklyn: Autonmedia.

Herbst, Jeffrey. 1990. *State Politics in Zimbabwe*. Harare: University of Zimbabwe Press.

Hill, Kevin. 1996. "Zimbabwe's Wildlife Utilization Programs: Grassroots Democracy or an Extension of State Power?" *Africa Studies Review* 39(1):103-121.

Hindess, Barry. 1996. *Discourses of Power: From Hobbes to Foucault*. Oxford: Blackwell Publishers.

Hirsch, Susan F. 1998. *Pronouncing & Persevering: Gender and the Discourses of Disputing in an African Islamic Court*. Chicago: University of Chicago Press.

Hirst, Paul. 1979. *On Law and Ideology*. London: MacMillan Press.

Hirst, Paul. 1985. *Marxism and Historical Writing*. London: Routledge and Kegan Paul.

Hodder-Williams, Richard. 1983. *White Farmers in Rhodesia, 1890-1965: A History of the Marandellas District*. London: Macmillan Press.

Holleman, J.F. 1958. "Town and Tribe." In P. Smith (ed.) *Africa in Transition: Some BBC Talks on Changing Conditions in the Union and the Rhodesias*. London: Max Reinhardt.

Holleman, J.F. 1968. *Chief, Council and Commissioner: Some Problems of Government in Rhodesia*. Assen: Koninklijke Van Gorcum.

Howman, Roger. 1962 (1953). *African Local Government in British East and Central Africa*. Pretoria: University of South Africa.

Hughes, David M. 1998. "Refugees and Squatters: Immigration and the Politics of Territory on the Zimbabwe-Mozambique Border." *Journal of Southern African Studies* 25(4):533-552.

Hutchinson, Sharon. 1992. "The Cattle of Money and the Cattle of Girls among the Nuer, 1930-83." *American Ethnologist* 19: 294-316.

ILO (International Labour Office). 1993. *Structural Change and Adjustment in Zimbabwe*. Interdepartmental Project on Structural Adjustment Occasional Paper 16. Geneva: ILO.

Jeater, Diana. 1993. *Marriage, Perversion, and Power: The Construction of Moral Discourse in Southern Rhodesia, 1894-1930*. Oxford: Clarendon Press.

Joerg, W.L.G. 1932. *Pioneer Settlement: Cooperative Studies by Twenty-Six Authors*. American Geographical Society Special Publication No. 14. New York: American Geographical Society.

Kanji, Nanzeen, and Niki Jazdowska. 1993. "Structural Adjustment and Women in Zimbabwe." *Review of African Political Economy* 56: 11-26.

Kanyenze, Godfrey. Forthcoming. "Zimbabwe's Labour Relations Policies and the Implications for Farm Workers." In Dede Amanor-Wilks (ed.) *Zimbabwe's Farmworkers: The Policy Dimensions*. Panos Institute.

Kaspin, Deborah. 1993. "Chewa Visions and Revisions of Power: Transformations of the Nyau Dance in Central Malawi." In J. Comaroff and J. Comaroff (eds) *Modernity and its Malcontents: Ritual and Power in Postcolonial Africa*. Chicago: University of Chicago.

Kazembe, Joyce. 1986. "The Women Issue." In I. Mandaza (ed.) *Zimbabwe: The Political Economy of Transition 1980-1986*. Dakar: CODESRIA.

Kennedy, Dane. 1987. *Islands of White: Settler Society and Culture in Southern Rhodesia, 1890-1939*. Durham: Duke University Press.

Kinsey, B.H. 1983. "Emerging Issues in Zimbabwe's Land Resettlement Programme." *Development Policy Review* 1: 163-196.

Kirkwood, Deborah. 1984a. "The Suitable Wife: Preparations for Marriage in London and Rhodesia/Zimbabwe." In H. Callan (ed.) *The Incorporated Wife*. London: Croom Helm.

Kirkwood, Deborah. 1984b. "Settler Wives in Southern Rhodesia: A Case Study." In H. Callan (ed.) *The Incorporated Wife*. London: Croom Helm.

Kopytoff, Igor. 1987. "The Internal African Frontier: The Making of African Political Culture." In I. Kopytoff (ed.) *The African Frontier: The Reproduction of Traditional African Societies*. Bloomington: Indiana University Press.

Kriger, Norma. 1992. *Zimbabwe's Guerrilla War: Peasant Voices*. Cambridge: Cambridge University Press.

Ladley, Andrew. 1982. "Changing the Courts in Zimbabwe: The Customary Law and Primary Courts Act." *Journal of African Law* 26: 95-114.

Ladley, Andrew, and David Lan. 1985. "The Law of the Land: Party and State in Rural Zimbabwe." *Journal of Southern African Studies* 12: 88-101.

Laing, Richard. 1986. "Health and Health Services for Plantation Workers: Four Case Studies." *Evaluation and Planning Centre for Health Care.* London: London School of Hygiene and Tropical Medicine.

Lan, David. 1985. *Guns & Rain: Guerrillas & Spirit Mediums in Zimbabwe.* London: James Currey.

Lancaster, Chet. 1974. "Ethnic Identity, History, and 'Tribe' in the Middle Zambezi Valley." *American Ethnologist* 1: 707-730.

Lancaster, Chet. 1987. "Political Structure and Ethnicity in an Immigrant Society: The Goba of the Zambezi." In I. Kopytoff (ed.) *The African Frontier: The Reproduction of Traditional African Societies.* Bloomington: University of Indiana Press.

Lancaster, Chet, and A. Pohorilenko. 1977. "Ingombe Ilede and the Zimbabwe Culture." *International Journal of African Historical Studies* 10: 1-30.

Leys, Colin. 1959. *European Politics in Southern Rhodesia.* London: Oxford University Press.

Leys, Roger. 1986. "Drought and Drought relief in southern Zimbabwe." In P. Lawrence (ed.) *World Recession and the Food Crisis in Africa.* London: James Currey.

Loewenson, Rene. et al. 1983. "Evaluation of the Mashonaland West Farm Health Worker Scheme." Unpublished paper.

Loewenson, Rene. 1986. "Farm Labour in Zimbabwe." *Health Policy and Planning* 1: 48-57.

Loewenson, Rene. 1988. "Labour Insecurity and Health: An Epidemiological Study in Zimbabwe." *Social Science and Medicine* 27: 733-741.

Loewenson, Rene. 1992. *Modern Plantation Agriculture.* London: Zed Books.

Lowry, Donal. 1997. "'White Woman's Country': Ethel Tawse Jollie and the Making of White Rhodesia." *Journal of Southern African Studies* 23(2):259-281.

Macpherson, C.B. 1962. *The Political Theory of Possessive Individualism: Hobbes to Locke.* Oxford: Oxford University Press.

Malkki, Liisa. 1995. *Purity and Exile: Violence, Memory, and National Cosmology among Hutu Refugees in Tanzania.* Chicago: University of Chicago Press.

Mamdani, Mahmood. 1996. *Citizen and Subject: Contemporary Africa and the Legacy of Late Colonialism.* Princeton: Princeton University Press.

Manicom, Linzi. 1992. "Ruling Relations: Rethinking State and Gender in South African History." *Journal of African History* 33: 441-465.

Marcus, Tessa. 1989. *Modernizing Super-Exploitation: Restructuring South African Agriculture.* London: Zed Books.

Marx, Karl. 1987 (1852). *The 18th Brumaire of Louis Bonaparte.* New York: International Publishers.

Mazonde, Isaac. 1991. "Vorsters and Clarks: Alternative Models of European Farmer in the Tuli Block of Botswana." *Journal of Southern African Studies* 17(3):443-471.

May, Joan. 1987. *Changing People, Changing Laws.* Gweru: Mambo Press.

Mbembe, Achille. 1992. "Provisional Notes on the Postcolony." *Africa* 62(1):3-36.

McClintock, Anne. 1992."Screwing the System: Sexwork, Race, and the Law." *Boundary 2* 19:70-95.

McClintock, Anne. 1995. *Imperial Leather: Race, Gender and Sexuality in the Colonial Context.* London: Routledge.

McIvor, Chris. 1995. *Zimbabwe. The Struggle for Health: A Community Approach for Farmworkers.* London: Catholic Institute for International Relations.

McKenzie, John A. 1989. *Commercial Farmers in the Governmental System of Colonial Zimbabwe, 1963-1980.* Ph.D. thesis. University of Zimbabwe.

Mitchell, Timothy. 1988. *Colonizing Egypt.* Cambridge: Cambridge University Press.

Mitchell, Timothy. 1991. "America's Egypt: Discourse of the Development Industry." *Middle East Report* March-April: 18-36.

Mitchell, Timothy. 1998. "Fixing the Economy." *Cultural Studies* 12(1):82-101.

Mittlebeeler, Emmet. 1976. *African Custom and Western Law: The Development of the Rhodesian Criminal Law for Africans.* New York: Africana Publishing Company.

Mohanty, Chandra Talpade. 1983. "Under Western Eyes: Feminist Scholarship and Colonial Discourse." *Boundary 2* 12: 333-358.

Moodie, T. Dunbar (with Vivienne Ndatshe). 1994. *Going for Gold: Men, Mines, and Migration.* Berkeley: University of California Press.

Moore, Donald. 1993. "Contesting Terrain in Zimbabwe's Eastern Highlands: Political Ecology, Ethnography, and Peasant Resource Struggles." *Economic Geography* 69 (4):380-401.

Moore, Donald. 1994. "Optics of Engagement: Power, Positionality, and African Studies." *Transition* 64: 121-127.

Moore, Donald. 1998. "Subaltern Struggles and the Politics of Place: Remapping Resistance in Zimbabwe's Eastern Highlands." *Cultural Anthropology* 13(3):344-381.

Mosse, David. 1994. "Authority, Gender and Knowledge: Theoretical Reflections on the Practice of Participatory Rural Appraisal." *Development and Change* 25:497-526.

Mosse, David. 1997. "The Ideology and Politics of Community Participation: Tank Irrigation Development in Colonial and Contemporary Tamil Nadu." In R.D. Grillo and R.L. Stirrat (eds) *Discourses of Development: Anthropological Perspectives.* Oxford: Berg.

Mouffe, Chantal. 1993. *The Return of the Political.* London: Verso.

Moyo, Nelson. 1988. "The State, Planning and Labour: Towards Transforming the Colonial Labour Process in Zimbabwe." *Journal of Development Studies* 24: 203-217.

Moyo, Sam. 1995. *The Land Question in Zimbabwe*. Harare: SAPES Books.

Moyo, Sam. 1998. "The Land Acquisition Process in Zimbabwe (1997/98): Socio-Economic and Political Impacts." Mimeo. Unpublished paper.

Moyo, Sam, Blair Rutherford, Dede Amanor-Wilks. 2000. "Land Reform and Changing Social Relations for Farm Workers in Zimbabwe." *Review of African Political Economy* 84:181-202.

Muchena, O.N. 1980. *Women's Participation in the Rural Labour Force in Zimbabwe*. World Employment Programme. Lusaka: International Labour Office.

Mugwetsi, Thokozani, and Peter Balleis. 1994. *The Forgotten People: The Living and Health Conditions of Farm Workers and their Families.* Silveira House Social Series No. 6. Gweru: Mambo Press, with Silveira House.

Muir, K., M. Blackie, B. Kinsey, and M. de Swardt. 1982. "The Employment Effects of 1980 Price and Wage Policy in Zimbabwe Maize and Tobacco Industries." *African Affairs* 81: 71-85.

Muir, Kay.1994. "Agriculture in Zimbabwe." In M. Rukuni and C.K. Eicher (eds) *Zimbabwe's Agricultural Revolution.* Harare: University of Zimbabwe Press, pp. 40-55.

Muir, Kay and Malcolm J. Blackie. 1994. "Maize Research and Development." In M. Rukuni and C.K. Eicher (eds) *Zimbabwe's Agricultural Revolution.* Harare: University of Zimbabwe Press.

Murombedzi, James. 1992a. *Decentralising Common Property Resources Management: A Case Study of the Nyaminyami District Council of Zimbabwe's Wildlife Management Programme.* Harare: Centre for Applied Social Sciences, University of Zimbabwe.

Murombedzi, James. 1992b. *Decentralization or Recentralization? Implementing CAMPFIRE in the Omay Communal Lands.* Harare: Centre for Applied Social Sciences, University of Zimbabwe.

Murray, D.J. 1970. *The Governmental System in Southern Rhodesia.* Oxford: Clarendon.

Naldi, Gino. 1993. "Land Reform in Zimbabwe: Some Legal Aspects." *Journal of Modern African Studies* 31: 585-600.

Ncube, Welshman. 1989. *Family Law in Zimbabwe.* Harare: Legal Resources Foundation.

Nyambara, Pius. 1999. *A History of Land Acquisition in Gokwe, Northwestern Zimbabwe, 1945-1997.* Ph.D. thesis. Northwestern University, Chicago.

Oakeshott, Michael. 1962. *Rationalism in Politics and Other Essays.* London: Methuen.

Page, Sam, and Helán Page. 1991. "Western Hegemony over African Agriculture in Southern Rhodesia and its Continuing Threat to Food Security in Independent Zimbabwe." *Agriculture and Human Values* 8: 3-18.

Palmer, Robin. 1977. *Land and Racial Domination in Rhodesia.* London: Heinemann.

Peters, Pauline. 1994. *Dividing the Commons: Politics, Policy, and Culture in Botswana.* Charlottesville and London: University of Virginia Press.

Phimister, Ian. 1986. "Discourse and the Discipline of Historical Context: Conservationism and Ideas about Development in Southern Rhodesia." *Journal of Southern African Studies* 12: 263-275.

Phimister, Ian. 1988. *An Economic and Social History of Zimbabwe, 1890-1948: Capital Accumulation and Class Struggle.* London: Longman.

Pigg, Stacey Leigh. 1992. "Inventing Social Categories Through Place: Social Representations and Development in Nepal." *Comparative Studies in Society and History* 34: 491-513.

Pratt, Mary Louise. 1985. "Scratches on the Face of the Country: or, What Mr. Barrow Saw in the Land of the Bushman." *Critical Inquiry* 12: 119-143.

Raftopoulos, Brian. 1992. "Beyond the House of Hunger: Democratic Struggle in Zimbabwe." *Review of African Political Economy* 54:59-74, 55:57-66.

Raftopoulos, Brian and Ian Phimister (eds). 1997. *Keep on Knocking: A History of the Labour Movement in Zimbabwe, 1900-97.* Harare: Zimbabwe Congress of Trade Unions and Baobab Books.

Ranchod-Nilsson, Sita. 1992. "'Educating Eve': The Women's Club Movement and Political Consciousness among Rural African Women in Southern Rhodesia, 1950-1980." In K. Tranberg Hansen (ed.) *African Encounters with Domesticity.* New Brunswick: Rutgers University Press. pp. 266-289.

Ranney, Susan. 1985. "The Labour Market in a Dual Economy: Another Look at Colonial Rhodesia." *Journal of Development Studies* 21(4):505-524.

Ranger, Terence. 1985. *Peasant Consciousness and Guerrilla War in Zimbabwe.* London: James Currey.

Ranger, Terence. 1993a. "The Communal Areas of Zimbabwe." In T.J. Bassett and D.G. Crummey (eds) *Land in African Agrarian Systems.* Madison: University of Wisconsin Press. pp. 354-385.

Ranger, Terence. 1993b. "The Invention of Tradition Revisited: The Case of Colonial Africa." In T. Ranger and O. Vaughan (eds) *Legitimacy and the State in Twentieth Century Africa.* Basingstoke, UK: Macmillan. pp. 62-111.

Ranger, Terence. 1999. *Voices from the Rocks: Nature, Culture and History in the Matopos Hills of Zimbabwe.* Oxford: James Currey.

Richer, Pete. 1992. "Zimbabwean Unions: From State Partners to Outcasts." *South African Labour Bulletin* 16: 66-69.

Roberts, H. W. 1951. "The Development of the Southern Rhodesian Tobacco Industry." *South African Journal of Economics* 19: 177-188.

Rorty, Richard. 1989. *Contingency, Irony, and Solidarity.* Cambridge: Cambridge University Press.

Rose, Nikolas. 1987. "Beyond the Public/Private Division: Law, Power and the Family." *Journal of Law and Society* 14: 61-76.

Roseberry, William. 1989. *Anthropologies and Histories: Essays in Culture, History, and Political Economy.* New Brunswick: Rutgers University Press.

Roseberry, William. 1991. "Marxism and Culture." In B. Williams (ed.) *The Politics of Culture.* Washington: Smithsonian Institution Press.

Rostow, Walter. 1952. *The Process of Economic Growth.* New York: W.W. Norton.

Rubert, Steven. 1990. *You Have Taken My Sweat: Agricultural Wage Labour in Colonial Zimbabwe, 1904 to 1945.* Ph.D. thesis. University of California, Los Angeles, Los Angeles.

Rubert, Steven. 1998. *A Most Promising Weed: A History of Tobacco Farming and Labor in Colonial Zimbabwe, 1890-1945.* Athens, OH: Ohio University Center for International Studies.

Rukuni, Mandivamba. 1994. "The Evolution of Agricultural Policy: 1890-1990." In M. Rukuni and C.K. Eicher (eds) *Zimbabwe's Agricultural Revolution.* Harare: University of Zimbabwe Press.

Rutherford, Blair. 1996. *"Traditions" of Domesticity in "Modern" Zimbabwean Politics: Race, Gender, and Class in the Government of Commercial Farm Workers in Hurungwe District.* Ph.D. thesis. McGill University, Montreal.

Rutherford, Blair. 1999. "To Find an African Witch: Anthropology, Modernity, and Witch-Finding in North-West Zimbabwe." *Critique of Anthropology* 19(1):105-125.

Rutherford, Blair and Eric Worby. 1999. "Zimbabwe's Agrarian Answer: The Rhetoric of Redistribution." *Cultural Survival Quarterly*, Special Issue *Uprooted: Dispossession in Africa.* 22(4):56-59.

Rutherford, Blair and Rinse Nyamuda. 2000. "Learning about power: Development and marginality in an adult literacy centre for farm workers in Zimbabwe." *American Ethnologist* 27 (4).

Sachikonye, Lloyd. 1986. "State, Capital and Trade Unions." In I. Mandaza (ed.) *Zimbabwe: The Political Economy of Transition 1980-1986.* Dakar: CODESRIA.

Sachikonye, Lloyd. 1993 "Structural Adjustment, State and Organised Labour in Zimbabwe." In P. Gibbon (ed.) *Social Change and Economic Reform in Africa.* Uppsala: Nordiska Afrikainstitutet.

Sachikonye, Lloyd. 1997. "Trade Unions, Economic and Political Development in Zimbabwe since Independence." In B. Raftopoulos and I. Phimister (eds) *Keep on Knocking.* Harare: Zimbabwe Congress of Trade Unions, Baobob Books.

Said, Edward. 1978. *Orientalism.* New York: Random House.

Scarnecchia, Tim. 1994. *The Politics of Class and Gender in the Formation of African Communities in Salisbury, Rhodesia, 1937-1957.* Ph.D. thesis. University of Michigan, Ann Arbor.

Schimdt, Elizabeth. 1991. "Patriarchy, Capitalism, and the Colonial State in Zimbabwe." *Signs* 16: 732-757.

Schmidt, Elizabeth. 1992. *Peasants, Traders, and Wives: Shona Women in the History of Zimbabwe, 1870-1939*. London: James Currey.

Scott, David. 1995. "A Note on the Demand of Criticism." *Public Culture* 8:41-50.

Scott, Joan. 1992. "Experience." In J. Butler and J. Scott (eds) *Feminists Theorize the Political*. London: Routledge.

Scott, Peter. 1954. "Migrant Labor in Southern Rhodesia." *Geographical Review* 44: 29-48.

Seidman, Gay. 1984. "Women in Zimbabwe: Postindependence Struggles." *Feminist Studies* 10: 419-440.

Shenton, Robert, and Michael Cowen. 1996. *Doctrines of Development*. London: Routledge.

Simmel, George. 1978. *The Philosophy of Money*. London: Routledge.

Sloterdijk, Peter. 1987. *Critique of Cynical Reason*. Tr. M. Eldred. Minneapolis: University of Minnesota Press.

Smith, Dorothy. 1990. *Texts, Facts, and Femininity: Exploring the Relations of Ruling*. London: Routledge.

Southern Rhodesia. 1944. "Post-War Land Settlement in Southern Rhodesia." *Rhodesian Agricultural Journal* 41:87-97.

Spurr, David. 1993. *The Rhetoric of Empire: Colonial Discourse in Journalism, Travel Writing, and Imperial Administration*. Durham: Duke University Press.

Stewart, Susan. 1984. *On Longing: Narratives of the Miniature, the Gigantic, the Souvenir, the Collection*. Baltimore: Johns Hopkins University Press.

Stoler, Ann. 1989. "Rethinking Colonial Categories: European Communities and the Boundaries of Rule." *Comparative Studies in Society and History* 31: 134-161.

Stoler, Ann. 1997. "Sexual Affronts and Racial Frontiers: European Identities and the Cultural Politics of Exclusion in Colonial Southeast Asia." In F. Cooper and A.L. Stoler (eds) *Tensions of Empire*. Berkeley: University of California Press. pp. 198-237.

Sylvester, Christine. 1995a. "African and Western Feminisms: World-Traveling the Tendencies and Possibilities." *Signs* 20(4):941-969.

Sylvester, Christine. 1995b. "Women in Rural Producer Groups and the Diverse Politics of Truth in Zimbabwe." In M. Marchand and J. Parpart (eds). *Feminism/Postmodernism/Development*. New York: Routledge. 182-203.

Sylvester, Christine. 2000. *Producing Women and Progress in Zimbabwe: Narratives of identity and work from the 1980s*. Portsmouth, NH: Heinemann.

Taussig, Michael. 1992. *Nervous System*. London: Routledge.

Thomas, Nicholas. 1991. "Against Ethnography." *Cultural Anthropology* 6(3):306-322.

Thompson, C. and H. Woodruff. 1954. *Economic Development in Rhodesia and Nyasaland*. London: Dennis Dobson.

Thornycroft, Peta. 1991. "A High Risk Harvest." *Parade* (Zimbabwe). February.

Thornton, Robert. 1995. "The Colonial, the Imperial, and the Creation of the 'European' in Southern Africa." In J. Carrier (ed.) *Occidentalism*. Oxford: Clarendon Press. pp.192-217.

Torres, Gabriel. *The Force of Irony: Power in the Everyday Life of Mexican Tomato Workers*. Oxford: Berg.

Trouillot, Michel-Rolph. 1989. "Discourses of Rule and the Acknowledgement of the Peasantry in Dominica, W.I., 1838-1928." *American Ethnologist* 16: 704-718.

Tsing, Anna Lowenhaupt. 1993. *In the Realm of the Diamond Queen: Marginality in an Out-of-the-Way Place*. Princeton: Princeton University Press.

Turner, Victor. 1967. *The forest of symbols: Aspects of Ndembu ritual*. Ithaca, NY: Cornell University Press.

Turner, Victor. 1979 [1964]. "Betwixt and Between: The Liminal Period in *Rites de Passage*." In W. Lessa and E. Vogt (eds) *Reader in Comparative Religion: An Anthropological Approach*. 4th edition. New York: Harper & Row. pp.234-243.

Tyler, Stephen. 1987. *The Unspeakable: Discourse, Dialogue, and Rhetoric in the Postmodern World*. Madison: University of Wisconsin Press.

Vaughan, Megan, and Graham Chipande. 1986. "Women in the Estate Sector of Malawi: The Tea and Tobacco Industries." *World Employment Programme Research Working Papers*. Geneva: International Labour Office.

Vickery, Kenneth. 1989. "The Second World War Revival of Forced Labor in the Rhodesias." *International Journal of African Historical Studies* 22: 423-437.

von Blanckenburg, Peter. 1994. *Large Commercial Farmers and Land Reform in Africa: The Case of Zimbabwe*. Aldershot, England: Avebury.

Wade, Peter. 1993. "'Race,' Nature and Culture." *Man* (n.s.) 28:17-34.

Watts, Michael. 1992. "Capitalisms, Crises, and Cultures I: Notes Toward a Totality of Fragments." In A. Pred and M. Watts. *Reworking Modernity: Capitalisms and Symbolic Discontent*. New Brunswick: Rutgers University Press.

Weiner, Dan. 1988. "Land and Agricultural Development." In C. Stoneman (ed.) *Zimbabwe's Prospects: Issues of Race, Class, State, and Capital in Southern Africa*. London: MacMillan.

Weiner, Dan, et al. 1985. "Land Use and Agricultural Productivity in Zimbabwe." *Journal of Modern African Studies* 23: 251-285.

Werbner, Richard 1989. *Ritual Passage, Sacred Journey*. Washington: Smithsonian Institution Press.

Werbner, Richard. 1991. *Tears of the Dead*. Edinburgh: Edinburgh University Press.

Werbner, Richard. 1996. "Multiple Identities, Plural Arenas." In R. Werbner and T. Ranger (eds) *Postcolonial Identities in Africa*. London: Zed Books. pp. 1-25.

Werbner, Richard. 1999. "The Reach of the Postcolonial State: Development, Empowerment/Disempowerment and Technocracy." In A. Chater (ed.) *The Anthropology of Power*. London: Routledge.

White, J.D. 1971. "History and Customs of the Urungwe District." *Native Affairs Department Annual* 10: 33-72.

White, Luise. 1990. *The Comforts of Home: Prostitution in Colonial Nairobi*. Chicago: University of Chicago Press.

Wolff, Richard, and Stephen Resnik. 1987. *Economics: Marxian versus Neoclassical*. Baltimore: Johns Hopkins University Press.

Worby, Eric. 1992. *Remaking Labour, Reshaping Identity: Cotton, Commoditization and the Culture of Modernity in Northwestern Zimbabwe*. Ph.D. thesis. McGill University, Montreal.

Worby, Eric. 1994. "Maps, Names, and Ethnic Games: The Epistemology and Iconography of Colonial Power in Northwestern Zimbabwe." *Journal of Southern African Studies* 20(3):371-392.

Worby, Eric. 1995. "What does Agrarian Wage-Labour Signify? Cotton, Commoditisation and Social Form in Gokwe, Zimbabwe." *Journal of Peasant Studies* 23 (1): 1-29.

Worby, Eric. 1998. "Tyranny, Parody, and Ethnic Polarity: Ritual Engagements with the State in Northwestern Zimbabwe." *Journal of Southern African Studies* 24(3): 561-578.

Worby, Eric, and Blair Rutherford.1997. "Law's Fictions, State-Society Relations, and the Anthropological Imagination: Pathways Out of Africa." *Anthropologica* XXXIX:65-69.

World Bank. 1981. *Accelerated Development in Sub-Saharan Africa*. Washington: World Bank.

Young, Robert. 1990. *White Mythologies: Writing History and the West*. London: Routledge.

Zimbabwe. 1984. *Labour & Economy: Report of the National Trade Unions Survey, Zimbabwe, 1984. Volume One*. Harare: Ministry of Labour, Manpower Planning and Social Welfare.

Zimbabwe. 1991a. *Second Five-Year National Development Plan*. Harare: Government Printer.

Zimbabwe. 1991b. *Zimbabwe: A Framework for Economic Reform (1991-95)*. Harare: Government Printer.

Zishiri, O.J. 1998. *An Inquiry into the Squatter Problem and Possible Solutions in Mashonaland West Province*. Working Paper No. 24, Economic Advisory Project. Harare: Friedrich Ebert Stiftung.

ZTA. 1992. *Zimbabwe Tobacco Year-Book*. Harare: Zimbabwe Tobacco Association.